The Making of Modern Nevada

Wilbur S. Shepperson Series in Nevada History

T0303611

THE MAKING OF

Hal K. Rothman

ada

MODERN NEVADA

UNIVERSITY OF NEVADA PRESS   RENO & LAS VEGAS

Wilbur S. Shepperson Series in Nevada History
Series Editor: Michael Green

University of Nevada Press, Reno, Nevada 89557 USA
Copyright © 2010 by University of Nevada Press
All rights reserved
Manufactured in the United States of America
Design by Kathleen Szawiola

Library of Congress Cataloging-in-Publication Data

Rothman, Hal, 1958–2007.
 The making of modern Nevada / Hal K. Rothman ; foreword by
David M. Wrobel.
    p. cm. — (Wilbur S. Shepperson series in Nevada history)
Includes index.
ISBN 978-0-87417-826-5 (pbk. : alk. paper)
1. Nevada—History. 2. Nevada—Politics and government.
3. Nevada—Economic conditions. 4. Social change—Nevada—
History. I. Title.
F841.R68 2010
979.3—dc22   2010009968

The paper used in this book is a recycled stock made from 30 percent post-
consumer waste materials, certified by FSC, and meets the requirements of
American National Standard for Information Sciences—Permanence of Paper
for Printed Library Materials, ANSI/NISO Z39.48-1992 (R2002). Binding materials
were selected for strength and durability.

FIRST PRINTING
19 18 17 16 15 14 13 12 11 10
5 4 3 2 1

CONTENTS

FOREWORD
David M. Wrobel

HAL K. ROTHMAN held the title of distinguished professor of history at the University of Nevada, Las Vegas (UNLV), when he died in February 2007, at the age of 48, after a courageous battle with amyotrophic lateral sclerosis (ALS), Lou Gehrig's disease. A testament to his legendary scholarly productivity, *The Making of Modern Nevada* is Hal's third posthumously published volume, following *Blazing Heritage: A History of Wildland Fire in the National Parks* (2007) and *Playing the Odds: Las Vegas and the Modern West* (2007). Originally titled *A New History of Nevada*, the book was intended to be a comprehensive history of the state, organized around a direct and strongly argued thesis—that until very recently, Nevada has been controlled by forces outside of the state. But his worsening medical condition in the fall of 2006 prevented him from completing *The Making of Modern Nevada*. He wrote to the University of Nevada Press on November 11 of that year: "I have become so sick so fast that I will not be able to finish the Nevada History. I am attaching 8 chapters and an introduction. I would like you to find someone to finish the book. I really wanted to finish this one." Hal had planned to write a chapter on the Native Americans. Despite the absence of this chapter, the press decided that asking someone to finish the manuscript would, while making it more complete in its coverage, have made it less clearly and definitively a testament to the bold arguments and strong narrative voice of its author. As it stands, *The Making of Modern Nevada* is Hal's unique interpretation of Nevada's history. Here, then, is one of the final manuscripts crafted by a historian and public intellectual whose work influenced the fields of western American, environmental, cultural, economic, post-industrial, National Parks, and Las Vegas history and, at the close of his life, the history of the Silver State, the adopted home which he grew to care deeply about.

In his book *Counterculture Green: The Whole Earth Catalog and American Environmentalism*, Andy Kirk, my colleague and Hal's in the UNLV History

Department, described Hal as a "force of nature [with] abundant confidence and legendary energy . . . a true original." Andy's observation is spot on, hyperbole free. Hal was born on August 11, 1958, in Baton Rouge, Louisiana, and moved through life at a pace that was astonishing. He graduated from high school at age 16. After a stint as a roadie for the Eagles, the Rolling Stones, and other legendary rock 'n' roll bands, he earned a BA in 1980 at the University of Illinois, Urbana-Champaign, and then went to the University of Texas at Austin where he received his MA in 1982 and his PhD three years later, at age 27. He took a position as assistant professor of history and director of the program in public history at Wichita State University in 1987. In 1992 he joined the UNLV faculty as associate professor of history. Four years later he was promoted to full professor. A decade later he was awarded the university's highest honor, the designation of distinguished professor.

In Henderson, Nevada (the state's second largest city), where Hal lived, he played an instrumental role in creating the organized community spirit and raising the funds to build the Midbar Kodesh Temple, a process he wrote about with justifiable pride in *Neon Metropolis: How Las Vegas Started the Twenty-First Century*. Hal was certainly an active community member in the history profession too. He was editor of both the *Environmental History Review* (1992–1996) and its successor, *Environmental History* (1996–2002), and he edited the University Press of Kansas's Western Resources book series. At UNLV, he was chair of the History Department (2002–2005) and served as the faculty representative to the NCAA. And, of course, Hal was also an incredibly prolific and successful author on a wide range of topics.

In one short period Hal's book publications included, in addition to the widely acclaimed *Neon Metropolis*, *The New Urban Park: Golden Gate National Recreation Area and Civic Environmentalism* (2003), *LBJ's Texas White House: "Our Heart's Home"* (2001), *Saving the Planet: The American Response to the Environment in the Twentieth Century* (2000), and *Devil's Bargains: Tourism in the Twentieth-Century American West*, (1998). That remarkable half-decade's worth of fruits of his scholarly labors also saw the publication of two edited collections, *The Culture of Tourism: The Tourism of Culture* (2003) and *Reopening the American West* (1998). He also co-edited a collection with Mike Davis, *The Grit Beneath the Glitter: Tales from the Real Las Vegas* (2002). Reflecting upon this memorable total of eight books published in six years, I'm reminded of a morning in the very early 2000s, shortly after my arrival at UNLV, and in the middle of this period of Hal's heightened productivity. Hal passed me on the exterior staircase of the John S. Wright Hall, where the History Department is housed, and offered a beaming smile that suggested great achievement and seemed to beckon a question in that direction. "Well what is it, Hal?" I asked, "what's so clearly brightened up your day?" to which he responded, "Don't you love those two-book days, David?" He had just delivered two of his completed book manuscripts to the mail room in the same morning. My response, much the same as just about every other scholar's would have been, was: "I wouldn't know."

But those eight books in six years, including the two mailed off on one day, comprise only about half of Hal's scholarly record. His other authored books, in addition to the trio of posthumous works, are: *The Greening of a Nation? Environmentalism in the U.S. Since 1945* (1997), *"I'll Never Fight Fire With My Bare Hands Again:" Recollections of the First Forest Rangers of the Inland Northwest* (1994), *On Rims and Ridges: The Los Alamos Area Since 1880* (1992), and *Preserving Different Pasts: The American National Monuments* (1989). He also co-edited, with Char Miller, *Out of the Woods: Essays in Environmental History* (1997), and with Sara Dant-Ewert, *Encyclopedia of American National Parks* (2004). In addition, he authored eight administrative histories for the National Park Service, and published more than two dozen journal articles and a dozen book chapters.

But Hal's academic works were just one part of his tremendous output as a professional and public historian. He strongly believed that academic historians have a duty to render the past meaningful to contemporary audiences. He wrote for several publications including the *Los Angeles Times* and *Urban Ecology*, and was frequently quoted in and often appeared in national and international media outlets like *The New York Times*, the CBS *Evening News*, and *Public Radio International*. He was still writing a weekly column for the *Las Vegas Sun* up until the last few months of his life.

It should come as no surprise, given Hal's exceptional productivity as a scholar and public intellectual, that he was the recipient of a whole series of tremendously prestigious awards. But the many awards that he received were more than matched by his gifts to the profession. He was a dedicated member and supporter of numerous academic organizations and nurtured the careers of countless young scholars involved in them. He was a loyal friend and vigorous supporter of dozens of graduate students at UNLV and at institutions across the country, and his legacy will live on in their work as well as his own.

And, fortunately for scholars, students, and residents of the state of Nevada—indeed, for all those interested in the state's history—Hal's legacy is evident, too, in *The Making of Modern Nevada*. Never one to mince words, he describes Nevada, at the tail end of the Comstock era, as "the equivalent of a medieval fiefdom, where few possessed not only wealth but power, and everyone else simply existed, many harboring grievances against the power structure." The book's driving theme of the exploitation of Nevada is evident throughout the manuscript and finds particularly clear expression in the coverage of Hoover Dam: "[a]s did every previous venture in the state," he writes, "the dam in Black Canyon benefited interests outside the state ahead of Nevada residents . . . Boulder Dam was located primarily in Nevada, but it served California above all else." The dam, Hal is quick to point out, was built by six non-Nevada companies, but it was the federal government, he emphasizes, that really directed the fortunes and fate of the state through the provision of work programs and other forms of federal assistance and through the purchase of silver. On the whole, New Deal colonialism benefited the state, Hal suggests, even if, he wryly notes, its residents "had to swallow a little government assistance." He is quick to point out that when federal colonialism was less beneficial to the state its residents revolted against colonial authority in organized and effective fashion, as evidenced in the now more than two-decade-long, and almost certainly successful, struggle against the plan to store the nation's nuclear waste at Yucca Mountain, adjacent to the Nevada Test Site, north of Las Vegas.

The Making of Modern Nevada is a clear testament to Hal's bias in favor of the southern part of the state, where he lived and taught. Northern Nevada gets the bulk of its coverage in the first half of this study; the second half belongs to Clark County, which for him was the future of the state, the nexus of its demographic growth, and increasingly the barometer of its national significance. Hal was a historian of metropolitan Las Vegas first, and only later a scholar of the state as a whole; *The Making of Modern Nevada* bears that imprint. Moreover, he was a booster for Clark County and an ambassador for both the region's normalcy and its exceptionalism. He worked hard to transform common national and international perceptions of southern

Nevada as the weirdest, most anomalous, most conspicuous center of capitalist consumer excess on earth. He preferred to view the region as a center of cultural innovation, the "last Detroit"—the last haven of opportunity for working-class Americans to secure their piece of the American dream. But he also contended that the region was becoming more like the rest of the United States, in part because of its profound influence on the nation.

Conceptually, it was quite a tightrope act for Hal. The emphasis in *The Making of Modern Nevada* on the territory and then the state as a colony of a series of outside interests that controlled its fate is very much in the vein of what is probably his most important and influential book, *Devil's Bargains*, which bemoans the loss of community as places sell out when faced with the prospect of outside corporations offering quick profits and steady employment. What those places sell or trade in the devil's bargain, he argues, is their community cohesiveness or authenticity and their ability to control their own fate and chart their own future. Yet Hal's deep affection for the Las Vegas metropolitan region prevented him from viewing his home place as a typical part of the landscape of such lamentable trade-offs. For him, greater Las Vegas was a place that knew what it was and what it was selling. In *Neon Metropolis* he calls Las Vegas "a center of the postindustrial world . . . [and] the first spectacle of the postmodern world." The "old pariah," he continues, "has become a paradigm, the colony of everywhere, the colonizer of its former masters."

That is the paradigm shift that marks this book, his history of Nevada, the shift from colony to colonizer, from blank slate in the desert to postindustrial, postmodern pacesetter, not just for the nation, but for the globe. Only he could have finished *The Making of Modern Nevada* and only the bravest of souls would seek to finish it for him. Nonetheless, the occasional comments from members of the UNLV history community suggest that Hal had his finger very squarely on the pulse of the Las Vegas metropolitan region, the state, and the nation in his last months of life. One doctoral student recalls Hal advising him in spring 2006 to sell the condo he had purchased at the beginning of his studies, in the early 2000s, cash out on the equity and avoid the bust that would inevitably follow the remarkable housing boom that marked the first half of the 2000s nationwide, but nowhere more so than Clark County, Nevada, Phoenix, Arizona, and some parts of California and Florida. And the real estate bust that has followed the boom has been quite astonishing, with many properties in Clark County by mid-2009 losing more than 50 percent of their peak value in early 2006. Once again, the southern part of the Silver State has been at the cutting edge of national trends; once again Las Vegas dominates the national headlines as the recession focuses on the excesses of the real estate boom, the dangers of overbuilding new housing subdivisions, shady mortgages, and enormous expectations. Long the national symbol of American consumer cultural excess, Las Vegas has now become the symbol of speculative excess.

Having formerly shifted from pariah to paradigm, one wonders if Hal's home place and, since 2000, the home of more than two million residents and thirty-five million visitors per year, has become the pariah once more, or whether its economic failure in the late 2000s encapsulates the failure of a nation afflicted by real estate madness and its incessant bouts of consumer spending through home equity lines of credit, and the condition of economic stagnation that follows such flurries of exuberant purchasing. It would be good to have Hal's perspective on the real estate boom and bust, on the Democratic Party's near takeover of the state government during the 2008 election, the controversies surrounding the administration of Governor Jim Gibbons, the issue of whether a more reliable set of structures for generating state revenue might emerge from the current economic crisis that the state of Nevada is suffering from, and whether the Clark County, Nevada, that comes close to topping the nation in the unenviable area of unemployment rates at the end of the 2000s will ever again regain its mantle as the "last Detroit." We can only speculate on what Hal would have to say were he still with us, and be grateful for the voluminous body of work that he left us, including *The Making of Modern Nevada*.

The Making of Modern Nevada

Introduction

N E V A D A was always different from other American states. Larger in size and more varied in landscape than most of its peers, yet among the most sparsely populated, the state promised wide-open spaces but its people overwhelmingly clustered in urban areas. Arid in a society that valued humidity and wetness, and bleak by the visual standards of a culture that based its idea of fertility in the presence of trees, Nevada had little to offer the United States when it gained entry to the Union in 1864, although the discovery of gold and silver at the Comstock Lode in 1859 had started a population swell that would eventually enable Abraham Lincoln to declare the territory a state. From its founding, the state has always struggled to belong. It has had a series of masters—the mining industry, the railroads, the federal government, and now gaming and tourism—that have driven the state's economy and compelled its direction.

To survive, Nevada followed a different route than most states. Without the rich soil or developed manufacturing that could draw agriculture and industry, and with many of the profits of its mines directed out of state, Nevada embraced what society called vice. Beginning in the mid-nineteenth century and continuing through to the twenty-first, the state has sanctioned pleasures thought immoral elsewhere. In Nevada, you could be free of a spouse or see a professional boxing match when it was nigh on impossible to do either elsewhere. In Nevada, you could sit at the gaming tables or visit a brothel, all within the law. In Nevada, as nowhere else, you could be free of the constraints that the larger society put upon you. Such became the Silver State's promise, first to its detriment and later to its advantage.

The state's history reveals this pattern with a clarity unfamiliar in American history. Nevada's industries have always catered to the needs of outsiders ahead of residents of the state, and until recently, the dollars that developed it came predominantly from outside the state. In this pattern, Nevada remains a colony, a place that, despite its strong individualist leanings, bent to the will of the outside. Outsiders extracted the riches in its earth, leaving only scraps for the locals; many of the mansions of Nob Hill in San Francisco were built with profits from Nevada's silver mines. Railroads owned U.S. senators and set freight rates to impoverish the farmers, ranchers, and even miners of the state; the federal government regarded the state first as a storage tank for water and other resources and then as a sacrifice zone, a place to experiment in an unconscionable way with the power of the atom.

Gambling (or "gaming," an old term used to help reduce the activity's social stigma) gave Nevada a way to turn the tables. Thought immoral and debauched because it permitted games of chance, Nevada positioned itself ahead of the rest of the nation long before American culture began to liberalize. As personal freedom replaced delayed gratification as the purpose of life in American society, and as experience became a scorecard for personal accomplishment, Nevada's historic idiosyncrasies became valuable assets. The old pariah, the state that people shunned for its tolerance, became the new standard, the one people measured their success against as forty-eight states embraced some form of gaming.

As this process gathered momentum throughout the twentieth century, the people and the power in Nevada shifted from north to south and from rural to urban, setting off a series of tensions that had become full-blown political and social issues as the twenty-first century took shape. From 160,000 people in 1950, Nevada topped 2,000,000 in 2000, pressing an entirely new set of issues on the state. The result was a maturing of Nevada, a distancing from the individualist attitudes of the past and an embrace of the culture of the moment. Both novel and reflective of the state's ability to mimic the desires of the nation, this new shift suggested that twenty-first-century Nevada might be quite different than its nineteenth- and twentieth-century counterparts.

But Nevada's ways were deeply rooted in its history. The state's environment dictated the terms of human existence in it. For thousands of years, the only people who could live in Nevada were those who understood its limits, the lack of water, and the way that the seasons dictated what foods were available. Only when American society could provide the technology to transform those limits could Nevada become integrated into the larger nation. Only when Nevada could provide a reason for the rest of the nation to use its attributes did the state begin to enjoy the advantages of industrial America. In this complicated intersection of place and need, modern Nevada was formed.

1   A Light Hand on a Difficult Land:
European Exploration

AS THE NINETEENTH CENTURY DAWNED, the historic condition of much of Nevada remained as it had been for hundreds of years. The major native groups that lived in large parts of the region that would later form the state continued their subsistence ways, largely without participating in the great changes taking place elsewhere in the West. Although most were part of extended networks of trade, they rarely saw the Europeans and Americans who put so much pressure on native people elsewhere on the North American continent. Beyond the mountains to the west, Spaniards arrived in the late eighteenth century and began a chain of missions, forts, and ranchos along the coast. East of the deserts of the interior West, competition between the Spanish, French, British, and later Americans transformed the lives of native peoples. If the Southern and Northern Paiute, Western Shoshone, and Washoe people knew of these great political upheavals, evidence came only from the trade goods that appeared in their world.

Yet geopolitical forces far from Nevada soon affected the lives of its peoples. The 1803 Louisiana Purchase gave the new United States an enormous but largely undetermined holding west of the Mississippi River. President Thomas Jefferson established a century-long pattern when he sent out William Clark and Meriwether Lewis and their Corps of Discovery to discern what the nation had acquired. A few years later in 1812, the U.S. found itself in another war with Great Britain, this one ending three years later, culminating in the battle of New Orleans, an American triumph that propelled the new nation westward. By the end of the 1810s, the U.S. had established itself as an important player in the West, a threat to the interests of European nations.

A struggle between the United States and Spain led to grim realities for the Spanish in the New World. Faced with internal strife in Spain and lacking resources to combat the American onslaught in the Southeast, the Spanish foreign minister, Luis de Oñis, agreed to a treaty with U.S. Secretary of State John Quincy Adams. In the Adams-Oñis Treaty of 1819, the Spanish ceded Florida to the United States, allowing the new nation to remove the last European power east of the Mississippi River. In return, the U.S. agreed to pay up to $5 million in claims to Spanish citizens, and ceded its claims to Texas west of the Sabine River. In addition, the treaty drew boundaries for the Louisiana Purchase, terminating U.S. jurisdiction at the Arkansas River and assigning lands south of that to Spain. In exchange for receiving all of the Far West, the Spanish gave up their claims to Oregon. With one signature, the lands that later became Nevada were codified as part of the failing Spanish empire. The U.S. ended its battles with Spanish Florida in the east, bringing to a halt the ongoing hostilities in the American South that dated from the War of 1812.

Yet that cession was fiction, the result of the arrogance of both the U.S. and Spain and their insistence that they could control a great deal more land than their explorers had visited. Since they arrived in the New World, European powers had claimed far more land than they had ever seen, oblivious to the ways of living and sometimes even the existence of native peoples upon it. Americans followed the pattern, both in completing the Louisiana Purchase and in signing the Adams-Oñis treaty. Once again, representatives of the new nation did not know what they ceded. As the ink on the treaty dried, neither Americans nor Spaniards had yet seen the lands that became the state of Nevada.

Adams-Oñis was only paper, an agreement that obscured a larger picture of on-the-ground realities in the western deserts. Even before Mexico became an independent nation in 1821, the treaty was more meaningful in national capitals than in the region it governed. With or without an international agreement, with little regard for jurisdiction, travelers and traders between Mexican California and the province of New Mexico became more common. Many were Mexicanos, engaged in conveying goods back and forth; others were wanderers and still more were native peoples, using the route for transportation and to reach the often vulnerable settlements of the California coast. But after American trappers and traders reached Santa Fe in the 1820s, they heard of California beyond and within a few years they became more frequent travelers on the Old Spanish Trail, an existent trade route between Santa Fe and California.

As such travelers arrived on the fringes of the Paiute world in the 1820s, they encountered a changed Southern Paiute community. The greatest vulnerability of the Southern Paiute had little to do with any choices they made; instead, it resulted from a specific addition to the regional repertoire that they did not acquire. One major consequence of the arrival of the Spanish was the spread of the horse. The peoples who acquired them—the Apache, the Comanche, the

Cheyenne, and the Lakota—became the dominant native groups, imposing their will on others.

Those who did not so quickly adapt were forced into a subservient role. The Southern Paiute were in a particularly disadvantaged position. Paiute lands possessed little to sustain a domestic animal population, and for them the horse became as much a liability as an advantage. In the Paiute world, horses were competitors for scarce food resources and were relatively easy game to hunt. Simply put, Paiute ate horses instead of riding them.

The inability to turn the horse into an asset hurt the Paiute. Without horses, the Southern Paiute quickly became prey for their neighbors, native and new-comer alike. North and east of the Sevier River in what is now Utah, the Ute people shared much with the Southern Paiute, but lived in a world of more lush grasses. They could keep the horse and feed it, and over time they captured wild horses and domesticated them. Soon these turned into large herds, which in turn granted mobility, advantages in warfare, greater range in search of food, and the ability to avoid exploitation of their immediate surroundings. In particular, the horse allowed for better military organization, and the Utes became skilled at warfare and predatory behavior. The more sedentary Southern Paiute became a prime target for the newly horsed and lethally aggressive Utes.

The combination of the horse, the Utes, and the Spanish trade placed the Southern Paiute at the center of a changing world for which they were poorly equipped. The Utes mirrored the patterns of Spanish trade, exchanging horses in Mexico and bringing slaves for the labor market. Utes brought Paiute slaves to California and to Santa Fe in the province of New Mexico as a trade in slaves grew up in the Mexican provinces. The Southern Paiute often became the bait.

Astride animals that appeared enormous, the Utes captured slaves among nearby people. Sometimes they simply took people, often women and children. Ute preference for younger and weaker people reflected the Spanish assumption that women and children would be easier to keep as slaves. This predatory behavior took many forms. Ute horsemen might have appeared in a Southern Paiute village and used their horses as tools of intimidation to coerce people into surrendering their children to slavery. The image of a man using his horse to push another around for the purpose of intimidation, to take a family's future, offers a painful reminder of how hard life could be for the native people of southern Nevada.

For a generation, the Southern Paiute consistently lost members to the slave trade, forced upon them by their distant cousins from the north. Ute power increased and the Southern Paiute suffered. Population decline, social disorganization, and an inability to secure resources were all direct consequences of the slave trade. The relationship between Southern Paiute and slavery became so firm that a standardized scale of cost existed for Paiute slaves. By 1850, the standard value ranged from $50–$200 depending on their gender, age, and health.

After a generation or more of suffering, the Southern Paiute had devised strategies to protect themselves from hostile raiders. They learned to avoid places where resources were abundant, for such places drew the heaviest travel and the human predators who stalked their world. The Old Spanish Trail, which passed at the base of the Spring Mountains west of modern Las Vegas, and the springs at Las Vegas ceased to provide sustenance and became risky places to replenish their supplies. The largely peaceful Southern Paiute community had little recourse as other native groups and Mexican outlaws raided their communities. In some instances, the Southern Paiute fought back, but successful battles of this type were not the norm.

As a result of this constant pressure, Southern Paiute numbers dwindled. They could not maintain the resources that had long sustained them; they were poorly prepared for warfare against men on horses—some of whom had guns— and slavers depleted their numbers and their future. By the end of the 1820s, scarcely half of Southern Paiute children reached adulthood with their native band, creating a crisis of enormous proportions. Not only were hunting and gathering limited by these powerful intruders, the population became so small and so spread out that agriculture, their other staple, suffered as well. By 1830, the Southern Paiute were under great duress. They had become prey for many. They were too close to the peoples of the Mojave in ways of life to successfully defend themselves against more aggressive cultures.

Even as their lot worsened in the 1820s, the Southern Paiute had not yet encountered the most powerful culture that later influenced them. Despite the enthusiastic rhetoric of American exploration, the young nation had not yet reached the lands that became Nevada. Their multipronged westward movement took many forms. First came government representatives, men such as Lewis and Clark, who headed west in 1804 in the aftermath of the Louisiana Purchase. The addition of these lands gave the young nation an enormous stake in the West, but no one knew exactly what the new territory contained. Lewis and Clark set out to explore and to discern what was out there so that government officials could make policies for settlement. This pattern of exploration continued even beyond the Civil War.

American expansion took other forms as well. The mountains of the West were well stocked with fur-bearing animals, and a new breed of protocapitalist, the mountain man, set out to bring them in. The beaver became the most highly valued, their pelts a commodity prized for hats—from the standard tricorner of the Revolutionary War era and beyond to broad-brimmed hats to keep off the rain to the high-crowned "Beau Brummell" that gentlemen of the era preferred. High fashion in the capitals of Europe, these hats of beaver skin created an unparalleled economic opportunity, but only for those bold enough to brave the high elevation winters of the American West.

The beaver trade and the mountain men who plied it were in the forefront of an entrepreneurial revolution. A handful of men, many of whom initially knew little of the West or even the outdoors, headed out into the lands of the Louisiana Purchase and beyond in search of beavers to trap. They found the animal in abundance in the mountains of the West—the Rockies, the Wasatch, the Sierra Nevada, and elsewhere. Despite the image of mountain men as people who chose to be apart from their society, most were unmarried economic entrepreneurs who, if asked, would likely say that their goal was to make enough money to live well in an eastern city.

By the 1820s, 100,000 beaver pelts a year were used in the hat trade, prompting a rush to the mountains by many who intended to profit from the opportunity. These entrepreneurs fanned out all over the mountains of the West and as they trapped, they served a dual function as explorers. They saw a great deal, drew maps for their own use, shared information with one another and with outsiders, and a few even wrote about their experiences, paving the way for subsequent settlement.

Mountain men led dangerous, hard, often miserable and lonely lives. They usually worked in pairs, wading in cold streams to lay traps. Most did not see anyone except their trapping partner for months at a time. If they did encounter anyone else, it was almost certain to be Native Americans, unlikely to welcome Anglo-Americans taking animals from their rivers. Although many mountain men integrated into native culture, many others found that positive relationships with the people around them remained out of reach.

By the time trappers reached the lands that became Nevada, they had a twenty-year history in the West that created the beginnings of a social structure. It centered on the annual rendezvous, when trappers would meet at an agreed-upon place on a specific day, often the Fourth of July, to trade their furs and enjoy themselves. The location and time had been selected months before when the factor, the representative of the trading company, supplied them for the coming season. Affiliated in loose organizations and funded by outside backers, trappers needed to be assured of resupply in the middle of the season. The factor would meet them at the predesignated time and place to take the furs they had already harvested and provide them with supplies to finish the trapping season. As the rendezvous developed, it became a week-long trade fair that simultaneously mimicked Indian trade fairs and the growing commercial markets of the East. The partying was legendary.

Possibly the first Anglo-American to see Nevada was a trapper, Jedediah Smith, an experienced mountain man and entrepreneur when he arrived at the Cache Valley Rendezvous in the summer of 1826. Twenty-seven years old at the time, Smith had just purchased the Rocky Mountain Fur Company along with William Sublette and David Jackson. Seeking to expand his new company's business, Smith left the Great Salt Lake on August 16, 1826, accompanied by seventeen men. They headed along the Sevier River, which disappeared into a dry lake bed; so they traversed a mountain range and found the Virgin River, entering present-day Nevada near Bunkerville. The Virgin led to the Colorado River, but food was scarce; they got pumpkins and other food from the Paiute, but they noted that these new people had much less to give than the mountain peoples they had earlier met. The constant assaults on them as well as the limits of the land they lived on had already begun to take a toll on the Southern Paiute.

When they reached the Colorado River, Smith recognized it as an important source of sustenance, not only for him and his men, but for the people whose lands they crossed. The party followed the river as their supplies ran short, getting hungrier and hungrier and finding no sign of beaver. As fall began to change to winter, Smith decided the expedition was a failure. He prepared to return to the Great Salt Lake, but then spoke to some Mojave people he encountered and decided to continue on to the west. Eventually, his party was attacked, most likely by Utes or Navajos returning home after raiding California, but possibly by Southern Paiute, who by that point had good reason to fear all newcomers.

Smith's party spent time in the California desert with the Mojave, and he compared these people favorably to the Southern Paiute. The Mojave lived better than the Paiute; they possessed horses, and they sowed fields in the floodplain of the Colorado River. The Mojave told Smith that a ten-day journey to the west would bring them to the Mexican settlements in California. Smith pushed on, astonishing the Mexican authorities when he arrived at Mission San Gabriel near Los Angeles. Mexican officials were rightly upset by the appearance of an American trapper and they ordered the party to leave immediately. Smith and his men pleaded with the authorities and were allowed to stay into January. As ordered, they departed by the route they came, then took a sharp left and headed north. With fresh horses and stores, they once again crossed the San Bernardino Mountains and went north to the San Joaquin Valley. The party reached the American River, but could not find a way to cross the Sierra Nevada. They caught plenty of beaver and made plans to return in time for the rendezvous at Cache Valley.

Returning was more difficult than the men imagined. Smith and two men began a remarkable journey that took them along the south shore of Walker Lake and then east to Hot Creek. From there they made their way back to the Great Salt Lake roughly following what is now U.S. Highway 6 through Nevada. The trek took them by the Pancake Range, in the shadow of White Pine Peak and past Mount Wheeler. Smith reached the Cache River Rendezvous, where he had started the year before, on July 3, 1827. The journey had been an ordeal, but Jedediah Smith could rightly claim to be the first American in the land that later became Nevada.

Although Smith did not stay long in Nevada and never returned, he served as a harbinger of a new culture with different values than the Spanish. American culture, first and foremost, was a settler culture. When Thomas Jefferson sent Lewis and Clark on their expedition, he asked for an inventory of the lands of the Louisiana Purchase to see what could be made of them. By the 1820s, Americans had shown their expansionist streak and anyone who looked would have seen a culture chafing to settle more land. Spanish and Mexican patterns of settlement were different. Rather than populate with their own people, they sought to convert and harness native peoples for their purposes. Their primary institutions—the mission, the source of faith, and the presidio, the garrison—differed greatly from the American emphasis on individuality, cloaked in the language of democracy. If the old axiom "to populate is to govern" held true, then the question of who would populate the Silver State was already answered.

Smith initiated a process of opening the way for future endeavors, but he was not alone. Peter Skene Ogden of the Hudson's Bay Company, a competitor of Smith's Rocky Mountain Fur Company, may have entered the northeastern tip of what later became Nevada a few months before Smith. Ogden explored more substantially in 1828 and 1830, part of a move by the British company to keep Americans out of the Pacific Northwest by challenging them in the southern mountains. Ogden came into Nevada from the north, likely entering near modern Denio, and proceeded to the Humboldt River Valley. He called it the "Unknown River," and he and his men trapped along the river long enough to find out that it did not reach the Pacific Ocean. When the weather got rough, they retreated to the Great Salt Lake, where they knew they could find buffalo to sustain them through the winter.

Ogden returned to Nevada in the spring of 1829 and again in the fall, furthering his own claim to be the leading explorer of the Silver State. He was followed by other explorers: Ewing Young in 1829, Antonio Armijo in 1829–1830, and William Wolfskill and George C. Yount in 1830–1831. Their efforts led to the first "road" across Nevada. The Old Spanish Trail was a Mexican internal road: it traveled from Mexican New Mexico across lands ceded to Mexico and on to Mexican California. The presence of Americans on that road was the same sort of threat Mexican authorities experienced in Texas, as the Anglo-American population grew in numbers and began its revolt. Subsequent English-speaking travelers found Mexican California no friendlier than had Smith.

At this early stage of American expansion, the primary motivation for most individuals who reached Nevada was economic gain. Finding lands for which there was yet little competition—at least among Europeans—they worked to exploit the resources of the state. Trapping parties came in numbers; hunters followed. They too collided with native peoples, worsening the lot of the already threatened Southern Paiute. One trapping party in 1832 with which mountain man Joe Meek traveled shot a Southern Paiute "to keep him from stealing traps," an extreme act that smacked of the contempt that Anglo-Americans in that era often felt for Indian people.

From the point of view of these economic entrepreneurs, the Nevada they found offered them little. Most found the area barren and unappealing. Game was scarce and hard to track, especially in the higher mountains. The region was dry, except alongside the rivers, and in general its promise seemed limited to people who looked with nineteenth-century eyes that placed value on timber and grasslands. But this wide expanse of desert and mountains stood between the American Republic and the Pacific Coast. It would have to be addressed, dealt with in some fashion, if the United States was to carry out what more and more people believed was its continental destiny.

That destiny took some unusual forms. In 1831, Capt. Benjamin Bonneville of the U.S. Army requested a leave of absence to head a fur-trapping expedition in the Rocky Mountains. Bonneville's change of role, from Army officer to trapper, has led to questions about his motives. Clearly he constructed a story that made him simply an economic actor, not one tied, at least at that moment, to larger American goals of exploration. Whether anyone representing Mexico who he or his men encountered would believe that story was quite another question.

Bonneville's exploring expedition sent a group headed by Joseph Walker ostensibly to explore the western shore of the Great Salt Lake. In reality, Walker had been asked to spy on Mexican California. When he followed Ogden's Unknown River—which the group renamed the Barren River—Walker and his men found a climate that repelled them. One wrote of the region: "everything here seems to declare that, here man shall not dwell," a fitting description of a place that challenged the skills of even these hardy explorers.

The party proceeded down the Humboldt River, finding an area of ample grass for grazing that immensely pleased them. They thought they could simply take it, but as many as nine hundred Northern Paiute blocked their way. The grass was theirs and they intended to defend it. Walker and his men piled their baggage up to build a barricade and refused Paiute entreaties to smoke a pipe. The situation seemed dire until Walker's men fired their guns at some ducks in a nearby marsh. At the sound, the Indians fell to the ground. When they saw that the ducks were dead, they were astonished. The trappers then shot holes through a beaver skin that the Northern Paiute held as a target. The power of technology extricated Walker and his men from a dicey situation.

After this impressive display, the party continued the next day, with the Indians trailing Walker and his men. Walker felt threatened by a group of about one hundred who wanted the party to stop and smoke with them, and Walker decided to assert his power. "We must kill a lot of them, boys," Walker told his men, and the party of thirty-two trappers surrounded the following Indians and fired at them. About thirty-five Paiute fell, many dying on the spot. Walker's men put the wounded out of their misery, and the action started an intense hatred of Walker by the Paiute as well as announcing Americans as the new predator.

Walker and his men continued west toward California, arriving on November 25, 1833, at Mission San Juan Bautista, located south of modern San José and just west of Hollister. The Mexican priests and officials were certainly dismayed to find yet another group of Americans who had managed to cross the Sierra Nevada. They provided hospitality to Walker and his men, who remained for about six weeks, traveled to the ocean, and departed on their return trip in January 1834. Six men stayed behind, entranced by the prospects. They were perhaps the first Americans to succumb to the California dream, but certainly not the last.

Walker's expedition disrupted the geopolitical structure of expansion. It was a wake-up call, part of a growing pattern that deeply concerned Mexico. The entire northern frontier of Mexico seemed in upheaval. In Texas, agitation for independence from Mexico had begun. Smith had earlier shown up in California, and now here came another American. The scent of the American military was not far from Walker or Bonneville. Mexican authorities in California had to wonder if an invasion of some kind or another was imminent. The potential for an international incident was high.

Walker's expedition also illustrated an ongoing theme in early Nevada history. California, not Nevada, was the goal. The Golden State was then perceived as a land of abundance, where wealth could be easily made and where ordinary people lived well. The lands that became Nevada were merely the harsh and barren reality that had to be crossed to reach that promised land. This stark contrast explained not only the behavior of explorers and others, but began the historic relationship between the Silver State and its vastly larger golden cousin to the west.

Walker's return trip demonstrated this principle in clear relief. The party left the Owens Valley and headed due east instead of going north to the Humboldt River. This route took them across Death Valley and toward modern Tonopah, Nevada. The inauspicious choice of a route was largely without water and by early April, the weather had grown increasingly hot. Game was almost nonexistent. Short of food and water, the party suffered. The stock fared worst. In April alone, sixty-four horses, ten cows, and fifteen dogs died. Some dogs gazed into their master's faces in anguish, howled at the top of their lungs, and fell over dead. The men fought among themselves as they tried to decide whether to go forward or return to California. In the end, they determined to return to California, but the party could not find its own tracks from just a few months earlier to retrace their route. They stumbled around on the Eastern Sierra until they found landmarks from the previous year, reached the Humboldt River, and had to fight their way through to Captain Bonneville's camp on the Bear River. If the harsh nature of this vast expanse of desert had at all been in doubt, Walker's party conclusively proved that the area was unlikely to yield easily to nineteenth-century humans.

Travelers continued to come, in search of California. Some, such as the thirty-two-person John Bartleson party that sought to reach California in 1841, were told that they should be careful "not to go too far south, lest we should get into a waterless country without grass." Nevada's vaunted arid character was already evident to emigrants. The party had to reduce the loads on its wagons because the animals could not pull the weight through the desert; on one occasion, they had to burn a few of their wagons for fuel. They covered eighteen to twenty miles each day down the Humboldt River, surrounded by what one member of the party, John Bidwell, called "the interminable sagebrush." This hardy plant grew in such abundance and became so dense that it made it difficult to cut trails and even caused light wagons to overturn.

Bartleson proved inadequate to the task of leadership. The portly leader took seven men and some oxen and went ahead of the party. When they reached Carson Lake, the heavyset Bartleson had become a slim man whose clothes hung upon him. He and his men were happy to take food from the friendly Paiute near the lake, who offered fish and pine nuts. Bartleson had had enough. "Boys," he insisted, "if I ever get back to Missouri I will never leave that country. I would gladly eat out of the troughs with my dogs." While it would be hard to classify Bartleson as a prominent explorer, his experience reinforced the perception of the harshness of Nevada's climate. The stories of the brutal passage spread, and travelers became wary of the lands that later became the Silver State.

A new kind of exploration began in the 1840s, driven by imperial aspirations of the American Republic. The noted explorer and sometimes renegade John C. Frémont explored Nevada in 1844 and 1845 as part of his efforts to spy on California for the Manifest Destiny contingent in Congress, headed by his father-in-law, Missouri Senator Thomas Hart Benton. As Americans aggressively pursued not only the exploration of the Louisiana Purchase, but also surrounding lands that the nation had earlier ceded, Frémont became a pivotal player. He cut a dashing figure in the mid-nineteenth century, and his accounts, likely penned by his wife Jessie Benton Frémont, captivated the public. Frémont gave the first full-fledged accounting of Nevada.

When Frémont left St. Louis in 1843, he was no longer part of a vanguard of discovery. Instead, he was a pioneer in a mass movement—the first great migration to Oregon and California. There were parties ahead of his men, some seeking more than land in the distant West, but no other had quite the political positioning of Frémont. His journey was as much of conquest as exploration, part of nation-building and expansion even more than individual economic gain.

On New Year's Day 1844, Frémont's party of twenty-five men reached the Black Rock Desert. They were a hardy bunch, including such veterans of the fur trade and exploration as Christopher "Kit" Carson and mountain man Thomas "Broken Hand" Fitzpatrick. Even these experienced men were stymied by Nevada. They saw the white vapor plumes of nearby hot springs and made their way down a creek that seemed otherworldly. The terrain was burnt, and it looked to the men like heaps of coal and cinders. Ice, snow, and salty soil made travel difficult. Frémont's party packed a twelve-pound howitzer, and the mules struggled to pull its weight. They encountered a dense fog, so thick that men who went after horses got lost and struggled to find the party. "We were evidently on the verge of the desert which had been reported to us," Frémont wrote. "The appearance of the country was so forbidding that I was afraid to enter it."

With imperial designs, Frémont's men stumbled around, in search of the mythic Rio Buenaventura, the fictitious river that was supposed to reach the Pacific Ocean from the interior. They went south, reaching the Granite Creek Desert. No relief was in sight, and the prospects for finding a way to California seemed ever slimmer with each passing day. Nevada remained as it had always been—an obstacle to the goals of people with bigger horizons.

Miraculously, the party's fortunes changed. Frémont and Carson came upon a deep green-blue lake, an oasis amid the dried-out brown of the desert. They saw herds of mountain goats, more ducks than they could imagine, and trout they described as being as big as the salmon of the Columbia River. When the rest of the party arrived, local Paiute gave them fish and a terrific feast ensued. Frémont named this body of water "Pyramid Lake." Excited about the prospects of the region, the party continued along the Truckee River and crossed to the Carson River. Kit Carson looked for signs of beaver, sure that if he sighted evidence of this furry animal, it would point the way to a water route to the coast.

The party persisted, with Frémont taking them over Carson Pass in the middle of winter, an attempt so foolhardy that even the nearby Washoe people tried to discourage him. In sign language, they told him the snow was too deep. The crossing was brutal. It took a full thirty days and exhausted the party. Some Indian guides deserted; others simply sat down and sang their death songs. One man lost his wits; another disappeared into the snow and was presumed dead. Years later, he appeared one spring day in Jefferson, Missouri. Frémont persevered, and his men made it to John Sutter's ranch along the American River in late winter. This far north and nearly one hundred miles inland, the Mexican authorities held little sway. Sutter let Frémont stay the winter.

In April Frémont and his men left California, once again crossing the Sierra Nevada, this time through the lower San Joaquin Valley to Tehachapi Pass, and explored the Mojave Desert and Southern Nevada. The party found little to recommend the area. The route was as rough and rocky as any Frémont had followed in the West, and the party's pack animals suffered. They reached the Old Spanish Trail and thought their travails were over. But even on known roads, the way was difficult. At the water holes along the Old Spanish Trail, the grass was scarce. Too many travelers had depleted the resource. Some springs contained bad water, bitter to the taste and heavy with minerals. The party struggled until they reached the meadows, "Las Vegas" in Spanish, where they met Joseph Walker, who served as a lieutenant on the Bonneville expedition. Walker's vast knowledge of the mountain geography helped them find their way back.

Frémont's report on his journey was a galvanizing moment in American expansion. With the help of Charles Preuss, who drew the first great map of the West to accompany Frémont's report, and with the writing skill of Jessie Benton Frémont, a mere chronicle of exploration became romance and art. Frémont told of the lands he'd seen with vigor and passion. His report was widely hailed as a monumental effort, one that powerfully transformed the young nation's vision of its possibilities. Even more telling, it was widely influential. Frémont's work reached many who looked to the West to settle, to make new lives, to fulfill the increasingly powerful notion of the Manifest Destiny of an American continent.

Nevada's bizarre topography was an important part of the Frémont report. Here was a land he described as unlike any other, not easily settled, and lacking the attributes that the nineteenth century valued. Yet at the same time, the conquest of this harsh and forbidding land was not only an objective, it was part of a national mission. This remote and wild place inspired many who looked west, and as they turned their dreams into actions, they depended on Frémont and his assessments. Exploration had been the vanguard. Now, it became the blueprint for further national expansion, the symbol of an aggressive policy of conquest that persuaded Americans of their destiny. Before Frémont, the question of a continental republic inspired debate. After Frémont, a nation that stretched from coast to coast seemed inevitable.

Frémont returned to Nevada in 1845, but this time, his motives were entirely different. With a bellicose Polk administration already gearing up for war, Frémont was ordered back in February, one of three military expeditions sent to prepare the way for conflict. Frémont's orders confined him to exploring the Arkansas River basin in modern Colorado, Kansas, and Oklahoma, but he defied them and took a company of sharpshooters across the central Rockies to California. From the Great Salt Lake, he headed across the Great Basin, first reaching Pilot Peak and then the Humboldt Mountains. There he divided his party and cut diagonally to the southwest to reach the Humboldt Sink. Frémont had made a new transcontinental route. He reported that he could reach Sutter's ranch from what is now Colorado in just thirty-five days. This route, he announced, would also accommodate wagons.

Frémont's defiance was arrogant and provocative. Not only had he ignored his orders, he blatantly crossed the international boundary to California, daring the Mexican authorities to respond to this incursion. Frémont's men moved leisurely through the Salinas Valley, proceeding to Klamath Lake in what is now Oregon. After a visit from Marine Lieutenant Archibald Gillespie, Frémont and his men returned to California to take part in the ill-fated Bear Flag Revolt, a poorly organized attempt to seize the Golden State and establish an English-speaking government. Historians have debated whether Gillespie brought Frémont an order to return to California or Frémont took this bold step of his own volition. It makes little difference. Frémont's return hastened the American takeover of California and the ultimate organization of Nevada, first as a territory and then as a state.

The 1845 expedition meant a great deal less than its immediate predecessor, but it continued the pattern of American exploration and the subsequent consolidation of control. The most important thing that Frémont did in Nevada in 1845 was to discover the shorter route. He made it possible for the emigrants streaming up the trail toward Oregon and California to have confidence in their ability to cross the desert with speed and relative safety. Their confidence was not always rewarded, as the experience of the Donner Party—whose members were forced to resort to cannibalism as they were frozen in the snows of the Sierra in the winter of 1846–1847—so graphically illustrated.

Frémont did something else important for Nevada. He made it real in a way that earlier explorers had not. His maps and especially his measurements of time suggested that the place could be tamed, that people could first safely traverse it, and in the aftermath, find reasons and places to stay. Although Frémont's adventures set off no rush to Nevada in the way that occurred in California and Oregon, it did create the possibility that the bold and the innovative might very well find a way to take this harsh land and make it their own.

And come they did, in ever greater numbers, headed for the rich farmlands of Oregon and California. Soon, a few spilled over and stayed in the lands that became Nevada. Few in number and closely tied to water sources and overland routes of travel, they became the first Euro-Americans to settle Nevada, and their presence was a product of geopolitical forces. Their motives were varied, their objectives equally diverse. Conversely, they created first an American territory and then a state.

2 Making a Territory and a State

THE ROAD to territorial and eventual state status for Nevada began far away from the remote deserts and mountains of the West, in the excitement of an expansionist nation feeling its newfound strength and trying to manage the tension associated with its growth. This path was neatly wrapped in national sentiments about expansion, about the growth of the American nation and its manifest destiny—a term that became popular and soon acquired capital letters and quotation marks as "Manifest Destiny," the idea not only that the continent belonged to the new American nation, but that the nation's future was its ability to expand. Along with the issue of slavery tearing at the fabric of the nation, Manifest Destiny determined American policy throughout the 1840s and 1850s.

Three catalytic events—the Mexican-American War, the Mormon exodus, and the California Gold Rush—defined the future of the land that soon became Nevada and linked it to the rest of the nation. Each of the catalysts brought greater attention to the area that became Nevada, changing political power, population, and economic opportunities. Separate from one another but close in time, the three created enough emphasis on the region that the settlement of the area followed—an outcome that was as much a response to economic forces and political needs as it was to the demands of American expansion.

The Mexican-American War had been brewing for a while when it finally exploded in the spring of 1846. The election of James K. Polk, an avowed expansionist, helped create the conditions that led to the war. In his first message to the U.S. Congress, Polk announced that he would not tolerate European powers in North America without American consent. Spoiling to challenge Great Britain, he claimed all of the disputed Oregon territory in a move that became the basis of his policy, the "Polk Doctrine." Polk loudly put European powers on notice that the West belonged to the United States. An articulation of the concept of Manifest Destiny, Polk's vision of the U.S. role in the West opened the way to military conflict. The United States would dominate the continent, and beware any nation, European or otherwise, that challenged American sovereignty.

In March 1846 conflict began, albeit not with Great Britain or another European power, but with Mexico, the U.S.'s neighbor to the south. In the newly added state of Texas, Gen. Zachary Taylor took his troops to the Rio Grande, an area claimed by both Mexico and the U.S., and built fortifications. The Mexican army in Matamoros treated this maneuver as an act of aggression and responded in kind. Tensions mounted. Taylor was warned to retreat to the Nueces River, the established boundary between the two countries. Mexico tried to resolve the dispute, but the warlike Polk administration refused diplomatic options. On April 24, 1846, a Mexican cavalry troop inflicted a few casualties on U.S. troops blockading a Mexican town. Two days later, Gen. Taylor reported that a war had begun.

The war was a rout. Despite opposition at home from a wide cut of American society, including the writer Henry David Thoreau and a young congressman named Abraham Lincoln, the well-armed American army overran the weaker Mexican forces. The war spread to California, where the famous explorer John C. Frémont had again managed to intrigue. Frémont helped orchestrate the Bear Flag Revolt, in which at Frémont's prompting, a number of Americans seized the rancho of Mariano Vallejo, a Mexican citizen who was nevertheless sympathetic to the American cause, and proclaimed the short-lived Bear Flag Republic. Although the revolt failed, American troops did take California, and in the Treaty of Guadalupe Hidalgo that followed the U.S. received California and all or part of six states. All other Mexican claims to the north were extinguished. As a result of the war, Nevada became an unorganized part of the United States.

The Mexican-American War established the United States as a transcontinental republic, the most powerful in North America, and began a pattern of dominance in hemispheric affairs that persists today. It also reignited the free state-slave state controversy that had dogged the Union since its founding in 1776; for by adding new land that could become states, the Mexican Cession, as the lands acquired under the Treaty of Guadalupe Hidalgo were formally called, upset the delicate equilibrium of slave and free states that allowed the Union to function. Equally important, it cleared the way for westward expansion inside the United States. When Americans went west before 1846, they often passed into lands held or claimed by other nations. After the war, and by the time the Gadsden Purchase of 1853 resolved boundary issues, the United States held authority over the entire American Southwest, including the lands that became Nevada.

There were challenges to the newly proclaimed American sovereignty in the West, but the most potent came not from a European nation, but from the most successful of the new religions that sprang up in the fertile soil of the rapidly urbanizing nation early in the nineteenth century. Nevada's first European settlers were part of a larger migration that transformed the Intermountain West. The westward movement of the members of the Church of Jesus Christ of Latter-Day Saints after the murder of their founder, Joseph Smith, in Nauvoo, Illinois, in 1844, was the first systematic migration of English-speaking people to the Far West. Unlike the settlers who headed out along the Oregon Trail, the Mormons moved as a community, en masse and for communal goals, as they had before when they faced violent resistance to their way of life. They sought places that would not be attractive to others, finding on the front range of the Wasatch Basin a sufficiently hospitable location to settle that they expected others would not want. Brigham Young, Smith's successor and a hard-nosed leader who kept the flock together, fashioned a new nation in the western desert. Called Deseret, this Mormon nation would be composed of the Great Basin and an outlet to the Pacific Ocean near San Diego. In it, these Latter-Day Saints intended a kingdom of God on earth.

As they began to forge a society in the desert, the Mormons looked for ways to expand their frontier. Hostile to the American nation and its all-inclusive expansionist goals, the Mormons planned a periphery around their Salt Lake City core. Young soon dispatched Mormon settlers to create viable communities that would shield the nascent State of Deseret from intrusion from the "Gentiles" around it. As initial settlements prospered in southern Utah, in what became known as "Mormon Dixie," the Mormon community became sufficiently prosperous to support additional outlying communities. Young sent groups farther from Salt Lake City to establish missions and trading posts, crossing into what became Nevada and reaching as far as modern San Bernardino, California. Several of the earliest communities in what became the state of Nevada started as the offspring of Mormon expansion.

In the meantime, the discovery of gold at Sutter's Mill in California in 1848 put Nevada in the direct path of the most diverse and disorganized migration in American history. If the Mormon migration was comprised of a community of religious refugees seeking freedom from the institutions of what they regarded as an oppressive society, the Gold Rush was individualistic to the core. It drew masses of entrepreneurs, adventurers, ne'er-do-wells, and nearly everyone else who could walk, ride, or crawl across the country to the Golden State in search of riches. They created American California in a heartbeat, using their numbers to swamp the Spanish and Mexicans who preceded them. Wealth was the primary goal of most, making the society they spawned more than a little bit harrowing. The goldfields proved a chimera for the overwhelming majority. As always, the real wealth for nearly everyone was not in the goldfields, but in supplying the goods that miners needed. No less an American institution than Levi Strauss got its start in the Gold Rush, becoming a leading source of apparel and more. The lesson that Strauss taught was not lost on many others.

The town frequently considered the first in Nevada, Mormon Station—later Genoa—perfectly followed this service model. Situated on the eastern flank of the Sierra in the Carson Valley, very close to the Carson River route over the Sierra Nevada, the place was a natural resting and refueling stop before wagons headed across the Sierra Nevada to the goldfields beyond. A Mormon party led by Joseph DeMont and Hampton S. Beatie arrived in the Carson Valley in June 1850, and the two men recognized that the location was an excellent spot from which to supply wagon trains planning the brutal trek across the High Sierra. The men built a cabin, set up a trading post, and imported goods from California to sell to passersby at exorbitant prices. Their peak season was in the spring and summer; as winter approached and the emigrant trains slowed and finally stopped, they sold to a man named Moore. Some of the party went on to California; others, including Beatie, returned to Salt Lake City. As 1850 ended, permanent settlement in the Carson Valley seemed unlikely. Despite its roots in a communitarian society that needed outlying settlements to protect its aspirations, Mormon Station looked to be another of the countless trading posts that sprung up along western trails and rapidly faded into oblivion.

The Carson Valley's fate turned out to be considerably different. Upon Beatie's return to Utah's capital, he found work in a general store run by two brothers, Enoch and John Reese, who became excited at Beatie's tales of the Carson Valley. In April 1851, John Reese loaded a wagon train with supplies and set out for the Carson Valley. When he arrived in July, he purchased the trading post from Moore, built a permanent structure, and with other families in the party, planted seeds they brought from Salt Lake City. Soon they had a small version of the kind of communities Mormons created all over the interior

West. Reese's endeavor soon drew others who dreamed of similar success. They arrived throughout the year, starting farms in the Carson Valley and in Jack's Valley and Eagle Valley to the north.

An established businessman even before he left Salt Lake City, Reese did not limit his efforts to catering to passing wagon trains and growing crops. Placer miners in an area called Gold Canyon, some twenty-five miles northeast of the Carson Valley, became consistent customers and Reese recognized them as an ongoing and possibly lucrative market. A passing emigrant train had discovered gold in Gold Canyon in 1850. Although it was not enough to distract men headed for the supposedly infinite wealth of California, any tale of gold attracted notice in the goldfields of the Golden State as the best claims played out and the yields fell. Through with California, some miners returned to Gold Canyon early in 1851. As John Reese passed by on his way to the Carson Valley that same year, he saw the miners and began a commercial relationship with them.

This little settlement on the Carson River was somewhere between Utah's Zion and California's Eden. The proximity of goldfields in California and the migration they spawned had a powerful cultural influence on the Carson Valley. Wagon trains brought news and goods; migrants exposed the Mormon community in the Carson Valley to exactly the kinds of secular and nationalistic influences its leaders feared. Utah exerted a powerful counter influence. The region's leading citizens were Mormons, and the Carson Valley and surrounding areas were nominally attached to the Utah Territory in law. The Carson Valley was so far from the capital at Salt Lake City, more than 650 miles away in a time when twenty miles a day was a great deal to cover, that such ties were scant. Salt Lake City cared little for its remote outlier; on the rare occasions that some official representative arrived, the trip was so long and the stay so comparatively short that the influence was even more limited than might be anticipated. As a result, the Carson Valley seemed torn between the close-at-hand secular world and its promise of individual riches and the more distant but spiritually powerful communitarian world of early Mormonism. A battle between secular influence and Mormon control seemed to loom in the shadow of the Sierra.

It came to a head in November 1851, when more than one hundred settlers met to create a squatter government in a series of meetings at Reese's Mormon Station. The very idea of a squatter government showed the influence of California. Such governments became the method of choice in mining camps throughout the Sierra. Adapting the model to the Carson Valley was a simple task. The group took three substantive actions: the squatters created a set of regulations regarding surveying, buying, and selling real estate; they elected officers to govern their community; and they crafted a petition addressed to the U.S. Congress to ask for an independent territory for the Carson Valley and its surroundings.

The missive to Washington, D.C., was a threat to Mormon control of the Carson Valley that stemmed in no small part from the frustration of Mormon settlers far from the core of their spiritual world. It was also a political move that upset the existing power structure in the newly settled American Far West. In response, Brigham Young incorporated the Carson Valley into the Utah Territory's political structure. He extended existing county lines all the way to the California border, creating vast horizontal counties that encompassed the settlements at the base of the Sierra Nevada but left enormous empty spaces in between. Young's response satisfied Utah far more than the settlers in the Carson Valley. Despite the extension of political domain, the new arrangement did not lead to a greater presence by the territorial government and frustration grew. Mormons and their Gentile neighbors began displaying an early version of the tension that would plague the routes through Deseret for decades.

The solution for non-Mormon settlers was self-rule, and they soon closely considered that alternative. In 1853, a group of forty-three Carson Valley residents petitioned the state of California to annex the valleys and provide government. The reasons for this entreaty have been interpreted in different ways. Some suggest that Gentile settlers sought California affiliation as a result of frustration with their Mormon neighbors. Others believe that the desire for a functioning government crossed religious boundaries and stemmed from neglect by the Utah territory. Either way, it was impossible to interpret the petition as anything other than a rejection of Utah's political control of the Carson Valley.

Hearing of the effort, Brigham Young sought to keep the far edge of his budding empire under his sway. In January 1854, he formed Carson County, Utah, encompassing most of what is now Nevada, as a separate county in Utah Territory, but this declaration had little effect on day-to-day life in the Carson Valley. No actual governance was attached to it. Young and the settlers continued to parry back and forth until summer 1854, when a group of citizens in the Carson Valley drew up a constitution for an independent "colony" government. In their view, neither California nor Utah would act on their behalf. Although no evidence demonstrates that this constitution was presented for a vote of the settler community, its very existence may have persuaded the Utah territorial legislature to begin to create actual government in and around the Carson Valley.

Young faced a difficult choice. Only on-the-ground institutions could establish the Utah Territory's firm claim on its distant periphery, and with a near revolt on his hands—undertaken by perfectly legal means by a secular group—Young used the mechanisms of government to keep the Carson Valley under his jurisdiction. Quickly, the rudiments of government appeared. In January 1855, the Utah legislature created a separate U.S. judicial district in the Carson Valley, with Young appointing church officials to county positions. Orson Hyde, one of the top officials in the Mormon Church, became probate judge and county judge for the new district. Yet difficulties remained. Hyde's jurisdiction was more than six hundred miles from his residence, necessitating a long and treacherous trip to prove Utah's control. In May 1855, Hyde's party left Salt Lake City to make the trek to Carson County and establish once and for all Utah's claim to the far reaches of its realm.

The mission left as Utah's hold on its periphery was at its weakest point. California had been ascendant since the Gold Rush of 1848, and after hundreds of thousands of miners found that the boom did not last, many settled in the valleys and mountains and searched for other ways to make a living. They created the beginning of towns and trade, catered to wagon trains, and built the kinds of ties that demonstrated greater permanence than the appearance of miners might otherwise have suggested. In the creation of this regional network, they connected with the Carson Valley, bringing local economic influence to bear that was no less than equal to and likely considerably greater than the political influence of the distant Utah Territory. It was a classic American dilemma: did law or common practice hold sway?

Hyde's mission to the Carson Valley was part of the wave of missionary expeditions Young sent out to create the nation-state of Deseret. These endeavors stretched through southern Utah, beyond the Colorado River in the south and to San Bernardino in the west. Young planned de facto colonization of the Great Basin; his representatives seemingly occupied every water hole, well, and wet spot in the desert. One of those was a little oasis called Las Vegas, ("the meadows" by the Spanish). In 1855, Young appointed William Bringhurst to lead an expedition to the Las Vegas Valley and establish a mission there. The route to San Diego had been buttressed by a $25,000 appropriation to build a road from Salt Lake City to the California border and regular mail service began in 1854.

Young hoped that the community, then technically in New Mexico Territory, would not only provide supplies along the trail, but also help extend Mormon influence to the Pacific Ocean. Another Mormon settlement in Nevada began, this one far from the secular influences of the California Gold Rush.

When Hyde arrived in the Carson Valley in June 1855, he immediately took steps to establish Utah's claim to the area. Looking every bit the part of a government official, Hyde ordered a survey of the California boundary to ascertain that the Carson Valley was located in Utah. Once he established that the community fell within his jurisdiction, Hyde called for local elections. Mormon settlers were so dominant in the area that they nearly swept the election. Only one Gentile was elected to a county office. Local Gentiles responded with indignation, shouting of a Mormon coup d'état. They filed another petition asking California to annex them, which state officials there received more favorably than before. The California state legislature passed a resolution asking Congress to grant the settlers' petition, but no changes in jurisdiction or state boundaries followed. In Washington D.C., officials believed that the Utah Territory was addressing its prior neglect and should be allowed to continue. A large portion of Congress was also opposed to making California any larger than it already was.

Yet the request for annexation spurred Young to even more substantial measures. Then as now, battles over territory were settled with facts on the ground, by populating regions so as to affect control. Young sent more Mormon families to the area, creating the overwhelming dominance so common in settlement when the majority population gains political and governing power. Family after family came, creating not only social mores, but also an overwhelming political majority. By 1857 political and social control of the Carson Valley firmly resided in the hands of the Latter-Day Saints.

Utah's hold on this far edge soon became complicated by tension between the Mormon territory and the United States. In mid-July 1857, frustrated by nearly a decade of bad relations between Utah and the federal government, an exasperated President James Buchanan dismissed the officials of the Utah Territory, who were essentially the hierarchy of the Latter-Day Saints Church and included church leader Brigham Young, and replaced them with Gentiles. Howls of outrage shook Utah. In the view of the people of the territory, a horrible injustice had been done. Legitimate leaders had been replaced by the whim of faraway masters. From the point of view of the American government, they had replaced an illegal regime. The political climate disintegrated so badly that one British observer noted that the Mormons regarded the United States "pretty much as the states regarded England after the War of Independence." Insurrection loomed. Utah clamored against the change and threatened the safety of the new officials. In December, Buchanan requested that the U.S. Army be sent to Utah to protect his officials and assure the enforcement of federal law. Young perceived the action as an invasion of Deseret; the Mormons felt that they were to be persecuted again, as they had been in Missouri and Nauvoo. Young issued a call for all loyal Mormons to return to Salt Lake City and defend the faith.

Young's message affected the settlements in Nevada. The little Las Vegas colony that further established the Mormon claim to the land that became Nevada had already fallen into disarray. Hampered by withering heat, raids by local Paiute, and infighting in the group, the colony was coming apart even before Young's call to the members to return from their mission in 1857. It disintegrated as most of the settlers returned to Salt Lake City. News of Young's call arrived in the Carson Valley in September 1857, and an exodus immediately followed. Newspapers were told that the colony was moving to the Salmon River in the Washington Territory to allay suspicion, and within weeks nearly 450 Mormons in the area, almost two-thirds of the population, returned to Salt Lake City. About two hundred people, mostly miners, remained. The departing Mormons took court records back to Salt Lake City, and the Utah legislature abolished the independent judicial district in Carson County, costing the Carson Valley its representative in the territorial legislature. Those left in the Carson Valley and surrounding areas took advantage of the Mormons' situation, buying property for extremely low prices or simply appropriating it outright once the Mormons were gone. Mormon leader Orson Hyde cursed those who profited from the Mormons' departure, but there was little he could do. The crisis in Utah drew the Mormon community inward and the concept of an expansive nation-state of Deseret was at least temporarily abandoned.

As Utah waited to meet the Utah Expedition, the military force that was sent to quell the perceived rebellion, the people left in the Carson Valley pounced upon the opportunity to forever sever their ties to Utah. Squatter meetings again sought a functional government, and political chaos ensued. Gentiles did not want to participate in what some called the "spiritual despotism" of the Mormons, and they agitated for a separate territory. The military arrived in Utah and the Utah crisis ended with nominal American control of the institutions of government. The new governor of Utah territory, Alfred Cumming, who was not a Mormon, sought to keep the Carson Valley in Utah Territory. He appointed Carson Valley resident John S. Child as probate judge of the Carson Valley. In October 1858, Child called elections, but Gentiles charged fraud in four of six precincts to stave off a sweep by the Mormon candidates. Soon after, in January 1859, the Utah legislature again tried to reassert its authority. It restored Carson County's judicial independence as the Second Judicial District, attaching to it St. Mary's County and Humboldt County. John Cradlebaugh, a tall, lean Ohio lawyer with impeccable Yankee credentials, became federal district court judge.

Cradlebaugh's appointment suggested a new turn for Utah's remote county. Throughout the early 1850s, Mormon Utah had been the primary political influence on the territory's far edge. Political institutions were scant; instead social conditions determined political power and as long as Mormons remained the majority in the Carson Valley and ran the territory, Mormon political influence was stronger than any other. Even the repeated calls for annexation by California ultimately paled in comparison, and by the mid-1850s the possibility of an enormous and rebellious Mormon-run Utah that reached the Sierra Nevada seemed possible.

After Young's call and the departure of most of the Mormon population, the religious nature of the community dissipated and a more conventional American ethos took hold. The premise of Carson County became economic instead of community-based. Miners created customs as they did in the California goldfields, and these soon acquired the force of law. Even though an Ohio Yankee such as Cradlebaugh could be expected to be sympathetic to the miners, in many ways his presence or that of any authority was a threat to the independence they had enjoyed since the Mormon departure.

Before Cradlebaugh arrived, the settlers in the area attempted to create political realities that the new judge could not circumvent. On June 6, 1859, a public meeting in Carson City yielded a "provisional territorial constitution," created voting precincts, and set a date for a July election to ratify the constitution and elect officers and a legislature. When Cradlebaugh arrived in midsummer, he catered to the distrust of Mormonism, impaneling a federal grand jury to hear the complaints of Gentile settlers. After the July election, a representative, James M. Crane, went to Washington, D.C., to argue for independent territorial status. A constitutional convention opened in Genoa on July 18, yielding a document that included a declaration of cause for separation from Utah loosely modeled on the U.S. Declaration of Independence. A September 7, 1859, election was certified in December under unusual conditions, and Isaac Roop of Susanville, now in California, was elected governor. He was the only official among the electees who attempted to serve. Also in September, Cradlebaugh completed his report, which catalogued the Gentiles' grievances against Mormon government but failed to offer indictments.

The Carson Valley had erupted in a full-scale political struggle for power. On one side of a growing social and political divide, Cradlebaugh and the non-Mormon miners and settlers of the region pushed for secular order. Cradlebaugh quickly became comfortable as the official standard-bearer for this perspective. On the other, Brigham Young and Mormon Utah still tried to exercise control through the territorial legislature. Judge Child reasserted Utah's authority when he called for new elections, claiming that these would replace the previous ones, which he believed were tainted by charges of fraud.

The second set of elections was no more representative than the first, with only three of ten precincts opening to voters. Despite the borderline fraudulent conditions, Utah Territorial Governor Cumming and Child were so determined to reestablish Utah's sovereignty over its far western edge that they issued commissions to the victors in the elections. A situation that bordered on civil war grew even more threatening. Americans of the era were experienced with civic unrest; "Bleeding Kansas" was fresh in people's memories. Cooler heads prevailed along the eastern slope of the Sierra Nevada. The election winners wisely declined their commissions, refusing to serve without real electoral victory.

As 1860 began, two separate sets of elected officials could claim to represent this far western edge of the Utah territory, one sanctioned by the federal government and the other by Deseret, the name the Mormons had chosen for their home in the Utah territory. Neither side truly enjoyed legitimacy. When Roop's provisional legislature met in December 1859, it adjourned for lack of a quorum and never reconvened. President Buchanan removed Judge Cradlebaugh and appointed a replacement, but Cradlebaugh argued that the president had no right to remove a federal judge. R. P. Flenniken, Buchanan's choice for the position, arrived in Nevada and for six months two people in Carson County claimed exclusive federal judicial authority. At the same time, Child held an election for county office and territorial representative and opened the probate court for the first time in three years. The winners were certified, but their representation was local, and if they added legitimacy to Utah's claim to Washoe, it was soon superseded by a revolutionary change that altered the entire direction of the region's history. After June 1859, the focus of nearly everyone, regardless of religion or political persuasion, was the discovery of a tremendous lode of precious metals on nearby Sun Mountain. The eastern slope of the Sierra Nevada faced an onslaught similar to that of California a decade earlier. Political chaos lasted in no small part because there was no need to replace it, but the impact of the Comstock Lode created a tremendous need for effective government.

AMERICANS CAME FROM A CULTURE that by the mid-nineteenth century could best be described as rapacious. Americans saw in the New World the opportunity to get ahead, initially by owning land that gave them independence from the kind of tyranny that had been so common for so many in Europe, and later by other means. The America of farms and fields was already being outdone by its urban proto-industrial counterpart even before the Civil War, for land alone did not provide the aspiring nationalists with enough to accomplish their objectives. As commerce became the currency of the American nation, the rush for riches took other forms. Chief among them was the pursuit of gold. Next was silver.

In this, Nevada's location beside California was fortuitous. As the waves of travelers passed through on their way to the goldfields, they saw Nevada and heard of its possibilities. Mormon settlers found placer gold, the dust left in alluvial sands, and despite their efforts to keep quiet about the find, the backwash from the California goldfields were drawn to the western edge of the Utah territory. As the number of miners in California diminished, the easily accessible gold played out, and people looked for new places to mine, Nevada received the benefit of extra people, and in a few cases, new skills. They came in force, adding greatly to the population of the Carson Valley and its surroundings. Mining dominated the horizons of these newcomers, for the proximity of the Washoe front to the Sierra Nevada seemed to promise similar riches. Many were bitten by the gold bug, an expression of the obsession with the get-rich-quick ethos of mining.

For most such individuals, the move to Nevada did not improve their economic status. While California lent itself to individual prospecting in the easy harvesting of widely dispersed gold in streams and rivers, Nevada's enormous wealth was buried deep in the heart of a huge mountain. For most, there were no easy pickings in Nevada—no panning gold in the stream that led to great riches, no successful small claims that an individual could work by himself or with a friend, and few stories of individuals who simply wandered out of town and came back wealthy. Nevada mining was industrial mining; it required capital, organization, and equipment. It employed a labor force rather than serving as an entrepreneurial enterprise. It was for the big companies, not for the little guy. Geology made it so and the practice became institutionalized in the history of the state that was not yet born.

By 1859, the presence of precious metal in the western edge of Utah territory was known to many. Gold had first been discovered in Gold Canyon, Nevada, in 1850 by a passing group of emigrants, but with California and the prospect of wealth so near, they did not stop to develop their find. The word spread, and in 1851 miners who failed in California came back across the Sierra Nevada to see if they might fare better in its environs. Most were typical of the earlier miners who rushed to "see the elephant," as the expression went that described going to California—individuals who lacked resources but who had acquired a reasonable understanding of geology by the standards of the day from their experience and believed they knew where to find precious metals in the ground. They found more placer gold in the alluvial sands washed down from the mountains, discovering the ore in the same way that James Marshall did at Sutter's Mill just a few years before. Since most of the early miners in Nevada brought knowledge and experience from the California goldfields, they conceived of their new find in Gold Canyon much as they had in the initial phase of mining in the Golden State. "Color," as they called the specs of gold dust, drew them to the new location.

Miners divided up the goldfields according to the customs they developed in California. Typically, placer gold was evenly distributed over a wide area in shallow concentrations. By custom, a miner could claim only what he could work, a specific area of terrain. This prevented individual miners from tying up large claims. Under this practice, each miner got a piece of the wealth. It was evenly distributed among them, and no one miner was entitled to any more ground than he himself could profitably develop. This distribution promoted informal record-keeping that only minimally described boundaries between properties. All of the ground was more or less equally profitable, and the gold was generally spread widely over an area. Claims did not have to be precise—a few yards one way or the other did not make a considerable difference in the fortunes of individuals.

The real battle in mining was over the water, always scarce in the desert and made even more valuable by the high stakes of gold mining. Water washed the sand away from the heavier gold, allowing for great success with very little technology for fortunate individuals. When water was scarce, mercury could be used to separate the gold, but this method was considerably more expensive. It cost more than most miners could afford, placing a premium on water. As in western agriculture and ranching, whoever controlled the water supply controlled production, in this case, of gold. From these circumstances, the doctrine of prior appropriation—the concept of "first in time, first in right"— became enshrined in western water law, setting the stage for much of the conflict that seemed endemic in regional life.

Throughout the 1850s, placer miners worked Gold Canyon and neighboring Six Mile Canyon, finding enough gold to justify continuing their efforts. These miners, numbering somewhere near 150 men at the peak of production in 1852 and again in 1854–55, supported several saloons and a roadhouse. They were also the primary market for the produce of Mormon farms in the valleys along the Sierra Nevada. They greatly contributed to the agitation for governmental structure, as they needed officials to record mining claims and survey property, and demanded judges to hear the inevitable disputes. Unlike their Mormon neighbors, miners preferred a secular government from California or modeled closely on Californian patterns, such as the squatter or "provisional" government. Their demands stemmed from a combination of factors, including the tremendous distance to Salt Lake City and the general neglect of the Washoe by the territorial government, the general discomfort of the miners with theocratic Mormon decision making, and the fact that California's governmental institutions codified into law the traditions by which miners organized their activities. They played a significant role in the ongoing tension about governmental institutions in the far western Utah Territory.

While Mormon families settled and established what they hoped would become enduring communities, miners pushed hard to mine all the gold they could. By 1857, they had depleted the richest placer gold deposits, the total yield falling from a high of $118,400 in 1855 to $18,000 in 1857. The year of 1858 was even worse. Prospectors were accustomed to the easier mining at the base of mountains. There, they only needed to shovel placer sands into rockers to extract gold. Forced to look for more gold at higher elevations in the surrounding mountains, they faced a more intensive process. Gold found on the mountains proved even more difficult to obtain, for it had to be crushed into sand-sized particles before it could be washed through the placer tools miners used to recover the gold. This level of effort sent many miners in search of an easier way to make a living.

A drought in much of the western U.S. in 1857 and 1858 further limited mining in what later became Nevada. Drought diminished the already scant water supply, slowing production even further. Miners left the area in droves. Those who remained recognized that an era had come to an end. They needed more water to be able to do more work, and that water would not be available without capital. Investors required proof of rich deposits to make their expenditure worthwhile, but no such deposits had been found. Mining in Nevada seemed confined to small areas and a smaller scale. Especially in comparison to the wild California adventure of the preceding decade, the prospects for mining on the Washoe front seemed slim. The area needed some kind of major discovery to reverse its diminishing prospects.

Mining remained seasonal, especially at higher elevations. Winter snow and cold made prospecting and panning nearly impossible, and most miners went into town and spent the winter in the saloon, awaiting the promise of spring. Occasionally, if the weather broke, they could get out for some early exploring. In January 1859, a warm spell, called a "false spring," brought miners out in search of new goldfields. A group consisting of James "Old Virginny" Finney, John Bishop, Alexander Hamilton, and John Yount prospected a mound on the rocky slopes of Sun Mountain, at the head of Gold Canyon. They chose the spot because mining there was easy; the site was already sufficiently decomposed and did not require the heavily milling that they expected at such elevations. The men found a valuable deposit that promised to yield about $12.00 per day per miner, more than enough to bring other miners to the area. They and other miners, including Henry T. "Pancake" Comstock, James Rogers, Joseph Plato, William Knight, and Alexander "Sandy" Bowers, dug small shafts, eight to twenty feet in depth, which yielded more of the same kind of mineral content, enough to justify building a flume to carry water to the site from a creek a considerable distance away. Throughout the spring, the diggings remained profitable, and the lure of wealth attracted more miners. Californians crossed the Sierra in droves as soon as the winter snows receded, and a small-scale mining boom on Sun Mountain took shape, fueled by promises of $4,000 to $5,000 per share.

The same spring, miners working in Six Mile Canyon also ascended the slopes of Sun Mountain. In June 1859, Patrick McLaughlin and Peter O'Riley found a rich site well above other miners' diggings that contained a kind of blue-black crumbly rock not seen at lower elevations. This "annoying blue stuff," as they referred to it, was very heavy, and it impeded the separation of gold from rock with flowing water. Even though the work was an ordeal, the two men extracted great wealth that day. As they put away their equipment, one of the Gold Hill miners, Comstock, appeared and loudly insisted that he previously claimed the site that McLaughlin and O'Riley worked. No one really knows whether he had previously claimed the site, but the canny Comstock relied on the common response of miners in such situations. Because of the communal and informal nature of mining, when challenged, miners typically ceded part of their claim. Comstock's appearance also provided an advantage for McLaughlin and O'Riley: the presence of additional names allowed the group to claim a larger area, playing to the preconception of the time that mineral wealth was diffuse and a larger claim was necessary for greater wealth. The two Irishmen, out of a mixture of a generous spirit and a desire to avoid any potential trouble, agreed to split their claim with Comstock. In the end, Comstock bluffed his way into a share of the claim for himself and his partner Emanuel "Manny" Penrod, in the process providing future folklorists with a source of endless tales.

With the California goldfields long since depleted, the discoveries at Gold Hill and on the side of Sun Mountain brought many more miners to Nevada. The growing population required governmental mechanisms. In June 1859, as the struggle for control of Utah's far western frontier heated up, the miners called a meeting and established a compact, the legal structure for a mining district. They elected J. A. "Kentuck" Osborn justice of the peace, James Rogers constable, and V. A. Houseworth recorder. They expected a small-scale mining situation, hardly a boom of the scope of California in 1848.

About ten days later, the mining camp was stunned with news of the value of the find. A ranch hand from the Truckee Meadows had taken some of the blue rock from Comstock's claim to Placerville, California, to be assayed. The assay showed that the ore would yield $876 per ton in gold, but more importantly, it also held $3,000 per ton in silver, an almost inconceivable amount. The claim that Comstock had bluffed his way into held unparalleled wealth. Its form, silver, surprised many.

Silver had been discovered in the region before. In 1856, two brothers, Hosea Ballou Grosh and Ethan Allen Grosh, identified a silver ledge, but bad fortune prevented them from spreading news of their discovery. After finding the ledge, the brothers were beset by a series of accidents. Hosea Grosh struck his foot with a pick in August 1857 and died of blood poisoning a few weeks later. In November of the same year, Ethan Allen Grosh's legs froze during a mountain blizzard in the Sierra Nevada, and he died because he refused to have them amputated. These pioneers of silver never experienced the benefits of their insight.

The appearance of silver in the Placerville assay was the first confirmation of the bimetallic character of the Sun Mountain ore. Most of the wealth in California had come from gold, and now on its eastern fringe, the prospect of almost four times as much per ton from silver whetted the appetites of all kinds of people. This was real news in mining country and the rush was on. During summer 1859, it remained mostly local, as westerners had been disappointed time and again by the announcement of new gold strikes. Many chose to wait, but the newcomers who risked disappointment were well rewarded; by July 1859, the *Territorial Enterprise* abandoned its skepticism and announced that the find, "incredible as it seems, ha(s) not been overestimated." The first miners to respond to the call found themselves sitting on veritable gold mines in more ways than one. Newcomers paid considerable sums, as high as $12,000, to purchase claims from the initial placer miners. Such a sum amounted to three or four years work for the average miner, but was far less than eventually came from the claims. Most of these original miners surely believed they received the better end of the deal, for they could not know that the boom would last, and more importantly, they lacked the expertise in quartz mining or in silver mining to fully develop the new ores.

This individualist, entrepreneurial community depended on an interpretation of the nature of mining that stemmed from California. These miners regarded Nevada much as they had California, where their experience taught them that surface claims controlled the land beneath them. Squatter government had been designed to affirm this perception, creating the opportunity for many people to profit in a strike. The design of their law was based in the concept of decentralization, with no one permitted under rules and regulations to hold more than they could work. In some ways, this was an individualist's paradise, a nearly pure capitalist environment in which people succeeded based on how hard they were willing to work and how rich their particular patch of dirt happened to be.

The newcomers provided this rag-tag bunch at the edge of the world of miners with the ingredients to form the most basic level of community. Towns sprung up from tents; the first name given to the cluster of tents was Mount Pleasant; soon after the area was dubbed the Town of Ophir, after the fabled biblical gold mine. Finally in September, the miners named the town growing around the McLauglin-O'Riley strike "Virginia City," after "Old Virginny" Finney, one of the area's first residents. A popular legend asserts that Finney, in the midst of one of his frequent drunken stupors, tripped while walking down the street carrying a full bottle of whiskey. Not wanting to let the elixir go to waste, he declared that he thereby baptized the town and christened it after the state of his nativity. Fiction more than fact, such legends were at the core of the mystique of Comstock mining.

Even more remarkable, by fall 1859 the predictions of unparalleled wealth were on the way to coming true. In September, one of the leading mine owners sent 3,150 pounds of top-quality ore to San Francisco to be milled, where it yielded $4,871 in gold and silver. Thirty-eight more tons were shipped to San Francisco, at a cost of $512 per ton, over the following weeks. Even the extraordinary cost was worthwhile, as the ore yielded $114,000. Astounding wealth did not go unnoticed. Allsop and Company, a San Francisco banking firm, displayed the bullion in their window as proof of the importance of the lode. The word spread from San Francisco and soon people flocked to the area. Sun Mountain was on the way to becoming a mining town.

The haphazard nature of mineral discovery and the chaos that ensued left the people of the region vulnerable when winter set in. A storm in early November shut down the mountain passes for the winter, providing fitting closure to the events that began with the false spring of the previous January. Ore could not get out; newcomers could not get to Sun Mountain until spring. Food was in short supply. Nearly all the local farmers abandoned their fields to get at the diggings earlier in the year, and as winter fell, the shortage seemed likely to have serious repercussions. Nor were there places to live on the mountain for the roughly two hundred people who remained. Many miners burrowed into tunnels they sunk into the side of the mountain. Tents, brush hovels, and caves comprised the rest of the accommodations. The frozen ground made mining impossible and firewood was scarce. Most of the population spent the winter in the local saloons, as much for the wood-burning stove that glowed with heat as for the liquid refreshment. The rest headed to farming valleys below in search of scarce food.

Even as winter locked the mountain in its cold embrace, Virginia City and Mount Davidson were already in the throes of a rapid transformation. The nature of the find made placer mining, the kind of mining best suited for individuals with few resources, obsolete. The old-time prospectors could not thrive in an environment that demanded not only the capital to provide water, but also the technological sophistication necessary to extract valuable gold and silver from rock. They sold their claims for sums that seemed huge at the time, but looked small in comparison to what later owners took from the earth. Most were happy with what they got, for they recognized how tentative mining really was.

The newcomers who arrived before winter and those who were poised across the Sierra awaiting spring were different from Comstock and his breed. When the snows melted in the mountains in spring 1860, miners rushed to the area to bring the experience of California with them. The prospects were better in the Washoe, as the area was called in California, than in the Golden State. Miners in California had been reduced to working for $1.50 a day for large companies. Anyone with any gumption chased opportunity to the Comstock. Equally, many followed to provide goods and services to the miners or to make a quick fortune in speculation in mining stock. A boom that appeared to mirror the original California Gold Rush took shape.

The influx of people as spring 1860 began changed more than the nature of the mining community. The advent of mining had wide-ranging impact on the native peoples of the region. Living close to this unforgiving land, the Washoe, Northern Paiute, and Western Shoshone peoples moved through the regional landscape, pulling subsistence from different places at different times of the year. Each time a mining boom began and people came to work the ground, the newcomers cut into the already limited opportunities of prior inhabitants. Hunters who fed miners took game that native peoples had historically captured, destroyed food, and impinged on trade routes, and in a number of cases, engaged in battles with natives. The original inhabitants of what became Nevada recognized the threat to their very existence and fashioned a strong and powerful response.

Across the border in California, the gold rush had decimated many native groups, destroying their livelihood and social structure and diminishing their chances of survival. Perhaps the native peoples of the Comstock knew of the fate of their cousins to the west; perhaps the circumstances simply repeated themselves. In either case, the native peoples responded with fury. In May 1860, after a couple of young Indian women were attacked at a stage station, local Paiute and Shoshone had had enough of the random depredations of settlers, travelers, and others, and responded with fury, including killing six whites. An angry mob-like army of 105 was formed in Virginia City to exact retribution, but when the ill-prepared whites met the Paiute on May 12, the Native Americans trounced the loose militia. Seventy-six whites died, and almost all of the rest were wounded. Only nightfall, which brought an end to fighting, saved the fortunate survivors.

The battlefield fiasco threw the entire Washoe front into a panic. No community, even Virginia City, seemed safe as the bedraggled and beaten stragglers streamed home. Comstock residents fled the district, their gold fever suddenly cured by the circumstances. In Virginia City, a man named Peter O'Reilly was constructing a stone hotel. Women and children especially swarmed to it as a place of refuge. Anglo-Americans rallied, bringing reinforcements from California with a bloodlust to avenge the defeat. The U.S. military stood ready to help as well. As May ended, a force of more than 500 men set out from Virginia City to meet 260 regular U.S. Army troops just south of Pyramid Lake. In a series of small battles, the troops decisively defeated the outnumbered Northern Paiute and Shoshone. Yet the native peoples successfully resisted long enough to allow them to evacuate their women and children into the desert, beyond the army's reach. Starving in the desert, they eventually asked for peace and returned to Pyramid Lake.

In the larger struggle between native peoples and the incoming American nation, the Pyramid Lake War was a small battle, made more important by timing. The early 1860s were full of similar battles, most prominently in Minnesota in 1862 when Lakota people, resentful of their treatment and aware that the Civil War had taken many whites from their area, attacked and destroyed homesteads, farms, and killed hundreds of settlers. Most of these episodes resulted from the appearance of large numbers of settlers or miners and their impact on native ways. Unlike the later Indian wars, these battles were largely between free peoples, not those who escaped reservations. In this sense, the Pyramid Lake War more resembled the earlier battles between Americans and Native Americans than they did later battles such as George Armstrong Custer's debacle at Little Bighorn.

This "Pyramid Lake War" slowed the commerce of the Comstock, but within months, the lure of riches outweighed the perception of risk. Conflict with native peoples was typical on the frontiers of the time. The miners in Virginia City agreed to preserve the status quo as long as the conflict persisted. The mining district was frozen as it was. No new claims were allowed to be filed and people who did not work their claims did not run the risk of forfeit. In the absence of genuine local government, the miners did as they had in California during the Gold Rush. They created their own rules and laws on the ground and made them hold by the virtue of custom. Common agreement superseded written law as it must have for hundreds of thousands of years in human history. By the 1860s, such experience was unusual in the United States, but it had grounding in culture and custom.

This feature further illustrated the lack of institutional development on the Comstock. The chaotic local government, six hundred miles distant from Salt Lake City, could not handle the pressure created by the influx of people in search of wealth. Their values envisioned a society increasingly different from that of Mormon Utah, and the history of attempts to create a separate entity inspired those who sought independent territorial status for the Comstock region. The agitation had grown in intensity. In December 1859, the Comstock District sent a symbolic message to the nation's capital: the citizens shipped a block of silver ore weighing 163 pounds and inscribed "NEVADA" to the nation's capital for inclusion in the Washington Monument. Such a gift coupled the economic promise of the region with the aspirations of a growing number of its residents.

Despite such efforts, the petitions of the Comstock for territorial status went unrealized, caught up in the brewing sectional crisis. Throughout the 1850s, the Southern bloc in Congress stymied the creation of new territories in the West that might become free states. The battles over such territories, especially after the Compromise of 1850, were sometimes bloody and always contentious. As relations between the sections frayed throughout the 1850s, the people who wanted an independent Nevada territory waited for the best opportunity. After South Carolina and other southern states seceded in the winter of 1860–61, the Comstock District's delegate in Washington, D.C., John Musser, increased the pressure for independence for western Utah. Shortly after secession and the creation of the Confederate States of America, bills were introduced in both houses of Congress to create a new "Nevada Territory." President James Buchanan signed the bill into law on March 2, 1861, two days before he left office.

The importance of this measure had much to do with the mineral wealth of the new territory. With war imminent, the Union needed to secure a way to pay for its military. Nevada's riches were essential in that quest. The new president, Abraham Lincoln, promptly appointed James W. Nye, a former New York City Police Commissioner and staunch Republican supporter from New York who was also a close friend of Secretary of State William Seward, as territorial governor. His instructions were simple: keep the territory in the Union. Nye complied, squashing any pro-Confederacy sentiment. Nevada was Union from the moment of territorial status.

Among the many people who came to the Nevada Territory was a staunch Missouri abolitionist named Orion Clemens who had been appointed Territorial Secretary. He brought his younger brother along, a man whose name became synonymous with American literature. Samuel Clemens took a job writing for the *Virginia City Territorial Enterprise*. When he covered the territorial convention, he first used the byline under which he became famous: Mark Twain. Although the younger Clemens soon moved on to California, his formative experiences in Nevada shaped his writing for the rest of his life.

The Nevada Territory was part of a revolution that began the moment southern representatives walked out of Congress. Throughout the 1850s, the solidarity of the Southern voting bloc in Congress had stymied efforts to seek a route for a transcontinental railroad, to provide free land to people who would work it, and to provide land grant colleges to promote agriculture. After their departure, there were few barriers to the free soil agenda. One of the first examples of the exercise of this new power was the creation of the Nevada Territory. It was part and parcel of later actions such as the Homestead Act of 1862, the Morrill Land Grant Act of 1862, and even the Railroad Act of 1862. Together, these actions showed a new republic, devoted to something entirely different than stasis with the slave-holding South.

The Nevada Territory was closely tied to the Lincoln administration from its inception, and a wedge between it and the Utah Territory grew. The economic energy of the Comstock, the heart of the new territory's population, was so secular, individualistic, and entrepreneurial that it challenged everything about the Utah experience. Its particular economic importance to the Union during the Civil War guaranteed that the Lincoln administration would carefully eye the new territory. As people rushed from California, Nevada Territory underwent a cultural shift. From its onset, Nevada looked west to California, not east to the Great Basin.

Nevada's fortuitous birth in the Civil War led to a rapid transition from territory to statehood. As the 1864 election approached, Nevada's value as a state increased to the sometimes struggling and even unpopular Lincoln administration. The territory's population remained very small, but Lincoln supporters in Congress pushed through legislation that allowed Nevada to apply for statehood. The road to rapid statehood seemed clear. Lincoln wanted Nevada in the Union, both for its three additional electoral votes for the 1864 election and for future debates over Reconstruction. Local machinations derailed what should have been an easy achievement.

The problems began with William Stewart, a big, brawny, Yale-educated bully of a lawyer who argued mining claims and who represented wealthy California mine owners. Stewart was not above intimidation, and even resorted to physical violence in the courtroom. Since the transition from individualist mining, large companies backed by enormous sums of money gobbled up claims in the Nevada Territory. Legal disputes mounted, and Stewart became the champion of the large companies. He favored the "single ledge" theory of mining, which said that a vein of ore extended beyond the surface boundaries of a claim as long as it was connected to the initial find by "all its dips, angles, and spurs." This perspective, precisely opposite that of the squatter government and the individualist miners who established the territory, helped large mine owners because it allowed them ownership of great parts of the Comstock Lode from single claims. The single ledge theory granted the purchaser of a single claim ownership of any part of the underground wealth to which that initial claim was connected underground.

This also led to a definitional problem. What was connected and what was not? This question spurred enormous controversy and a series of lawsuits between differing mine owners. One of the most important, Ophir Mining Company vs. the Burning Moscow mine, illustrated the problem. The two mines were adjacent, and the Burning Moscow claimed ownership of mineral rights to the west of the Ophir Mining Company's holdings. As the claims were exploited, the men of the Ophir discovered that the two claims ran together. Since the Ophir was first in time, the Burning Moscow was jumping its claim. Sorting this out in the judiciary was both an economic and political matter of the greatest import. The future of the territory depended on such decisions.

For many, the problem with this point of view was that it ceded control of enormous portions of the Comstock to the first handful of claims. This had the effect of turning many neighbors into squatters, making their claims invalid for they encroached upon an existing prior claim, and centralizing the enormous wealth of the Comstock in a few hands. This was precisely Stewart's goal and he argued it loud and long in a series of court cases. Instead, Stewart's detractors advocated a "multiple ledge" theory, which said that each entry point was its own legitimate strike and such holders were entitled to their share of the ore.

A rivalry sprouted between Stewart and federal Judge John Wesley North, who changed the nature of law on the Comstock by ruling against the large owners and their "single ledge" theory. With one decision, North altered the architecture of Comstock mining. By ruling in favor of the multiple ledge theory, he gave the upper hand to the little guy. Stewart seethed. He saw in the drive to statehood an opportunity to rid himself of North. Statehood freed Nevada from territorial appointees, allowing the election of home-grown candidates. Stewart believed that with the resources at his disposal he could assure the election of judges and other officials who would favor his point of view once statehood was obtained. He worked to draft a state constitution and successfully manipulated the Storey County convention delegates to craft a slate that excluded Judge North.

The move for statehood was popular on the Comstock, for this new status was a much-coveted prize. A constitutional convention followed, but Stewart's actions soured the public. They saw the draft constitution as an effort to centralize power in the hands of Stewart and his friends. In January 1864, the proposed constitution was rejected by almost 80 percent of the population. The effort seemed to stall, caught up in the political machinations of powerful people in the territory.

An economic depression on the Comstock in 1864 changed the state's fortunes. Miners had to go deeper to find ore, a very expensive process, and the finds did not justify the expense. Many small mines were tapped out in a short time and their workers became unemployed. As is often the case, the change in economic conditions spurred a change in politics. Many began to view the multiple ledge theory as the cause of their problems. They were willing to shift their allegiances to larger corporations in an effort to secure employment and eventual prosperity.

The interest in statehood continued and Stewart found an opening in which to achieve his ends. He and his supporters claimed that the depression had been caused when the judiciary did not act quickly enough to resolve legal cases about mining claims. In essence, he blamed the depression on North in particular and the courts in general. The attack came from all directions and was withering. Newspapers loudly trumpeted Stewart's claims, individuals embraced the idea, and the currency of discussion pointed away from North and his two colleagues on the territorial supreme court. In August, North reevaluated and ruled in favor of the single ledge theory. It was too late for North and his colleagues, all of whom resigned on August 22, 1864, an event that the public took as admission of their guilt. A slander campaign had succeeded, paving the way to statehood.

The pace quickened. On September 7, 1864, the electorate accepted a revised constitution. In an amazing example of the power of nineteenth-century technology, Nevada officials telegraphed the entire constitution to Washington, D.C. Lincoln needed to review the document and there was not time to send it any other way. The message has gone down in history as the longest telegraph ever sent up to that time, perhaps a commentary on Nevada's glorious style and its ability to transcend unusual circumstances.

On October 31, 1864, President Abraham Lincoln signed the bill making Nevada the thirty-sixth state. In many ways, the new state could not fulfill the expectations of the Lincoln administration. Lincoln believed he needed Nevada to secure his reelection. He found himself caught between John C. Frémont, who advocated the Radical Republicans' harsh vision of postwar reconstruction, and General George B. McClellan, whose Democratic platform advocated settlement with the South. Lincoln worried about holding the center. But in September, Sherman's capture of Atlanta ensured Lincoln's reelection and the urgency for Nevada statehood evaporated. Despite the new circumstances, Lincoln followed through, and with a little more than 12,500 voters, Nevada became a state.

The future of the new state was by no means secure. In 1864, Nevada was a mining colony, a satellite of California power and wealth. Its transition from territorial status to statehood had been engineered for the purpose of consolidating that power. It remained to be seen how democracy in the state would develop.

3

The Comstock and the Railroads

BY THE STANDARDS OF THE DAY, the new state of Nevada, birthed in the tumult of the Civil War, had few of the attributes of previous entrants to the Union. Its population was small and its institutions poorly developed. Nevada was ripe for aggressive power brokers, those who thought that control of a state could lead them to greater wealth and national power. In that, the early state resembled the most corrupt fiefdoms in the Union, states where small cabals could control the workings of the entire body politic. Nevada's predicament was how to maintain its integrity as a state.

For the better part of the late nineteenth century, the state failed at that task. From statehood in 1864 until 1900, Nevada was the captive of various industries. Until 1880, mining dominated the state; after the demise of the Comstock, railroads ran Nevada. Both exploited the state, kept political institutions in their infancy, and used Nevada as a platform for their economic needs. The Silver State was hardly a state even by the lax standards of the day; most of the time, it was a colony of the powers-that-be somewhere else.

At its inception, the new state of Nevada was simply a province of California mining. The events on the Comstock supported California entrepreneurs but did little to develop the social and political institutions of Nevada. The powerful California interests that ran the Comstock had little interest in the development of Nevada. A mining colony was fine with these men, for it gave them ample control of not only the riches that Nevada produced, but with political institutions in their infancy, two United States Senate seats and one place in the U.S. House of Representatives. In the years following statehood, Nevada remained something less than many other states in the Union.

This sad state was obvious to all. The resources that supported the state came from outside its boundaries. Throughout the era, no one who called Nevada home had enough wealth to exert power. The San Francisco Stock Exchange was the center for investment in the Comstock. The wealth the state produced built Nob Hill in San Francisco, that city's testimony to its success. This striking example illustrated the principle of Nevada's colonial status. The wealth from the depths of Nevada built beautiful monuments elsewhere while leaving the new Silver State to flounder socially and politically.

Nevada lacked the strong institutions that a more extended territorial period might have yielded. Everything about the process of statehood had been hurried, by those within the state and beyond its boundaries. There were many reasons to make the territory a state. Few of them had to do with the size of the population and the power of institutions. Democracy in the new state would be a challenge. Power tended to congeal around wealth, and in Nevada there were only a few sources of wealth. The new state looked like an oligarchy, with power concentrated in very few hands.

From 1860 to 1880, the Comstock was the key to Nevada. Since the discovery of this rich lode, the politics of the territory and the state revolved around the great wealth it generated. Other mining booms and industries, such as ranching, which had sprung up in the state paled in comparison. For the better part of its first decade as a state, Nevada was the Comstock and the Comstock was Nevada. The only community of any note was Virginia City, the epicenter of the lode. The only economy was mining and everything related to it. The state's prospects and those of the Comstock were inextricably linked.

No one had ever seen wealth like the Comstock produced. Even jaded veterans of the California Gold Rush were astonished at the remarkable quantities of ore found in its mines. Winners and losers in California's natural resource derby looked at the new state with covetous eyes, seeing an unmatched opportunity for wealth and power. As they tried to extract riches beneath Nevada's ground and to harness its weak political institutions for their own purposes, they not only laid the basis for the state, they also created traditions of weak institutional structure that persist even today.

The development of the Comstock made the new state of Nevada a satellite of the powerful Golden State to the immediate west. Territorial Nevada had been pulled between Zion-Mormon Utah to the east and the brilliant lure of California to the west. After statehood, Nevada became no more than a colony of California mining interests. The Bank of California became the dominant force on the Comstock. Founded in 1864 by William Chapman Ralston, a formidable West Coast businessman who had experience in Nevada, and Darius Ogden Mills, a Sacramento banker and businessman, the bank was capitalized with $2 million in gold. Despite its name and headquarters in San Francisco, a great deal of the Bank of California's attention was focused on Nevada. Ralston had served as treasurer for several mines, most prominently the Ophir and the Gould and Curry. The economic depression of the early 1860s presented Ralston and his bank with a tremendous opportunity. They set up in Nevada with a gleam in their collective eye.

The force of something like the Bank of California could not be matched in the mining colony that was Nevada. Two million dollars in gold was more than anyone could imagine. The wealth in the mines was certainly greater, but it was not easily available. It took capital to extract the wealth buried deep in Nevada's earth. In a state built on money, the power of the resources of the Bank of California inspired both awe and envy.In 1864, the Bank of California opened a branch office in Virginia City, hiring William Sharon as its manager. At 5'5" and 125 lbs, small even by the standards of that day, Sharon was an attorney who had come to California during the gold rush and become a merchant in Sacramento. After a setback, he opened a real estate operation in San Francisco. He made money, attaining a grub stake of $150,000. He invested in mining stock, where his money promptly disappeared. Sharon had a checkered track record, with most of the wealth he attained slipping from his fingers. The quiet reserved man made the most of his opportunity in Nevada.

The architects of the Bank of California picked a propitious moment to set up their new operation. The depression of the early 1860s had wiped out many mining fortunes. The Bank of California had money to loan and would typically do so below the going rate. When loans were between 3 percent and 5 percent, Sharon's bank loaned money at 2 percent. As a result, many operations, both mines and mills, came to this new and cheaper source of funding. But Sharon was underhanded in other ways. He often required much greater collateral than the amount of the loan. In need of cash, mine and mill operators flocked to his door, worrying little about the terms. Miners lived in anticipation of the next big strike, rarely thinking about the long term. The Bank of California offered a miner's paradise, cheap money and deferred terms, and quickly became the banker of the Comstock.

The Comstock was in dire straits in 1865 and being the banker there entailed great risk. The Bank of California had invested millions, but to many, it appeared that the source of capital had arrived too late. The Comstock seemed played out, not producing at the level it had in the early years after the first strike. Miners had to dig deeper and deeper, often down to five hundred feet, to find the quality of ore that had been closer to the surface. The cost was too much, and smaller mines and many mills closed. As Sharon scooped up the best, some observers wondered whether he and his powerful bank had undertaken a fool's errand.

The depression came to an end with new finds in 1866. This initiated a three-year boom that vindicated Sharon and the Bank of California and sustained its investors. The new strikes provided consistent if not spectacular profits, and this centralization of the entire process in the hands of Sharon and his confederates allowed them to earn higher profits than they would have been able to attain in a market with more competition. Monopoly served the Bank of California well and the Comstock continued.

Like other nineteenth-century captains of industry, Sharon used his economic power to achieve his goals. The setup was more than a little insidious. When the economy worsened, companies could not make their note payments. Some were forced to default, and the bank became the new owner of properties. Sharon quickly amassed a number of mines and mills, putting pressure on even solvent operators on the Comstock. The canny entrepreneur coveted other mines and mills and took steps to bring them under his control. His mills undercut competitors in the sort of cost-cutting common in competitive businesses even today. He directed the product of his mines to mills he controlled, leaving competitors without the product they needed to stay in business. By 1867, the Bank of California controlled seven mills.

This kind of monopoly was common in late nineteenth-century America, but Nevada's version was particularly onerous. The new state lacked the kinds of institutions that could combat such overarching economic dominance. Its elected officials were part of the same kinds of cabals. The Bank of California was very much in line with the political leadership and their personal goals. It was not too much to say that the Bank of California served as the treasury of the state of Nevada.

"The Bank Crowd," as the representatives of the Bank of California had come to be called, soon formed the Union Mill and Mining Company as a holding company for their assets. This achieved vertical integration, the nineteenth-century business practice in which one owner controlled every dimension of a business. With mines and mills, Union Mill and Mining dominated the Comstock. Their aggressive tactics destroyed many competitors, forcing smaller owners out and centralizing power in the Bank Crowd. Before 1870, every important mine and seventeen mills belonged to Union Mill and Mining. William Sharon, the failed merchant and lawyer, had attained control of nearly every valuable asset on the Comstock.

Beyond the Comstock, the tentacles of the Bank of California reached even further. Between 1863 and 1871, the company built its own railway, the Virginia and Truckee Railroad (V&T). Constructed at the expense of the two counties—Ormsby and Storey—through which it passed, the railroad was a technological marvel. It traveled twenty-one miles from Carson City to Virginia City. Thirteen of those miles required heavy construction. Six tunnels and seventeen complete turns around the mountain were required to arrive at the terminal in Virginia City. Chinese labor built much of the V&T as it did the Central Pacific. Much more efficient than the old system, the railroad replaced an entire economy of packers, teamsters, and haulers—almost two thousand in number. It dropped the cost of cordwood by almost 50 percent and reduced the cost of transporting ore from $3.50 to $2.00 a ton. After completion of the Virginia City-Carson City route, the V&T built a line from Carson City to Reno. The Bank of California also added a timber company and even helped establish the U.S. Mint in Carson City.

This centralization of economic power foretold the future of Nevada. While the Bank Crowd was the first, throughout the state's history one dominant economic source has characterized nearly every era. In the 1860s and 1870s, the Bank Crowd held sway. The decisions its leaders made not only influenced state political leaders, but often made their minds up for them. Weak governmental institutions—some of which were in the hip pocket of people like Sharon—allowed consolidation of not only wealth, but the mines, the mills, and eventually transportation networks. Although the United States had yet to make laws about monopolies, had national figures bothered to look they would have seen in Nevada a model that would have alerted them to the problems of monopoly capitalism a full two decades before the issue became a national concern.

Big money begat big money, and technological advances helped transform the Comstock and keep it profitable. The most grandiose was the Sutro Tunnel, which was a product of the creative mind of San Francisco entrepreneur Adolph Sutro, a Prussian-Jewish immigrant who cut a wide swath through Gold Rush—era California. Sutro was a trained mining engineer when he arrived on the Comstock. Mine owners grappled with the problem of water flowing into their mines. As they dug deeper into the mountain, water often drowned miners and ruined mining operations. They sought a way to get it out so that mining could continue. A 15-horsepower steam engine was the initial mode of pulling water from the mines. Next, operators tried Cornish pumps, enormous machines that were remarkable for their size. One pump had a 40-ft. in diameter flywheel that weighed 110 tons. It could drain a small room with one cycle. Mine operators tried other remedies such as tunnels to drain the water. The Union Tunnel, built by four mines at the 200-ft. level, opened in October 1860 and initially succeeded in removing the water, but miners went deeper and eliminated the tunnel's effectiveness.

In 1865, seeing the problem and thinking big as always, Sutro first proposed an enormous drainage tunnel that would empty the mountain of water from below. His grandiose plan did not seem feasible, but Sutro persisted. Eventually, the Bank Crowd supported him. It was an age that rewarded big ideas, and after he secured $3 million in capitalization, Sutro envisioned an even larger project. He proposed an adit, a horizontal entrance to the side of the mountain that extended more than three miles from the Carson River Valley to the base of the Comstock mines, 1,663 feet below the surface. Some described his commitment to the idea as an obsession.

For a number of years, Sutro's flamboyance embroiled his project in political controversy. The powerful Bank Crowd feared that Sutro would seize much of its power and would gain control over the Comstock, and they did everything they could to thwart the tunnel. Sutro envisioned a town at the bottom, populated with miners and a mill he owned, which would supplant Virginia City. After completion of the tunnel, it would be easier to bring the ore out through it, breaking the topside monopoly that the Bank of California had secured. With its enormous political power, the Bank Crowd began to strangle Sutro's dream.

In 1869, the opposition to Sutro and his tunnel evaporated. Although the railroad made his dream of controlling the Comstock unlikely at best, the tunnel had enormous implications for miners at a time when safety was a primary concern for the increasingly organized workers in the mines. In October 1869, Sutro swung a pick and began this enormous undertaking. An expensive operation that sometimes cost $1,000 a day in salaries, the tunnel required technical ingenuity to solve questions of flow and width. Ore carts had to be able to travel in both directions at the same time. Despite the problems of construction and financing, the Sutro Tunnel was completed in 1879. Sutro sold the tunnel and returned to San Francisco, becoming mayor in the 1890s and at one point, owning one-twelfth of the city. The tunnel Sutro built was an albatross, a brilliant but unwieldy idea that was completed too late in the game to change the nature of life for miners on the Comstock. Yet it was a model of thinking big in a time when big thinking was appreciated.

Other technological advances that improved mining on the Comstock included square-set timbering. Invented by Phillip Deidesheimer, an engineer, the practice was designed to cut down cave-ins in the mines. Deidesheimer created a series of interlocking squares in which vertical posts were supported by horizontal ones and diagonals completed the structure. Essentially full-formed cages, square-set timbering used a great deal more timber than previous methods, but gave miners a sense of security they had not previously experienced. In addition, these structures could be constructed underground while miners continued to remove ore. Square-set timbering created work place safety and efficiency at the same time.

The Comstock was the center of Nevada's economy and life from 1860 to 1880. The initial heyday came between 1860 and 1863. Following the mining downturn after 1863, during which the Bank Crowd snapped up valuable mines and mills, a revival of fortune took place between 1866 and 1869 that allowed the Bank Crowd to capitalize on these purchases. At a time when power was in very few hands, the revival allowed even further centralization.

The capstone moment of this brief revival took place on April 7, 1869, when a fire started in the Yellow Jacket Mine. The fire began at the 800-ft. level of the mine, possibly because someone left a candle burning. Underground timbers caught fire, spreading after the night shift left and before the day shift arrived. At 7:00 A.M., the timber holding up the rock collapsed, pushing smoke through the underground cavern. One observer called it a "gale force wind of poison." As many as fifteen men died instantly. The fire then spread through the corridors and tunnels that connected the underground world of the Comstock. At the neighboring Kentuck Mine, the smoke killed a number more. At another mine, the Crown Point, the cage operator lowered men directly into the fire, where they found dying men at the bottom and tried to load them all in the cage to come back up. They succeeded and went back again, to find only two men this time. Forty-five died in this mine alone. Four days later, workers found the fire still growing and they tried to seal it off. They succeeded in containing the fire, but when they opened up the burning mines a number of times during the next two months, they found the fire still hot. Three years later, the sealed area was open again.

The Yellow Jacket fire highlighted the terrible dangers associated with mining. Not only was dramatic fire an ever-present threat, working below ground had other risks. Cave-ins were a constant danger, as were floods of scalding water, poisonous air, collapsing support structures, and explosives that either detonated unexpectedly or brought down more of the mountain than was intended. Even safety innovations such as the cages that carried men down could be dangerous. In one instance, a shift boss from a mine died when the cable that held his descending cage broke and he fell to the bottom of the mine. The death rate was stultifying; between 1863 and 1880, 295 miners lost their lives on the Comstock. Another 606 were injured on the job.

Although safety remained a major concern, wages drove the development of unions on the Comstock. As was often the case, Nevada suffered from a labor shortage. There were simply not enough workers to fill the Comstock's enormous need. The result allowed miners to put pressure on management for higher wages. The first such organization, the Miner's Protective Association, was formed in 1863 with the express goal of preserving the $4.00 per day wage as the first depression set in. Companies had already sought to reduce the daily rate to $3.50, but the new association was not strong enough to combat the trend. The result was agitation in the streets of Virginia City, where on July 31, 1864, miners marched as they shouted for the $4.00 per day rate. They soon organized the Miner's League of Storey County, dedicated to securing a higher wage.

The Miner's League quickly overstepped its power base. After drafting a constitution and electing officers, they tried to dictate terms to the mining and milling industry. They insisted that after September 27, 1864, no one should hire any miner who did not belong to the union. The Bank Crowd and other mine and mill owners were worried, and they began to use the vast power they had accumulated to crush the union. They persuaded territorial governor James W. Nye to call out federal troops to suppress what mine owners were inclined to see as a revolt. The union was compromised. It had too few members to fill all the jobs in mines and mills, and with federal troops in Virginia City and elsewhere on the Comstock, the pressure on the union was too great. The wage fell to $3.50 a day, and the mine owners emerged victorious.

But the idea of organizing for their own benefit had much to recommend it to the workers who made the Comstock lucrative. The agitation for a voice for labor continued even as the initial attempt to organize was repulsed. Beginning in 1864, miners in favor of unionization used the best mechanism they had, democracy, to begin to establish their long-term credibility. After 1864, pro-union miners won a series of local elective offices, including sheriff and a number of seats on the county commission. With this important elective toehold, made possible by the sheer number of miners exercising the franchise of citizenship, the miners were able to develop unions that were broad-based and had membership from the many strata of laborers on the Comstock. The first two, the Gold Hill Miner's Union—organized on December 8, 1866—and the Virginia City Miner's Union—founded on Independence Day, July 4, 1867—became linchpins in the effort to secure high wages and better working conditions.

In the odd way that management and labor have always worked together in Nevada, the Comstock set the standard. As was always the case, labor was at a premium. It was not possible to go out and recruit new workers at the drop of a hat. The Comstock remained lucrative for its owners, and it was easier to accommodate the unions than to fight them. The success of organizing also contributed. After a certain point, almost every worker on the Comstock was a member of a union. Mines cooperated with the unions, sometimes deducting the $2.00 a month dues from the wages they paid and then transferring them to the unions' coffers.

By 1870, Virginia City was more than a mining town. It had a complex economy that had shifted away from mining and toward milling. As the new decade began, the diversity of the economy became more and more apparent. Milling employed 400 workers, 300 more worked in manufacturing, while 3,000 remained in the mines. Mining had declined from 70 percent to 43 percent of the workforce between 1863 and 1870. Although the number of miners had grown, the additional workers made up a much smaller percentage of the workforce.

As the community's economy diversified, another depression began. This one gradually changed the balance of power on the Comstock, replacing the old Bank Crowd with a new group, the "Silver Kings," also known as the "Big Four of the Comstock" or the "Bonanza Crowd." The four men who made up this group were John W. Mackay, William S. O'Brien, James C. Flood, and James G. Fair. Mackay and Fair arrived from California with mining experience in the Golden State. They initially worked for the standard wage of $4.00 a day. Mackay was perhaps the most enterprising. A frugal man, he engaged in the kind of speculation that was typical for miners at the time. As superintendent of the Caledonia Tunnel and Mining Company and later of the Milton Mine, he acquired a reputation for shrewd investment in the niches left open by larger competitors. With a partner, he bought a small 100-ft. claim between two producing mines that became the famous Kentuck that produced more than $3 million in a four-year period.

Another skilled operator on the Comstock, James G. Fair, became acquainted with Mackay after being subjected to the power of the Bank of California. In the late 1860s, the Bank Crowd was at the height of its power and most who challenged them were destroyed. William Sharon could drive the price of the stock of any mine so high that no one could compete, and on a number of occasions he did this to Mackay and Fair. The treatment drove the two closer together, in part out of common interests and in part, self-defense. Soon after, Fair and MacKay joined up with William S. O'Brien and James C. Flood, former San Francisco saloon keepers who had become important players in the financial community of the burgeoning Bay Area. They were building what was called a "syndicate" in that era, a combination of financial backing and on-the-ground expertise. Not quite homegrown, the new alliance had the ability to make an impact on the Comstock.

The Comstock had always been a speculator's paradise, somewhere that easy riches seemed possible to obtain. When the Comstock first burst on the scene in the early 1860s, a feeding frenzy took place in the stocks issued by mining concerns. Everyone caught the bug; from mine owner to char woman, everyone bought stocks with little regard for their real value. But as in most booms, the stocks were often without value. In 1867, four hundred mining companies issued stock. Three paid dividends. This pattern made such investment dangerous. In the heady climate of the mining world, even experienced men ran high risks.

The initial subject of Mackay, O'Brien, Flood, and Fair's speculation was the Hale and Norcross Mine, the subject of a classic Bank of California effort to drive the stock price through the ceiling. In the first two months of 1868, the share price peaked at almost $7,100, an unsustainable level. In March, it held steady at $2,950 a share, but bad returns drove it down to $41.50 a share in September. At that point, the four men went bargain hunting and bought into the lucrative property for much less than anyone imagined. They soon won control of the board of directors of the Hale and Norcross Mine, and their extensive skill in mining turned a profit very quickly.

Their success made the four a target of the old Bank Crowd, but being experienced at mining, MacKay and Fair recognized that the key to success was to buy properties that were undervalued and to develop new veins of ore. Instead of working the financial markets, Mackay and Fair remained mining operators. It served them well. In 1870, Fair found a new vein of ore, and the Hale and Norcross paid $500,000 in dividends. With this success to their credit, the four men searched for new opportunities.

The adventurous speculation of the Bank Crowd had left it ill-prepared when depression again hit in 1870. The Bank of California had paid more for many of its assets than they commanded at the marketplace, putting the dominant entity on the Comstock in serious financial jeopardy. Other speculators began to hover like predators, waiting for the right opportunity to contest for the most valuable pieces of the Bank Crowd's empire. Two of them, Alvinza Hayward, a California investor, and John P. Jones, the Welsh-born superintendent of the Crown Point Mine, brokered a savvy deal that left them in control of the Crown Point. Although the two men ceded the valuable adjacent Belcher Mine to Sharon, the Crown Point allowed them to not only open their own mill, but to shift their banking business away from the Bank of California. With this move, they began the consistent erosion of the power of the Bank Crowd. The downward spiral culminated when Jones defeated Sharon in the 1873 U.S. Senate race. A vacuum had been created on the Comstock and as nineteenth-century philosophers and crass observers of the social scene were inclined to observe, nature abhors a vacuum.

Mackay, O'Brien, Flood, and Fair were ready to seize the opportunity. They had already capitalized on some of the worst moments in Comstock history. In 1870, Consolidated Virginia dropped to $1.00 a share; the Bonanza Crowd bought it and neighboring mines for $100,000. They mined for a while and then below the depth of 500 feet, which had not yet yielded anything, they found the "Big Bonanza." Miners recorded gold and silver ore that paid from $93 to $632 per ton. They created an underground room that was 20 feet high, 50 feet wide, and 140 feet long, filled with this remarkable ore. Even beyond it, the ore was rich. The find yielded $150 million in ore and paid $79 million in stock dividends during a twenty-year period. It became the basis of the empire that the Bonanza Crowd built.

With the infusion of wealth from the Big Bonanza, an effort at vertical integration also succeeded in the vacuum. In 1871, the Bonanza Crowd bought into the Virginia and Gold Hill Water Company, giving them control of the primary water supply on the Comstock. They bought the Pacific Mill and Mining Company in 1874, the Pacific Wood, Lumber, & Flume Company in 1875, and opened the Bank of Nevada in San Francisco in 1875. They could now control their own destiny on the Comstock. They no longer needed anything but transportation, the most valuable piece of the Bank Crowd's monopoly. The V&T remained beyond the reach of the Bonanza Crowd, but the threat of the Bonanza Crowd building its own railway kept the rates that the V&T offered their rivals fair.

The Big Bonanza brought the Comstock its best years. The amount of wealth was unequalled; between 1859 and 1882, more than $292 million was produced on the Comstock. The heyday was in the 1870s, the reign of the Bonanza Crowd. Between 1873 and 1878, the Comstock yielded more than $166 million of ore at a time when $4.00 a day was a good wage. In 1873, the Comstock topped $20 million in production; in 1876 and 1877, the total approached $40 million. Investors fared very well. More than $125 million was paid out in dividends, more than half of that from the Bonanza Crowd properties. The enormous numbers attracted miners from around the globe. Virginia City enjoyed its heyday in this era, as the wealth from the mines spread throughout the community. No place in the American West shone more brightly in the 1870s than did Virginia City.

The silver from the Comstock also made San Francisco shine again. William Ralston, the founder of the Bank of California, was a civic developer as well as the financial overseer of Nevada mining. By the mid-1870s, the Bank of California's position on the Comstock had been usurped by the Bonanza Crowd. Ralston put much of the profit from the Comstock into the San Francisco Bay Area. He built the Palace and the Grand hotels, a sugar refinery, the Mission Woolen Mills, the Cornell Watch Factory, and many other economic and civic developments. But Ralston overextended the bank. In 1875, he was exposed for issuing shares without informing his board of directors. In an age when banks were not guaranteed, such an admission sparked rumors that led to a run on the bank. Ralston was forced out, and then while swimming in San Francisco Bay the same day, he drowned. Some said he had a stroke; others believed he drowned himself in shame. Either way, a powerful force behind Comstock development was in trouble, until Sharon took over and righted the bank's operations.

With the Bank of Nevada firmly in financial control of the Comstock, Nevada for the first time had something resembling homegrown wealth dominating its economy. Nevada silver built San Francisco. Ralston and his friends saw to that. They treated the Comstock like a cash machine, pumping its profits into the Golden State. The Bank of Nevada had a much deeper stake in the Silver State. Not only were Mackay and Fair truly miners at heart, they had a powerful affinity for their adopted home. More efficient and fair in financial terms, the Bank of Nevada brought a higher level of organization to the Comstock. More people benefited from the practices of the Bank of Nevada than did from the Bank of California. Even though the Bank of Nevada was organized by San Francisco capitalists, its very name showed a shift in emphasis from its predecessors.

But the Bank of Nevada was also a California entity, organized and chartered in San Francisco. Its financiers were San Francisco men, and as a result, it is hard to see the Bonanza Crowd as a genuine Nevada creation. Although the Bank of Nevada did more for Nevada than the Bank of California, like its predecessor much of the wealth it generated went to the Golden State. In this sense, the Bank of Nevada was as much a colonial endeavor as was the Bank of California.

By the mid-1870s, the Comstock began to play out. The peak production of nearly $40 million in 1876 fell swiftly. In 1881, the total production of the Comstock fell to $1.4 million, a dramatic decline in a very short period. Even though investors spent millions of dollars to sink shafts as far down as three thousand feet, they found no new major bodies of ore. While this slowed the growth of Nevada, it did not impede the four men who had done so well in the 1870s. O'Brien died in 1878. Fair left the Comstock in 1881, and Flood died in 1889. Mackay held on, finally selling his interests to San Francisco stockbrokers in 1895.

By the early 1880s, the Comstock was dead. When the yields dipped to $1.5 million, there was almost no reason for most to stay. Other mining strikes also went sour at roughly the same time. Two mining camps, Candelaria and Tuscarora, both showed promise. Between 1880 and 1883, Candelaria in Mineral County produced almost $5 million, leading believers in the power of bonanza to think that they had found the new mother lode. In 1884, reality returned as the camp produced roughly $25,000. In Elko County, Tuscarora jumped to more than $1 million in production in 1878, but the number was not sustainable. Throughout the state, mining slowed and the great bonanza came to an end. Many of the mining companies packed up and left, and the workers followed in number. From a peak of 19,528 people in 1875, Storey County fell to 16,004 in 1880. The decline after that point was precipitous. In 1890, 8,806 people called the county home. A decade later, 3,560 were all that remained in Storey County.

Storey County mirrored the state. Nevada's population spiked and then fell. In 1870, the state had 58,461 people; a decade later, it reached its nineteenth-century apex with 69,066. Then the decline began. In 1890, Nevada had only 47,355 people, a loss of more than one-third of its population a decade before. The trend continued. By 1900, only 42,355 people called the state home.

The loss of population meant two things: Nevada had been tossed on the scrapheap of economic history and another vacuum had been created. With almost no value in the terms of the economic marketplace that had previously defined it, Nevada's earlier masters abandoned it. The state was not worth the trouble required to manage it. With mining more lucrative elsewhere and nothing to replace it, the interest in the Silver State diminished. The result was the most colonial—perhaps the most corrupt—era in the history of the state.

The Comstock era had not led to the development of typical American political institutions. The electorate remained small and beholden, first to the Bank Crowd and then to the Bonanza Crowd. Both William Sharon and James G. Fair served in the U.S. Senate, reflecting the close way power was held. As a result, Nevada experienced little of the maturing process that characterized state politics elsewhere. Although the state harbored many forms of dissent, none of the political unrest and turmoil that was typical in developing states contributed to the broadening of the reins of power in Nevada. The result was the equivalent of a medieval fiefdom, where few possessed not only wealth but power, and everyone else simply existed, many harboring grievances against the power structure.

Only the cattle industry had some power to resist and to shape a future outside the narrow confines of mining. Nevada's cattle industry had grown and spread throughout the state. In 1874, 135,000 cattle grazed Nevada's grasses. Cattle had no value in the wilds of the Silver State. Their worth came from the connection to the markets of the rest of the nation. Communities such as Winnemucca and Reno became cattle centers during this era, using their railroad connections as a way to develop their standing as towns. Founded in 1859 as "Lake's Crossing," Reno took its name in 1868 when the Central Pacific Railroad located a stop on the Truckee River. In 1872, the V&T extended its track to the new town, creating a valuable economic intersection of mining, transportation, and animals.

Cattlemen were the dominant force in small communities throughout the state, but they were at the railroad's mercy when it came to shipping their product. When the state elected L. R. Bradley, a Mound Valley cattleman, as governor in 1870, a brief interlude began in which the state shifted toward the interests of cattlemen. Under Bradley, the state legislature amended state law to allow it power over the rates of narrow gauge railways such as the V&T. Bradley remained a staunch opponent of the railroads, vetoing a bill in 1873 that benefited the Central Pacific and assured that the railroads took much more direct interest in Nevada. Bradley also managed to antagonize the Bonanza Group that predominated on the Comstock and was in league with the railroad operators in pursuit of unfettered power and profits. Bradley was defeated by a minion of the railroad in 1878, creating an opening in the state's politics.

Into the vacuum stepped two railroads, the V&T of Comstock fame, and the Central Pacific, the railroad that crossed the Sierra Nevada. As the mines declined, the time to consolidate power had come. For most of the rest of the nineteenth century, the railroads were the dominant political force in Nevada. In different ways, they ran state politics. The V&T and the Central Pacific were separate but intertwined; they had different goals. The V&T was an in-state "short line" railroad. The Central Pacific was a California-run conglomerate that was essential to new industry in the state.

The V&T had a long history in Nevada and served as a colonial force. Its general manager was Henry M. Yerington, for whom the town is named. A dapper man with white hair parted in the middle and a bushy mustache that reached to his chin, Yerington was a skilled political manipulator who understood how to assure the results he wanted. After Bradley passed his anti-railroad measures, the V&T paid considerable attention to Nevada politics. Railroad officials wanted only one thing: no regulation of railroads by the state. Yerington would stop at nothing to achieve his goals. Effectively the state's first lobbyist, he literally purchased legislators. His power allowed him to control the state Republican Party. He hand picked delegates to the county and state Republican conventions, bribed officials, and liberally dispersed railroad passes as part of the perquisite of being in his sphere. Inside the state, no entity had more power than the V&T and no individual influenced the state more than Yerington.

The Central Pacific Railroad had been a product of the drive to build the transcontinental railroad. The Big Four—Leland Stanford, Collis P. Huntington, Mark Hopkins, and Charlie Crocker—had been Sacramento businessmen when they signed on to build a railroad across the Sierra Nevada. Their success made them richer and more powerful than any men in the western half of the United States. After the construction phase ended, the Central Pacific became the most powerful entity in California, virtually running the state. With a big state in its pocket, devouring a small and comparatively weak state like Nevada was child's play.

The Central Pacific had an eye on Nevada since the inception of the transcontinental railroad. Although it failed to obtain an operating subsidy from the Silver State, the railroad had ways of making Nevada its own. It had a resident agent in the state who pulled the strings, and for much of the last two decades of the nineteenth century, it controlled the state's two U.S. senators. The main operative for the Central Pacific was Charles "Black" Wallace, a tall and imposing man who cooperated with Yerington in controlling the legislature. At this time, U.S. senators were not selected by popular vote. Instead, state legislatures chose their U.S. senators. Control of the legislature guaranteed control of who represented the state in the U.S. Senate. Wallace behaved in a manner similar to Yerington. He took legislators out for expensive meals, did them favors, granted them passes on the railroad, and of course, bribed and otherwise assured their loyalty. He bought voters and legislators and kept senators on the payroll to do the company's bidding. Wallace used this control to assure that Nevada in no way competed with California. The second-class status of the Silver State continued.

Railroads were the villains of the late nineteenth-century American West, the source of woe for farmers, ranchers, and nearly everyone else. Railroads had monopolistic control of the region, dictating terms to every other entity in most western states. Occasionally, something like the Comstock would briefly wrest control of a state from the railroad, but mining typically had short-lived moments of glory, and in the background railroads bided their time. With tools such as rate gouging at their disposal, they were the focus of ongoing animosity. In states like Nevada, where the voting population numbered as few as twenty thousand, the hatred for the railroads was particularly fierce.

The railroad consistently squeezed farmers, often breaking their fragile economic position. Since industrialization, the position of farmers had declined, creating the delicious irony that at the very moment that land was easily available to people who had never had their own, owning your own farm no longer provided the freedom American mythology promised. Railroads made the predicament of farmers worse. They manipulated freight rates shamelessly, creating an inverted situation that was particularly damaging to small farmers. It often cost farmers more to ship their products short distances than long. The cost from Reno to Salt Lake City routinely exceeded that from San Francisco to Salt Lake City. Even worse for farmers, railroads functioned as middlemen, buying from strapped farmers at ridiculously low prices and claiming the profits for themselves. If farmers objected, freight rates simply rose.

Elsewhere, especially in the Midwest and near West, Populism, the agrarian revolt, followed railroad dominance. In states like Kansas, farmers united against the railroad, electing state-level officials and developing a response to the power of the railroad. Populism succeeded best in heavily agricultural states. Nevada was so bereft of agriculture that it barely participated. Only 126,000 acres out of the state's total of 110,540 square miles were farmed, an infinitesimally small percentage.

But farmers and Nevada shared an interest in one important idea in the late nineteenth century: the monetization of silver. In 1873, the "Crime of '73" passed Congress. It took silver out of the money supply, permitting only coins of smaller denomination and trade dollars for overseas use to be made of silver. This removal was part of a federal effort to contract the money supply. At the height of the Bonanza, with one U.S. senator a former silver mine foreman, the lack of resistance of the Nevada delegation was striking. Both senators were in chambers when the bill passed, but neither protested. The best explanation for their lack of action was that they simply did not bother to look at the legislation. Senator William Stewart later claimed that he had been duped by a "tremendous conspiracy."

The "Crime of '73" diminished the value of one of Nevada's greatest products and hampered the state's economy. Nevadans were not alone in their pain; farmers were equally damaged by taking silver from the money supply. Farmers always had to borrow to put in a crop and in an economy where silver counted as legal tender, money could be secured cheaply. When silver no longer counted as part of the amount in circulation, the money supply tightened and the cost of borrowing increased dramatically, further damaging farmers. The interests of farmers and silver-producing states like Nevada paralleled one another.

In the wilderness of gold, Nevada senators pushed for whatever concessions they could wring from Congress. In 1878, two senators from Midwest farming states sponsored the Bland-Allison Act, which committed the government to purchase between $2 million and $4 million of silver per month for a period of ten years. This kept a premium on silver production and helped the Comstock at a time when it was beginning to wane.

But Nevada's Washington, D.C., delegation could not make inroads against the "Crime of '73." The impetus for the monetization of silver slowly slipped back to the state level. In 1885, the Nevada Silver Association formed, seeking to count silver at the rate of 16 ounces for every one of gold toward the money supply. Called "Free Silver Coinage," the idea had a great deal of traction in the late 1880s. It simultaneously served the needs of silver miners and farmers. That point was driven home in 1889, when Nevadans were well represented at the St. Louis Silver Convention, which joined the budding Populist movement with silver advocates for the first time.

It was a strange marriage, or at least courtship. Farmers and the silver miners in the far West had very different interests, but they coincided over the single most important issue to both. Farmers needed cheap money; mining interests needed a reason to continue to dig the earth for silver. Free silver as an inflationary policy served both their interests and created the unusual affinity between individual farmers and the essentially corporate structure of silver mining. The relationship grew in the 1890s, as Populism became a significant political movement in the U.S.

As Populism gained momentum in the 1890s, "Silver Populism" took off in Nevada and other western silver-producing states. Nevada had always been susceptible to third-party efforts, for in a state with few people and one source of power, conspiracy theories abounded. Silver remained Nevada's secular religion and anything that helped increase its value was welcomed. The momentum surrounding silver helped diversify power in the state. Silver clubs organized in likely and unlikely places with Winnemucca, a cattle town, hosting the *Silver State* newspaper, the strongest pro-silver voice in Humboldt County. When General James B. Weaver, the Populist candidate for president in 1892, spoke in Virginia City during the campaign, it brought silver to political prominence in Nevada. In the 1894 elections, the Silver Party won a resounding victory in state elections. Nationally, silver gained momentum with the Populists. Nevadans cheered when Democratic and Populist Party presidential candidate William Jennings Bryan gave the famous "Cross of Gold" speech in 1896. The idea of silver as legal tender made Nevada viable once again.

Populism failed nationally, if only by a whisker, and with it went the revival of Nevada silver mining. Nevada politics became impaled on the question of silver and its officials were easily manipulated by outside interests such as the Central Pacific Railroad. There were few other economic options for the Silver State, and the state floundered. Some even questioned its charter. Eastern states had always railed against Nevada's equal representation in the U.S. Senate. A state with only 40,000 people did not merit the same number of seats as did those with millions, some prominent legislators insisted. Nevada was called a "rotten borough" by newspapers in New York, Connecticut, and other eastern states. The *Chicago Tribune* opined that "the silver mines which made [Nevada] all she was have been exhausted. She has no other mineral wealth. She has no agricultural resources. She has nothing to attract people; and as a consequence, she is flickering out." The paper wanted Nevada's statehood revoked; failing that, it proposed that the Silver State's senators be sequestered and denied their seats as had Southern senators after the Civil War.

A good deal of the animosity toward Nevada was a direct result of the state's willingness to accept what other states called vice. In Nevada, gambling had never been made illegal. Technically, it was not legal either. Nineteenth-century Nevada law did not address the question. In that era, if law did not forbid something, it was permissible. Mining towns were notorious for their tolerance of gambling and in Nevada, people tended to mind their own business. Gambling flourished in Nevada, much to the consternation of the pious and sanctimonious elsewhere.

Divorce, then rare in the U.S., also caused people in other states to look down on Nevada. Through a quirk in state law, divorce required only six months residency, the same as was required to become a resident of the state. For a long time, only Nevada residents used the law. After an Illinois Supreme Court decision in 1896, it became more difficult to secure a divorce west of the Mississippi River. Nevada began to become a divorce mill. Those who opposed the idea of divorce railed against the state.

Nevada's willingness to allow prize fights for money also inspired great ill will. In 1897, the Nevada legislature had run out of funds and it agreed to allow prize fights in the state for a fee of $1,000, one-tenth going to the county in which the fight took place. With professional prize fighting illegal in most other states, Nevada had found another way to capitalize on its openness and tendency to live and let live. Promptly, negotiations began to bring a heavyweight title fight to Nevada. The state needed the money and promoters needed a location. It was a match, if not one made in heaven.

In March 1897, Gentleman Jim Corbett was set to face Robert Fitzsimmons in Carson City. The six-foot-tall, 180-pound Corbett was the reigning champion, the best fighter of his generation. From San Francisco, Corbett was part of the new breed of gloved fighters, a technician who advocated speed and skill over brute hitting power. Thirty years old in 1897, Corbett was a skilled athlete who kept himself in top physical shape and with a constant training regime, he was in his prime. His opponent, Fitzsimmons, was a different kind of fighter. A former blacksmith, he was about the same height as Corbett, but a much lighter man. Some called him "a heavyweight from the waist up." At thirty-four, he was at the end of his career.

When the fight took place, it was the event of the year. Nevada law required that the fight take place inside an enclosure so that the general public could not view it. Sheriff Bat Masterson of Dodge City, Kansas, fame stood at the door and collected 400 guns from the people who had paid to watch the fight. Down on his luck, the aging Wyatt Earp of o.k. Corral fame stood in Corbett's corner, his six-gun visible as a promise that any trouble would be met. The fight was filmed—the first time that any prize fight had been committed to posterity. When Fitzsimmons knocked out the adept Corbett in the fourteenth round, Nevada had begun to become a center for what other states did not permit.

Nevada's limitations were obvious to its leaders. As the twentieth century approached, the state could barely provide even the minimal services it offered. The railroads had broken the legislature and after the defeat of the Populists in 1896, it was unlikely that a revival of silver mining would take place. The closeness of California gave the Silver State another option: offering the people of the Golden State and elsewhere exactly what they could not get at home. Other states dabbled in this idea, but few had the dramatic need of Nevada. To save itself, the Silver State risked ridicule; given the options, the choice made sense. Unless there was a new mining strike, Nevada would continue to provide what could not be had at home. Every time another economy failed, the state would turn to vice. As the twentieth century began, Nevada had begun to chart the course that would bring it to prominence before the new century ended.

4 The Second Mining Boom: 1900 to 1929

DESPITE THE GROWING INTEREST in forms of entertainment that neighboring states would not sanction, professional boxing, open gambling, and easy divorce requirements were not enough to sustain even a state with as few as 40,000 people. Such activities were just a sideline, a way to generate some revenue for a state that was essentially bereft of funds. Nevada no longer had a viable economy. The Silver State had been stripped of its best assets and left without the benefits it should have received. After all the wealth it had generated in the nineteenth century, Nevada had become a poor state, in search of its next bonanza.

By 1900, there had been no major mining strike in Nevada in more than two decades. The state existed on the hope and prayer that someone would find something big, a mining strike that would equal that of the Comstock. All the action was in mining, the one industry that had the power to rescue Nevada and turn its fortunes around. This one-horse model of statehood was all Nevada could muster. But the strike that everyone sought did not come . . . until the first year of the new century.

The twentieth century began with a new mining strike that offered hope for the future. An old miner named Jim Butler found gold near Tonopah Springs in May 1900. Butler sought to preserve his position before the goldfields were overwhelmed with people. He became partners with attorney Tasker L. Oddie, a transplanted New Yorker who had come to inspect Nevada for his employer, Anson Phelps Stokes, a mining entrepreneur and railroad magnate. The flamboyant Stokes was the owner of the famed Stokes Castle, an odd stone tower that he built for his sons' recreation in Lander County, one mile west of Austin, Nevada. Initially Stokes' representative, Oddie liked Nevada so much that he opened a law office in Austin. He had Butler's find assayed and it produced $200 per ton in gold, about one-quarter the value of the typical Comstock assay. The strike also produced 640 ounces of silver, again considerably less than the Comstock.

The Tonopah strike created a mining boom for a state in depression, but a boom it was. Tonopah became the hottest place in Nevada, marking the first time the population shifted to the southern half of the state. Within a year, Tonopah had thirty-two saloons, two dancehalls, two newspapers, two churches, a public school, and everything a mid-sized American community offered. Single men comprised the largest percentage of the population, and smart business people catered to their needs. If Tonopah was a little heavy on the entertainment, Nevada remained as it had always been: wide open. Mining had always been a predominantly male venture and there was money to be made in keeping miners well lubricated with alcohol and providing them with prostitutes.

Tonopah was neither an easy place to reach nor located in a region ripe with resources. The new bonanza contained the same problems as all of its predecessors. Water was scarce, transportation nonexistent, and capital to mine was always hard to secure. Speculation was rife, as all kinds of charlatans saw an opportunity to get rich and ply their trade. The rule of law was shaky in such places and community institutions were weak when they existed at all. The miners were at the edge of the known world; they had to make do with what they had. The problems paralleled those of the early days of the Comstock, for about one-quarter of the output. But it was a boom and hope was the miner's watchword. After two decades of nothing, even one-quarter of the Comstock was real value.

The boom in Tonopah spurred other exploration. Within months, new strikes dotted the region. About thirty miles from Tonopah, Harry Stimler and William Marsh made a discovery of gold in December 1902. A later rich strike in January 1904 led to the development of the Goldfield Mining District. Seventy miles to the south, Frank "Shorty" Harris and Earnest Cross made another strike on August 9, 1904. The two men found surface ore in the Bullfrog Mountains and a gold rush quickly ensued. Following his discovery, Harris, whose ore deposits assayed at $700 per ton, went on a three-week celebratory drinking binge. In a stupor, Harris supposedly sold the Bullfrog gold mine for $1,000 and three barrels of whiskey.

The boom sparked the development of two towns besides Tonopah—Goldfield and Rhyolite. Tonopah was the most stable of the trio; it rose more slowly than the others and its decline was gradual. It remained a community throughout the twentieth century, as it became the county seat of Nye County. Down the road about twenty miles, Goldfield sat atop the richest gold strike in the region. It rose like a shooting star and soon evaporated. As Tonopah began to stagnate, Goldfield took off.

When Goldfield hosted the Joe Gans–Battling Nelson lightweight championship fight on Labor Day, 1906, it had more than 15,000 people and was the largest city in the state. Gans was an African American, and Nevada's openness made it easier for him to fight a white man. Then as now, the edges of American society were softer as people moved away from the more settled areas. Heavyweight champion James J. Jeffries refereed the fight, adding more official sanction to this unlikely interracial match. In a boomtown, anything went. Gans won in a 42-round brawl, becoming the lightweight champion of the world. Goldfield grew to 20,000 before it began to decline, and as the mines played out, the population fell rapidly. In 1910, only 4,838 people lived in Goldfield, less than one-third than had been there four years earlier.

Rhyolite's rise and fall was even faster. Before leaving Bullfrog, Shorty Harris helped found the town, just west of today's Beatty, Nevada. From 1905 until 1909, Rhyolite was the center of its own universe. Based on a rich but shallow ore strike, the community almost immediately overstepped its bounds. The population rose as the mines produced, and estimates ranged from 3,000 to 12,000. A railroad station soon graced the town, as did an opera house, a symphony, a hospital, churches, and swimming pools. Three-story stone buildings dotted the main street, and electricity, running water, and telephone service were all common in the community. Rhyolite's decline was as swift as its rise. The mines started to close and the community lost its reason for being. By the time census workers counted the population in 1910, only 675 people remained there. A decade later, only fourteen were left.

The southern Nevada mining boom helped the development of transportation networks in Nevada and the West. Moving the proceeds of mining required rails, for without some kind of rail access, mining served little purpose. Initially, a freighting system much like the one that preceded the V&T on the Comstock conveyed the ore to the nearest railhead. Freighters found ways to reach the railroad; a route from Tonopah to the Sodaville stop on the Carson and Colorado Railroad provided a major connection. From Goldfield, freighters used a route to the old mining town of Candaleria, where they connected with the Carson and Colorado. The Bullfrog mines had a long haul to reach the San Pedro, Los Angeles, and Salt Lake Railroad at the newly established town that became Las Vegas.

As the value increased and freighters could not keep up with the production, the rails came closer. In July 1904, a narrow gauge railroad connected Tonopah with the Carson and Colorado. In September 1905, the Goldfield Railroad opened for business, advertising broad gauge connections to San Francisco. Two months later, the two railroads merged into the Tonopah and Goldfield Railroad. At Bullfrog, the railroad began to serve both Rhyolite and the Bullfrog district and began to capitalize on the development of borax mining in Death Valley, just beyond the state line. In 1907, the Bullfrog and Goldfield Railroad reached Beatty and Rhyolite. In 1906, the Las Vegas-Tonopah Railroad, a very long spur from the San Pedro, Los Angeles, and Salt Lake Railroad, reached Beatty. A year later, it arrived in Goldfield.

Goldfield served as the basis for the rise of George Wingfield, Nevada's most important power broker of the first three decades of the twentieth century. Born in Arkansas in 1876, he came to Nevada in 1896, already an experienced rancher and a proficient gambler. Wingfield was truly a product of western ranch culture. Raised in Lakeview, Oregon, he imbibed its values and mores, thinking of the world in terms of conquest. He was hired to bring 2,900 head of cattle from the Lakeview area to Winnemucca, a 215-mile trek. When he successfully delivered the herd, he was offered a permanent job with the cattle company, but the restless and ambitious Wingfield had had enough of the trail and decided to stay in Winnemucca. For the next few years, he bounced around, but he was adept enough at the poker tables to amass a stake of $40,000.

Like many a young man with newfound wealth before and since, Wingfield hastily invested his stake. He found a short-lived copper boom in Golconda, Nevada, about sixteen miles east of Winnemucca. In 1899, he opened the California Saloon in the town, promising "if you want a good drink or a good cigar, you must go to the California." He also purchased two lots and houses in Golconda. A year later, he owned the Banquet Saloon, close to the Adelaide Mine, the most important in Golconda. He also became a figure in the local newspapers, as his comings and goings were news as were those of other prominent citizens of the new and thriving community.

By the standards of the time and place, Wingfield was already wealthy and he lived the life of a rising young capitalist. A small man, he dressed well, looking the part of an up-and-coming entrepreneur. He could be a dandy. In one photo, he was dressed in white, hair slicked back, with his hands inside his belt, leaning back against the bar at the California Saloon. He developed a racing stable, entering horses in the state fair races in Reno in 1899, became a leading figure in the Golconda Jockey Club, and dabbled in a number of mining claims in the area. Wingfield had the makings of a good and prosperous life in Golconda—as long as the mine held out.

Golconda met the same fate as every mining town and it came in a hurry. Golconda existed because of its mines and mill. They were the economic engines that kept the community alive. The mill closed early in 1900, and the population began to decline from its peak of about 500. Wingfield closed the Banquet Saloon before the end of June and ended his involvement in the town. As quickly as he had come, he departed, seeking his next fortune.

But in Golconda, Wingfield developed one of the most important relationships of his life. He befriended Winnemucca banker George Nixon, already becoming a significant figure in Nevada politics. Nixon had been part of Nevada's splinter Silver Party and later became a Republican. He was first elected to the Nevada assembly in 1891 and ran unsuccessfully for U.S. Senate in 1897. He also served as the agent for the Southern Pacific and Carson and Colorado railroads, making him a part of the powerful cabal that ran the state. By the time Wingfield met him, Nixon was among the most influential people in the state. Together, the two men formed an unbeatable partnership that developed in mining and seeded the evolution of state politics.

In the spring of 1901, Wingfield arrived in the budding mining camp of Tonopah, not yet the burgeoning metropolis it would become. Wingfield had gotten in ahead of the rush. The silver Jim Butler found the year before had not yet caught the public imagination and Tonopah sported only 250 people, no frame buildings, and water was still hauled in by barrel. But the town had big plans, as mining towns always do. It was only a matter of time, residents told each other. Although he knew no one there well, George Wingfield intended to capitalize on the prospects and make the mining town his own.

Already a successful gambler, Wingfield utilized his skills as a way to make inroads. He dealt poker and faro at the Tonopah Club, the new community's most important joint, and his good nature whether he won or lost made him a popular individual. He was always handy with a good cigar for the men he gambled with, and most appreciated his jovial nature. Wingfield was also a remarkable student of gambling, seeking ways to increase the house's advantage. He moved to make gambling less risky for the house, establishing limits to betting and a solid enough house bank to assure that it could not be broken. Wingfield won enough money in a legendary unlimited game to move to the management side of gambling. He became the gambling concessionaire for the Tonopah Club.

As Tonopah took off, Wingfield found himself in a very different position than he had been in Golconda. In his first venture, he had arrived late; in Tonopah, he was well ahead of the curve. The gambling concession was like a license to print money. With ore strikes increasing in value daily and more and more beneficiaries of the finds, the high stakes action grew and grew. He managed gambling now, minimizing the risk to the club and to himself. He was remarkably successful; by 1904 Wingfield was worth $2 million and was credited with a profit of $200,000 that year.

Again Wingfield invested in the community. He bought one home and then another; filed on his first mine claim in Tonopah, the Reptile; and with his partners, formed the Boston-Tonopah Mining Company, of which he became president. Wingfield also became interested in politics, becoming a delegate to the Nye County Democratic Convention in 1902. Recognizing the importance of a network, he developed professional and personal relationships with people like future U.S. Senators Key Pittman and Tasker Oddie.

The Tonopah-Goldfield rush transformed Nevada politics. The railroads had dominated the last two decades of the nineteenth century, but the return of mining produced a new political order that had its roots in the center of the state. Like the Comstock before it, the Tonopah-Goldfield rush produced greater wealth than anything else in the state at the time. In Nevada, wealth has always created political power and politicians rose from the goldfields to shape the Silver State's political structure. For the next four decades, political power in Nevada was rooted in the Tonopah-Goldfield rush.

Key Pittman, who represented Nevada in the U.S. Senate from 1913 to 1940, was the primary political product of the Tonopah-Goldfield rush. He arrived in Nevada at the age of thirty in 1902 after some experience in the Klondike. He landed in Tonopah and opened a law office, diving headlong into politics at the same time. Successful in business, Pittman challenged George Nixon for the U.S. Senate seat in 1910, but lost. When Nixon died in 1912, Pittman won a popular ballot and was designated by the state legislature as the successor to Nixon's seat. He remained in the U.S. Senate until his death.

Nevada politics had always been a closed club. From the inception of the state, its political officials reflected the desire of the power brokers rather than the population at large. Men like Pittman were products of an elaborate system, one that kept power close. Despite his wealth, he had to earn a place on the Democratic ticket. Francis Newlands, the son-in-law of William Sharon who became U.S. representative from Nevada in 1892, was typical. Although he was the author of the Reclamation Act of 1902, which created opportunity for farmers by providing a way to bring water to arid land, Newlands was part of a cabal that ran state politics. Wingfield wanted to be close to such people.

In Tonopah, Wingfield helped Nixon fulfill his political aspirations. Their partnership began in October 1902 and quickly made both not only wealthy, but able to achieve much larger objectives. Nixon organized the Nye County Bank, capitalizing on his experience in that field. Nixon won a U.S. Senate seat in the 1904 election. Wingfield benefited from his partner's election. The new power base transformed him from an intrepid gambler into a nationally renowned businessman thought of as one of the most competent minds in the nation.

Tonopah was a better strike than Golconda. Its silver veins produced at a much higher rate and more consistently, creating real opportunities. Wingfield worked hard at business, paying special attention to mining. He was much admired for the close way he inspected claims before he purchased them. Wingfield owned a number of mining claims and stock in other mining companies, kept his gambling concession, loaned money at the rate of 2 percent per month, and bought property. He was the man with cash in an economy consistently short of it. The opportunities were endless.

In 1905, Wingfield relocated to the town that would become synonymous with his name: Goldfield. By the time Wingfield arrived, Goldfield had taken off. The mines were generating $1 million per month. The population had topped 10,000 and by some accounts, reached 15,000. Real estate on Main Street commanded $1,000 per foot of street frontage. Mining stocks in the district were valued at $150 million and even neighboring camps offered stock valued at $50 million. Bank deposits totaled $15 million. The town was in the throes of a boom, the likes of which had not been seen since the Comstock.

For Wingfield, thirty years old in 1906, this was the moment to shine. Called "a modern buccaneer" by the press in 1905 and already adept at financial dealings, he was soon labeled the "Napoleon of Nevada finance" for his skill at managing the complex world of mining stocks. His efforts created much of the paper value of the strike, for as always, the real wealth was to be found in the buying and selling of stocks. He also worked with his partners to acquire good claims in other boom towns like Rhyolite, Bullfrog, and Gold Center. Often, Wingfield and his partner Nixon opened banks in the communities as well. When Nixon took his seat in the U.S. Senate in 1905, the younger Wingfield adeptly managed not only their partnership, but also his own holdings. With the combination of wealth and access to political power in his partner, Wingfield was becoming an important actor on the Nevada stage.

As on the Comstock, Goldfield held opportunity for the astute. One Wingfield property, the Goldfield Mohawk Mine, yielded a phenomenally rich discovery in April 1904. The ore assayed at between $400 and $600 per ton, the best numbers anyone had seen for a while. Stock prices shot up; the claim on which the discovery was made sold for twenty-seven cents per share in January 1904. After the strike, it reached $27 per share. By that time, Wingfield owned a controlling interest in the company and profited from the mine and its stock.

The boom drew less industrious and even shady operators. The worst of these was George Graham Rice, whose book, *My Adventures with Your Money*, chronicled the experiences of this stock swindler. Born Jacob Herzig in New York in 1870, Rice came to Nevada in 1904, already an experienced criminal. He opened an advertising agency, parlayed that into a piece of the promotion of the Gans-Nelson fight, and built a trust to develop mining stocks. When the trust collapsed at the end of 1906, Rice promised to meet his obligations and then fled to Reno.

Rice's greatest contribution to the boom was the promotion of the Rawhide District, a limited strike that never produced the kind of wealth that Goldfield, Tonopah, or Rhyolite did. Rawhide had been established in December 1906, but only with Rice's skill as a promoter did it garner national attention. In conjunction with his partners Tex Rickard—the already well-known boxing promoter—and Nat C. Goodwin, Rice persuaded Elinor Glyn, author of the bestselling novel *Three Weeks*, to visit. The promoters had some success until Rice's involvement was disclosed, ending both Rice's career in Nevada and, along with a devastating fire, the prospects of Rawhide. Rice later tried the same type of stock run-up in the copper mines, but ended up serving one year in a federal penitentiary when his manipulations were exposed.

Goldfield continued to produce exceptional results. In January 1907, a single carload of ore from the Mohawk sold for $575,000, bringing national attention to the region. Wingfield continued to invest, building the great Goldfield Hotel, which cost $500,000 to build when it opened in 1908 and still stands. Even more importantly, Wingfield formed the Goldfield Consolidated Mining Company and built the huge mill that dominated the town after 1908.

His mill was part of an important change in the way mining in central Nevada operated. Unlike the initial generation of prospectors on the Comstock and in Tonopah and Goldfield, the miners who succeeded them were employees of increasingly large companies. They sought to unionize, bringing the Industrial Workers of the World (IWW) to Goldfield in 1905. Representing unskilled workers as opposed to the trade unionists of the other labor unions, the IWW supplanted two existing unions, an American Federation of Labor affiliate and the local chapter of the Western Federation of Miners. When the Western Federation of Miners merged into the IWW, the stage was set for a major labor showdown.

The tension focused on a practice called "high-grading." For complex geological reasons, the ore in Goldfield was very, very rich in spots, especially toward the surface. This was unusual among mining strikes. Most ore deposits have lower, more consistent values. The Goldfield mines had good overall values, allowing mining to continue there for more than a decade. The early miners exploited the pockets of very, very rich ore. The extremely rich ore was tempting and with gold climbing in value during the first decade of the twentieth century after nearly two decades of depressed market prices, miners easily stole hunks of rock that had considerable value. Shady assayers served as the conduit for getting this high-graded material into the market. They had the equipment to process the ore and turn it into metal bars. Assayers typically paid the high-graders only a portion of the gold's value, in exchange for doing the work of refining it and getting the result into the gold market. Some of the high-graded material was also used to "salt" mines or prospect holes in order to assist with the sale of worthless properties.

In Goldfield before 1906, mines were leased to people who would work them for a fixed period of time. This spared the claim owners, who usually had little capital, the expense of developing them. The leasers paid a percentage of all they produced to the owner and kept the rest. This meant that the leasers had considerable incentive to get as much value out of the ground as possible in the shortest amount of time. Miners did not believe that high-grading was much of a crime. Leasers knew that they did not own the ground and with a fixed amount of time, they typically turned a blind eye to high-grading.

High-grading lubricated Goldfield. The supplemental income it provided helped keep wages at a manageable level for the leasers by making the expense of living in a remote place like Goldfield possible for an average miner. As Goldfield boomed, prices rose and the prosperity of workers became an issue. High-grading kept a lid on any tension. Much of the social excess that characterized Goldfield in the early years—the huge number of bars, the fancy dinners, the gambling that so benefited George Wingfield—was fueled by high-grading. Such excess income could pay for other luxuries too, like union dues.

When Wingfield and Nixon began to consolidate the mines and run them in an efficient manner, they ran smack into the social customs of Goldfield. The push toward efficiency was characteristic of American business in the new century. Businessmen thought they could run on scientific principles, and Wingfield and Nixon embraced the philosophy. The miners resisted. High-grading was entrenched in the region, and Wingfield sought to root it out. Part of the difference in approach stemmed from the fact that Wingfield owned his claims. He faced no time limit on his exploration and was willing to battle both the practice of high-grading and the unions. At this point, Wingfield's political connections became instrumental.

Union labor remained a powerful influence in Goldfield, and Wingfield and the companies sought to break its back. In 1907, a series of labor battles began, starting with the death of an anti-union restaurant owner and climaxing with a battle over the changing rooms, where miners shed their work clothes and put on their street clothes. The practice of high-grading took place in the changing rooms. There miners secreted high-grade ore from the mines into their street clothes. The effort to stop this practice led to a strike on November 27, 1907, in the middle of the Panic of 1907, when a run on the American banking system threatened to topple the American economy. Miners demanded to be paid in real money instead of scrip, the paper promissory notes that mine operators offered instead of cash.

Headed by Wingfield, mine operators used the opportunity to try to break the union. They relied on the cooperation of Governor John Sparks, a cattle-man from the Humboldt Valley, who had no love for organized labor. Sparks wired President Theodore Roosevelt, asking for federal troops to quell what he termed "domestic violence and unlawful combinations and conspiracies." On December 6, a detachment from the Presidio in San Francisco arrived to put an end to the supposed uprising. The mine operators announced their intentions the following day. They lowered the wage scale by one dollar per day and insti-tuted a card system. Wingfield locked out the union miners and hired replace-ments. The new men were required to sign a card saying they would not join a union. The operators also recruited non-union workers from out of state to fill the positions of the strikers. With federal troops guarding the entrances, the mines reopened in January 1908.

Despite labor tension, prosperity had returned at least in part and Nevada's fortunes were on the rise. The first decade of the twentieth century saw a dou-bling of Nevada's population. From about 42,000 in 1900, the number of peo-ple in the state grew to 81,875. A larger population diminished the cries to take away Nevada's statehood, but the state's population was no more stable in 1910 than it had been in 1865. A mining boom brought temporary prosperity and hordes of people, but few of them put down permanent roots. Instead, they were off when the next boom began. Despite the rapid growth it created, the twentieth century mining boom did little to further the development of state institutions. In many ways, communities like Tonopah, Goldfield, and Rhyolite more resembled Virginia City of the 1860s and 1870s than a typical city of their era.

At the same time a new mineral, copper, began to be extracted from Nevada's earth. The copper boom was quite different from even the mining at Goldfield and Tonopah, for copper mining was a much more capital-intensive process than gold and silver mining. From the beginning, large syndicates controlled copper production. There was little room for the kind of entrepreneurial energy that was so typical of the goldfields. Copper was corporate from the onset; it required a higher level of organization and capital. It drew major corporations to Nevada in a way that the state had never before seen.

Copper was first discovered in Nevada in the 1870s. But it was not developed as an industry until Mark Requa, the son of a Comstock engineer, optioned a claim in the Robinson District in White Pine County in 1902. He secured a small amount of capital and created a company to mine copper. But Requa ran into the problem that dogged copper mining. Simply put, he needed more cash than he could raise. Requa's need brought the Guggenheims, the most prominent copper mining family in the world, into Nevada. They purchased Utah Copper in 1890, and helped Requa for a while before outmaneuvering him and gaining control of his holdings. In 1905–1906, the Guggenheims formed a new company, the Nevada Consolidated Copper Company, to make their western operation, centered in Bingham, Utah, more economically efficient. With incredible resources to support its work, the Nevada Consolidated Copper Company began to develop the copper resources of the Robinson District. By 1909, the company generated more than $6.5 million in copper and the numbers continued to rise.

The Guggenheims were among the most efficient operators in the mining industry. They organized four company towns: Ruth, McGill, Veteran, and Kimberly. Ruth was located at the mine; McGill was twenty-one miles to the north and it became the largest and most important of the towns. Unlike mining camps, company towns lacked the saloons and bawdy houses that so characterized places like Virginia City. The houses were nicely built and uniform. The streets were wide and generally well maintained. Underneath the veneer of order existed a world in which workers had few choices. There was no local government and businesses operated only with the permission of the company. Typically, the company permitted a pool hall and saloon; it often leased such concessions to friendly operators, using the amenities as a way to keep workers happy and to divest them of their paychecks.

Company control stemmed from its ownership of every inch of land in the communities. The company owned the houses, the stores, the streets, and the recreation facilities. The miners resented this control, for it made them feel less than free. The worst was the company store, the "pluck me" in the talk of miners. They hated the company store because they had no choice about whether to shop there, because their purchases were deducted before they received their pay in the form of scrip, and because the prices they paid were much higher than they would have been from an independent vendor. "St. Peter don't you call me 'cause I can't go," the song "Sixteen Tons" lamented. "I owe my soul to the company store."

Many of the miners were immigrants, contributing to Nevada's rank as the state with the highest percentage of immigrants in the population. In 1910, 19,691 of the 81,875 people in Nevada were immigrants, an astonishing number that approached one-quarter of the population. The miners came from all over: Greece; the failing Austro-Hungarian Empire; the little nation of Serbia, where the murder of the Austrian Archduke Franz Ferdinand in August 1914 set off World War I; and from faraway Japan. Like immigrants now, they were less inclined to challenge authority and unsure of their rights in a new country.

European countries had stronger traditions of trade unionism than did the early twentieth-century United States, and immigrant workers sought representation. The Western Federation of Miners obliged, calling a strike in 1912 over conditions in the Guggenheims' Bingham, Utah, operation. The company hired strikebreakers and violence ensued at its Nevada properties. Two workers were killed, inspiring Governor Tasker Oddie to declare martial law. In the end, the union won a small wage increase, but the killers of the two workers were never prosecuted. Immigrant miners found the taste of democracy just a little bit bitter.

When World War I began in August 1914, it provided a boost to the copper mines. Production increased from $7 million in 1914 to $25 million in 1916, all the result of wartime demand. New mines opened as well, as did older silver and lead mines in places like Pioche, Goodsprings, and Eureka. Although advertisements in Nevada newspapers called on the nationals of countries like

Austria, Serbia, and Montenegro to enlist in the battle, most Nevadans looked at the war in economic terms. With its small population, the state provided only 3,384 men for induction. Despite its economic success as a result of the war, Nevada had only a small role in the American part of the conflict.

Postwar Nevada was the scene of intense labor agitation. As the wartime boom came to an end, layoffs inspired unrest. Management strategy during the war had been to promise wage increases after the war, and when the time came and the market dropped, labor was angry. The iww had been criminalized in 1919, further raising the stakes. This gave management another tool: it could claim that any strike was an iww action, putting it beyond the law. The stakes were high and the tension mounting. Labor fought for its position and management sought to end its influence. Only one could win.

At Ruth in January 1919, the drama began to play out. One hundred and fifty men refused to go to work, demanding that they receive raises to make up for the high cost of living during wartime. They wanted the raises they had been promised during the war, but in the falling market after the war, wage increases were out of the question. The walkout was a typical effort, without ties to any national network. Essentially a wildcat strike, this effort was labeled an iww attempt to challenge capitalism. At a time when the public held negative feelings toward both organized labor and immigrants, such a label was devastating to the workers. The effort failed.

Throughout the year, labor problems dogged the mining industry. In July 1919 at McGill, a better organized strike took place. Almost immediately, Governor Emmet Boyle and the federal mediator J. Lord began working on an equitable resolution, which they reached on August 29, 1919. In Tonopah in August, another major labor situation developed. After being ignored throughout the war, workers were amenable to iww organizers who arrived in Tonopah. The union demands for raises were ignored, leading to a strike. Again, Governor Boyle, Lord, and Nevada Labor Commissioner R. F. Cole tried to find common ground. On September 13, a compromise plan was presented to the miners. Fearing iww influence, the operators insisted on a secret ballot. A convincing majority voted for the plan, but the iww refused to return to work. Other unions honored the iww picket line until the craft unions withdrew their support of the strike. Skilled workers were always suspicious of the iww and what it represented. A new union accepted the governor's plan, the iww strike committee was prosecuted under the new anti-union legislation, and the strike ended on November 8, 1919.

As the Jazz Age began, Nevada remained a producer of raw materials for the industrial economy, an increasingly disadvantageous position. In early twentieth-century America, raw materials lost value when compared to the value of finished goods. Copper and other minerals received a tremendous boost during the war, but like agriculture, mining returned to its slump in 1919. When European producers returned to the market, a glut of production depressed prices. Again Nevada leaders faced a difficult situation. They needed to bolster the economy of the Silver State, for much of the rest of the country was booming. If they did not, they risked a return to the doldrums of the late nineteenth century.

But mining was not going to be the salvation of the state any longer. As Tonopah declined in the aftermath of the war, peaking at a little over $9 million in production in 1914 and 1918, anyone who looked could see that Nevada needed to go in a different direction. Agriculture had never been truly viable, even with the Reclamation Act. Nevada's only urban center was Reno, the only non-mining town in the state. Reno had become an economic center, where much of the state's commerce and banking took place. It depended on production in the rest of the state. Without a new mining strike of considerable proportions, Nevada seemed doomed to reenact the tragedy of its past.

In the early twentieth century, travel began to change. Between the end of the Civil War and the turn of the century, trains were the primary means of interstate travel. After 1900, the rise of the automobile changed the patterns of travel. Especially after the introduction of the Model T in 1908, travel became democratized. If elites traveled by railroad car, ordinary Americans embraced the automobile. In rapidly growing numbers, they used it to go wherever they could find a road or track.

In Nevada, that was not always easy. The state had few roads that connected its cities, for most intrastate transportation took place by rail. The automobile posed a dramatic problem: what good was such a contraption if it could not travel easily between communities? This put pressure on the state to build roads, an expensive proposition by any measure. The solution, as so often was the case in the West, was federal involvement.

Beginning in the 1890s, Nevada's leaders recognized the importance of a road network in a large and sparsely populated state, but only as the 1900s boom began to fade did the state begin to build roads. In order to take advantage of the 1916 Federal-Aid Road Act, which introduced a federal dollar match for state road construction dollars, the state created a highway department in 1917 and outlined four routes that would comprise a state highway system. A few years later in 1921, the state benefited from a new federal law, which Oddie—then a U.S. Senator—was instrumental in passing, that made it easier for states with large percentages of federal land to match federal dollars. By 1926, as much as $10 million had been spent on Nevada roads. Many Nevadans considered their highway system complete at that time. Most of the roads were gravel.

One of the things that the new roads brought were people in search of divorce. Early in the twentieth century, divorce was uncommon in the U.S., permissible only in extreme situations. Nevada enjoyed relatively liberal divorce laws, allowing people from other states to reside in the Silver State for six months to achieve freedom from matrimonial mistakes. This remarkably liberal law was brought to public attention in 1906, when Laura Corey, the wife of New York City millionaire William Ellis Corey—the president of U.S. Steel, one of the most important components in the national economy—sued for divorce in Reno. The high-profile public action drew considerable attention to Nevada's easy divorce requirements and made the state an option for many who considered separating from their mates.

Nevada continued to host events that would not be sanctioned in other states. The Jack Johnson–James Jeffries heavyweight championship fight in Reno on July 4, 1910, pitted the two best fighters in the world. Johnson was the first African American heavyweight champion, a flamboyant man who flouted the rules of a segregated American society. He particularly flaunted his relationship with a white woman at a time when African American men were lynched for much less in the South. Johnson had beaten Tommy Burns in Australia in 1908 to claim the crown. The aging Jeffries was considered the best fighter of his era and was saddled with the label of the "Great White Hope." When Johnson knocked out Jeffries in the fifteenth round, he cemented his title and gave white America someone to hate. Arrested on trumped-up morality charges, Johnson fled the U.S., losing his crown to Jess Willard in Havana, Cuba, in 1915. Many said the fix was in, that the superior Johnson lost as the price of making his legal problems disappear. In 1920, Johnson surrendered to U.S. officials and served his jail sentence.

With this kind of entertainment, Nevada had something that nearby states would not match. In an era when African Americans were rapidly losing any rights that remained to them, they were able to fight not once, but twice for world championships in the Silver State. Nevada was hardly any more liberal than anywhere else. It was no beacon of equality. Economic need forced dramatic decisions. Boxing paid and that was enough for state officials. The question was how to find other activities that would bring people to Nevada.

As the 1920s began, Nevada seemed to run the opposite way from national trends. As the Jazz Age dawned, with its flappers and speakeasies and all the other trappings of new prosperity, Nevada stagnated. The state's mineral output in 1920 was half that of 1918. Agriculture was also hurt by the war's end. The high prices for crops disappeared as European farms returned to production. Nevada farmers grew less and received less for it. Even more telling, the state lost population. From 81,875 in 1910, Nevada remained home to only 77,407 in 1920. This first decline in more than two decades signaled a return to the economic depression that plagued the state during the late nineteenth century.

Nevada returned to its historic role as a producer of raw materials during the 1920s. In a time when the American economy was expanding and new frontiers were being broached in technology and commerce, Nevada lagged behind. During the 1920s, the United States engaged in an enormous speculative party. The radio became an everyday device, changing communication. The stock market shot up at an unmatched rate, generating millions upon millions of dollars in new wealth. The silver screen brought a new kind of entertainment to millions of Americans. Nevada barely participated.

In part this stemmed from the close nature of power in the state. Since statehood, only a few hands had held power. The mines of the Comstock had been first, followed by the railroad. The new century had brought new political power from the mines down state: from Tonopah, Goldfield, and Rhyolite. That political power was consolidated even as the mines diminished. Only a few held real power in the state. George Wingfield topped the list, and throughout the 1920s he continued to hold sway.

If ever a man owned Nevada, it was Wingfield. The savvy young man of the early twentieth century morphed into a stolid middle-aged broker. The dapper young man became stout, and his way of operating mirrored the change in his physique. The older Wingfield was less visible. Upon the death of his partner in 1912, Wingfield declined the opportunity to fill George Nixon's U.S. Senate seat. He contented himself with being the power behind the throne, a hidden but hardly invisible voice that made the most important decisions. Elected officials were no match for the canny operator. By owning the banks, Wingfield assured himself of ongoing influence over the affairs of the Silver State.

Wingfield built a machine in Nevada politics. He had migrated from his initial forays into politics as a Democrat to becoming the most important figure in state Republican politics. At the same time, he inaugurated the bipartisan system of Nevada politics, where party affiliation meant less than loyalty to the powers that be. During the time when Wingfield's power was at its zenith, one Democrat and one Republican represented the state in the U.S. Senate. Wingfield supported Key Pittman, a Democrat, in every one of his U.S. Senate races.

Wingfield's dominance left another aspiring Nevada politician out in the cold. Pat McCarran had become an adversary of the machine early in his career. Born on a ranch near Reno in 1876, he entered the state legislature in 1903. He served as District Attorney for Nye County, which included Tonopah and Goldfield, from 1907 to 1909 and soon found himself on the state supreme court. He became chief justice in 1917. Seen as a duplicitous person by his peers in Tonopah, McCarran was not popular in Nevada political circles.

McCarran was an ambitious man, but for a generation, his single objective, the U.S. Senate, was thwarted by his opponents. He and Pittman had near pathological hatred of one another and it spilled over in complicated ways. The antipathy dated from McCarran's time in Tonopah, where Pittman decided the younger man could not be trusted. Wingfield harbored similar feelings; McCarran had represented his common law wife, May, in their divorce proceedings in Tonopah in 1906. Pittman made no secret of his disdain for McCarran and declared that he would fight him for every nomination. When McCarran decided to run against Pittman for the Senate seat in 1916, the animosity hardened into a rupture in state Democratic politics that lasted for a generation.

For more than a decade, McCarran stewed as the Wingfield machine dominated Nevada politics. Throughout the first half of the 1920s, Wingfield and his operatives dominated every dimension of state politics. With the powerful Pittman in firm opposition, McCarran could get no traction. While on the state supreme court and afterward, he sought an opportunity to reinvigorate his political career and indeed his reason for being.

The Cole-Malley scandal of 1927 handed McCarran his opportunity. On the evening of April 27, 1927, two men walked toward George Wingfield's home, bundled up against the cold April wind. "We are in a hell of a fix," Edward Malley, the state treasurer, told Wingfield as his partner, George A. Cole, the former state controller, watched in dismay. Along with Harold C. Clapp, a hard-drinking man who had worked in one of Wingfield's banks but had been fired, the two men had embezzled more than $500,000. Wingfield felt his empire dissolving before his eyes.

Nevada had never seen a scandal quite like this one. At that time $500,000 was an enormous amount of state money, and the idea that state officials had stolen the sum was quite remarkable. It was easy to overlook the real problem—that Wingfield was the person to whom the men went when they realized that they were to be exposed. Wingfield's bank was the source of the problem, for the state funds were presented for payment there. If ever there was tacit announcement of where the power lay, it was when the men appeared at Wingfield's house to tell of their misdeeds.

Wingfield immediately began to control the damage. He was vulnerable, for the responsibility for the funds could have fallen on his bank. He faced two stark choices: repay the money himself and avoid public outcry, or make the problem public and risk damage to his empire. Neither was desirable. He was also vulnerable in another way. A company he owned had provided a $100,000 bond on Malley as the state treasurer. If Malley was convicted, Wingfield stood to lose that money on top of the $500,000 that was already gone. Wingfield set out to find a path that protected him and his holdings.

This led him to make the theft public and seek the prosecution of the three men. On Saturday, May 7, 1927, Wingfield sent an elaborate press release to all the major press outlets. He chose Saturday because that allowed almost two full days before the courts opened. Cole, Malley, and Clapp knew that they would be arrested and had time to get their affairs in order. They retained Pat McCarran as their defense counsel.

The trial was a grandiose affair, designed to shift the blame onto the defendants without exposing where the power lay in Nevada. Malley fought back, trying to cash the fraudulent cashier's checks on May 12, and McCarran went after his old nemesis Wingfield by trying to have the state bank examiner close Wingfield's bank. Correctly reading the politics of the state, the bank examiner declined. Clapp pleaded guilty in May, and after a month-long trial, Cole and Malley were found guilty in September. McCarran took considerable pleasure in attacking his longtime rival, and the trial brought added attention to Wingfield's dominance over the state.

Wingfield had run Nevada for more than two decades, but like everyone else, he was a product of the Tonopah-Goldfield economic regime. When power began to shift away from the center of the state, it became harder for Wingfield to maintain his iron grip. New forces were gathering, and they foretold a different Nevada. An inexorable shift had begun, driven once again by forces outside the state. Just a few months after the end of the trial, the contract for the construction of what would become the Hoover Dam was let. This contract, bigger in scope and scale than any previous one in Nevada history, marked the shift of power in the state to the south and to the then-struggling community of Las Vegas.

5 Hoover Dam and the Rise of Federal Power

THERE HAD NEVER BEEN A PROJECT in Nevada like the dam along the Colorado River. This enormous, expensive, and significant public works development brought the twentieth century to Nevada. The state was born as a byproduct of the Comstock mining in the 1860s; the dam reinvented a state that had spent the better part of the early twentieth century casting about for legitimacy and a new and broader economic survival strategy, and provided it with the tools of western modernity.

Boulder Dam, as the 726.4-foot-high dam across the Colorado River was called when Franklin D. Roosevelt spoke at its dedication in 1935, redefined the sources of the state's sustenance. As a result of the dam, railroads and mining ceased to pay the state's way, and the federal government became the source of the dollars on which Nevada depended. The dam simultaneously created modern southern Nevada, bringing technology to a regional population that subsequently grew with astonishing speed. Nevada was never the same.

The dam created the context for the north-south rivalry essential to understanding the state in the later twentieth century. It set in motion economic and demographic changes that greatly increased the number of people in the state, depositing ever more of them in the south and starting the shift of population from north to south. The arid and dusty collection of small towns and ranches that existed in southern Nevada before 1929 was replaced by the urban center that has come to dominate the state in every way.

The dam was the grandest public works project of its era, and the largest federal water development project yet undertaken. It symbolized the combination of hubris and ability to conquer nature that was central to the American attitude about deserts, and it illustrated the complicated colonial position of Nevada. The decision to locate the dam in the narrows of Black Canyon inaugurated a fifteen-year pattern of federal dominance in the state economy and set the tone for the subsequent use of the state as a testing ground for atomic weapons.

As did every previous venture in the state, the dam in Black Canyon bene-fited interests outside the state ahead of Nevada residents. The creation of this engineering marvel resulted not from any need in the Silver State, but from questions that originated beyond its boundaries and only incidentally con-cerned Nevada. Boulder Dam was located primarily in Nevada, but it served California above all else. The Silver State was to be home to the dam that imple-mented the "Law of the River," the complicated arrangement of rules and reg-ulations established to govern the distribution of the Colorado River's scarce water, called the Colorado River Compact. The Law of the River catered to states up and down the river, with nary a thought for Nevada. The lake that backed up behind it drowned towns such as St. Thomas and archaeological ruins such as the Lost City—also known as El Pueblo Grande de Nevada, the westernmost communities of the prehistoric Anasazi people—serving California and states further up the Colorado as it used Nevada for storage of this scarce and always precious commodity.

The dam resulted from two unrelated forces, urban California and its incred-ible imperial need for water, and the raucous Colorado River, which refused to submit to the technologies of the day. Los Angeles's ever-growing need for water pushed the city officials outward in search of new and dependable sup-plies. Los Angeles County grew from 170,000 people in 1900 to 2,785,000 in 1940, an astronomical growth rate that required consistent expansion of nearly every service. Following 1900, the City of Angels became a vacuum for every drop of water it could garner from any source. First, Los Angeles used its municipal status to drain the Owens Valley in eastern California's Inyo County. As their hopes faded, the farmers of the valley took out an advertisement in the *Los Angeles Times* that read: "We, the farmers of the Owens Valley, who are about to die, salute you." Los Angeles still needed more, ever more. The Colorado River, the lifeblood of the West, became the logical choice, and throughout the 1910s, the growing power of California grappled with entrenched interests in the upper basin. States such as Colorado and Wyoming had little need for that water at the moment, but they could see that their future, their chance at the brass ring of industrial prosperity, depended wholly on being able to reserve water from the Colorado River for their future growth.

At the same time, agriculturists seized on the dam as a solution to the peren-nial violent flooding of the Colorado River. Nineteenth-century Americans were certain that with technology, they could make the desert bloom. With the help of Nevada's Francis Newlands, irrigation became the tool of their desires.

In 1901 in the Colorado Desert, where about 2.4 inches of rain falls per year, the most famous private irrgationist of the era, George Chaffey, cut a diversion channel and brought the river into an area then called the Valley of the Dead. It soon was renamed the "Imperial Valley," and within one year, the area boasted two towns, 2,000 settlers, and 100,000 acres of crops. The Imperial Valley seemed a reclamation paradise, where the ingenuity of human beings could transcend the overwhelming limits of nature.

The year of 1900 began an exceptionally wet thirty-year period in much of the West. In some places, the moisture gave people unrealistic expectations; in others, it washed away hopes and dreams under a cavalcade of water. In 1904, spring floods ripped into irrigated land with a fury in the Imperial Valley. Homes were swept away, fields drowned, and people watched a strange wall of water moving backward at a slow crawl from the irrigation channels toward the original river bed. The destructive floods came time and again and left an imprint on people downstream. There was only one way to secure the region, to allow it to grow unimpeded, to protect crops and people from the river's destructive nature, they believed as they stood amid the wreckage of their lives. A dam had to be built upstream that could regulate the flow of the Colorado River.

The objectives of the Imperial Valley dovetailed nicely with those of Los Angeles, already well on the way to outstripping its latest water supply. To keep growing, California needed water and growth was religion in the southern Golden State early in the twentieth century. The Colorado River was the obvious choice. Two different kinds of development in the most populous and the increasingly most powerful state in the West joined forces in support of a dam.

Upstream, the growth of California and its need for water was a source of concern. Upper basin states rightly regarded California's grab for water as the end of their own aspirations. The Colorado River held a finite quantity of water; western water law, called the "doctrine of prior appropriation," sanctioned the ethos of first in time, first in right. If someone used the water first, they retained the prevailing right to that water forever. Southern California's rapid expansion meant that the Golden State used water before the slower-growing upriver states, and by using it had the first and—as a result—only valid claim to its future use. Even distant states like Colorado were paralyzed by the prospect of California's dominance and they fought the Golden State to a standstill for a decade.

In 1922, the U.S. Supreme Court destroyed their defense. In *Wyoming v. California*, the court ruled that states that used the prior appropriation doctrine when they allocated water within the state, as did all the Colorado River states, were bound by it in interstate disputes if they shared a common water source. The decision gave the water in the Colorado River to California at the expense of the rest of the states. The Upper Basin states soon sued for peace and the Colorado River Compact attempted to divide the river fairly, allowing water for California's growth without taking all of the water in the river from other states.

Western water was not that simple. After the signing of the Colorado River Compact in November 1922, states refused to ratify the legislation. No one liked it; every constituency felt shortchanged and the agreement was pilloried in the press and in statehouses across the West. Six year later, the bill still had not become law, and in 1928, Congress intervened. It authorized Boulder Dam and the All-American Canal for the Imperial Valley and limited California's share of the river to 4.4 million acre feet on the condition that six of the seven compact states ratify the agreement.

With Nevada's 300,000 acre feet and California's 4.4 million, Arizona received 2.8 million acre feet, less than it wanted. As a result, Arizona refused to sign, but six states ratified the compact and the congressional decision made the refusal meaningless. Nevada just took its lumps. The relationship between California and its neighbors, the junior partners in western growth, was made clear. Like it or not, California would do as it pleased. Nevada and Arizona would not affect the outcome of water distribution. The stage was set for western growth—with federally funded dams regulating water apportioned by the principle "might makes right." As early as 1929, when surveyors began to stake the Boulder Dam project, the axiom "in the American West, water flows uphill to money" was entirely true.

The decision to construct the Boulder Dam, now Hoover Dam—the largest public works project of its time—in Black Canyon about thirty miles from Las Vegas was the signal event in the history of southern Nevada. Las Vegas had been created by the San Pedro, Los Angeles, and Salt Lake Railroad. When the railroad prospered, as it did with the opening of the silver mines in Bullfrog and Rhyolite before 1910, so did the region. But the end of the mining boom and the railroad's removal of its Las Vegas shop to Caliente to punish the town for supporting the national railroad strike of 1922 marked an important transition for the town. As the population grew, doubling in size from 1920 to 1930, Las Vegans recognized that they could no longer rely on the railroad alone. The dam stood as a panacea, a salve for a destroyed railroad economy, but it remained a hope rather than a reality. Elsewhere south of Tonopah and Gold-field, a few small towns and ranches comprised the rest of southern Nevada's population.

The dam assured not only greater interest from the rest of the nation, but also an ongoing stream of people to increase the region's population. After the announcement of a timetable for construction, men streamed into the arid heat of southern Nevada in search of work. They arrived in box cars and dilapidated automobiles, on horseback and even on foot. A few had experience in construction and more came from the ranches of Nevada and Utah to wrangle the horses and mules they were certain would be necessary to move such a quantity of dirt, rock, and concrete. Most were simply unemployed, looking for salvation in a steady job.

The dam project's ramifications reached beyond state boundaries. Authorized in 1928, before the October 1929 beginning of the Great Depression, the dam became a de facto federal employment project. When Herbert Hoover was sworn in as president in 1929, he inherited a nation flush with prosperity. "We will be judged," he said in his inaugural address, "by the health of the economy." During his first year as president, the stock market crashed, sending the nation into the throes of economic depression. Although Hoover's credentials for the presidency were notable, his personal devotion to self-help and the ideas of laissez faire capitalism prevented him from conceiving of a broad-based federal response to disastrous times. As unemployment climbed, families crumbled, and people boiled shoes to have something to eat, Hoover and his cabinet played medicine ball on the White House lawn to show their physical and presumably psychic fitness to deal with the crisis. With government absent, business was not strong enough to take up the slack, and for the first time in their history, many Americans lost hope.

The dam project provided an answer for many. It fit Hoover's idea of useful activity for government and offered employment for thousands. On July 3, 1930, Secretary of the Interior Dr. Ray Lyman Wilbur ordered Commissioner of Reclamation Elwood Mead to begin construction of the dam. On January 10, 1931, prospective bidders could purchase the specifications for the newly named Hoover Dam project for $5.00. With only two months until the bids were opened on March 4, 1931, the bidders rushed to assemble their proposals for this enormous project.

When the bids were opened in the Bureau of Reclamation's office in Denver on that March morning, observers were stunned that only five organizations completed the bid process. Two bids did not meet the specifications; two others came in at more than $53 million. Six Companies, Inc., a collection of western construction companies that included McDonald & Kahn and Bechtel of the San Francisco Bay Area, Morrison-Knudsen of Idaho, Kaiser Paving Company of Oakland, Utah Construction Company of Utah, and J. F. Shea and Pacific Bridge of Portland, Oregon, offered the winning bid at $48,890,999, about $24,000 more than Bureau of Reclamation specialists estimated as the cost of the project. The project was too large and complex for any one builder; together, these six non-Nevada companies stood a genuine chance of building an engineering marvel.

Federal money underpinned the rise of southern Nevada, for in 1931, the dollars to build the dam were the only game in the southern part of the state. With this nearly total control, the new federal regime mirrored its predecessors in mining and transportation. It created power that came from outside the state and was beholden to influences beyond state borders. The new regime brought the expectation that its operators would profit from the resources of Nevada. Although dam dollars drove the state, the goals and aims of the project—like those of mining and the railroad before it—were not central to the needs of Nevada. Federal dollars provided Nevada with construction jobs, but not with the basis for an ongoing economy independent of subsidy. The federal government continued the colonial patterns that marked Nevada's history.

When construction began in 1931, it provided an influx of dollars that the state's economy sorely needed. Agriculture and mining experienced dramatic declines after the stock market fell, and little else in the state seemed solvent. Construction at the dam generated $19 million, an enormous sum by the standards of the day. At 726.4 feet in height, more than 45 feet across at the top, and as thick as two football fields at the base, the dam contained 4.25 million cubic feet of concrete poured in sections. The project took four years of three shifts a day, seven days a week, with Christmas off, to complete. The dollars from the dam, and the four years of paychecks to between 3,000 and 5,000 workers at the height of the Depression, were nectar to the depressed state.

Work on the dam was difficult and dangerous, but in the 1930s, hundreds of applicants for every position rushed to take the risk. Everything about the job was dangerous, and the canyon could safely hold only a finite number of workers. Construction superintendent Frank T. Crowe recognized the challenge of managing the project. "We had 5,000 men in a 4,000-foot canyon," he told people. "The problem was to set up the right sequence of jobs so they wouldn't kill each other off." The climate made the work even more difficult. Temperatures routinely reached 120 degrees in the canyon bottom, and heavy lifting, pouring concrete, and moving rock were staples of daily endeavor. One summer, the thermometer topped 138 degrees, and for an entire month, never went below 100 degrees Fahrenheit, day or night. Nighttime shifts were desirable in the hottest months; by moonlight, the work was equally dangerous but nowhere near as hot. When workers collapsed from the heat, they were packed in ice and taken out in ambulances. Some died from the heat; not even the ice could revive them. Suicides were common. Others were injured or killed in construction accidents. Official accounts give 96 as the death toll from industrial accidents during construction, but that figure does not include deaths from illness, heat prostration, heart attacks, carbon monoxide poisoning, and all the other maladies that workers experienced. Some old-timers insist that the actual total was higher than 240 when work-related illness was included. With at least 3,500 workers at any given time and a peak of 5,218 workers in July 1934, the mortality figures were staggering by modern standards, but more typical of a time when work was hazardous and federal workplace regulations did not exist.

When Franklin D. Roosevelt dedicated the dam on September 30, 1935, the 760-foot concrete face offered a technological miracle that only the twentieth century could produce: a holding tank for all the water in the river, distributed by legal agreement between haves and have-nots. "This morning I came, I saw, and I was conquered," the president told the audience at the dedication, "as everyone will be who sees for the first time this great feat of mankind. The transformation wrought here is a twentieth-century marvel." The dam divided the Colorado River, but even more it created modern life, an economy, infrastructure, business, and even tourism, in a region that had struggled since Anglo-Americans settled it some seventy-five years before.

Hoover Dam was a testimony to the power of modernity, an architectural achievement that captured the national imagination. Nothing like it had been built before and the Depression decade made it a valuable social project as well. In this sense, Hoover Dam linked nineteenth-century construction, which used human and animal sweat as its primary source of energy, with the construction of the twentieth century, far more reliant on computers and other technologies to lighten the load of workers. Americans at the time recognized Hoover Dam as a monumental and even transformative achievement. The southwestern writer Frank Waters, giddy at its prospects, labeled it "the Ninth

Symphony of our day, a visual symphony written in steel and concrete." Others heaped accolades equally as grand upon it, some labeling it the eighth wonder of the world.

The economic and social energy the dam created was tremendous. Not only did it resuscitate Las Vegas and breathe new life into Nevada, it also transformed the Bureau of Reclamation from a marginal federal agency into one of the most powerful. The success of the dam paved the way for the bureau to become a preeminent federal agency and a powerful engine of development until the 1970s, when nascent environmentalism halted big dam construction. After Boulder Dam, the Bureau of Reclamation engaged in a forty-year orgy of dam building until it controlled the distribution of most of the water west of the Mississippi River and created legions of dependent local communities throughout the West. As it revived Nevada, it also gave it a new master, one that carried other dependents in tow.

Hoover Dam was the first of the great dams. Its descendants can be seen across the West and around the world: in Aswan, Egypt, on the Nile River, and recently at Three Gorges on the Yangtze River in China. These later dams, technological marvels in their own right, owe their genesis to Hoover Dam. The technologies applied in the Nevada desert laid the basis for development of large dams throughout the world and gave humanity the ability to harness rivers for its own purposes. It also contributed to the arrogance of people who believed that they could find technological solutions to all kinds of problems. Even after the completion of the dam, Nevada was not yet through with such technological dreamers.

AS THE DAM FILLED BLACK CANYON, Nevada faced ongoing difficulties. In the late 1920s, the Silver State's prospects looked up, but the Depression hurt small states such as Nevada even more than the big industrial states. Dependent on markets for its crops and minerals, the state suffered when those markets collapsed. Gross income from crops and stock toppled from $22.1 million in 1928 to $6.4 million in 1932. A drought in 1930 and 1931 crippled the stock and feed industries in the state, and the collapse of the Wingfield banks, including the Riverside Bank in Reno in 1932, paralyzed the state's small financial community. As did much of the nation, Nevada found itself in dire straits as the presidential election loomed in 1932.

The Silver State enjoyed one important difference from other destitute states: it had already institutionalized the idea of providing people from other places with pleasures they could not legally obtain at home. Since the advent of legalized prize fighting in 1897, Nevada had toyed with this concept. It permitted gambling until 1910, and much of the state scoffed at restrictive gambling laws and even Prohibition throughout the 1920s. Nevada had both permitted people to marry without the three-week wait required elsewhere and let them get unshackled after a mere six-month stay to establish residency. When other states dropped their requirements to match the Silver State's in 1927, Nevada dropped its to three months. This response reflected the state's dependence on the dollars from divorce, another scorned activity. When the Depression hit, Nevada leaders simultaneously recognized their predicament and the way that the state's unusual status permitted them to forge a solution.

When the 1931 legislature met, its primary goal was to fashion a strategy to bring the state out of its economic doldrums. What other states regarded as vice provided the best option in the Silver State. In March 1931, a first-term assemblyman from Humboldt County, Phil Tobin, introduced a bill to again legalize gaming. Although Tobin always claimed that the idea was his own and his alone, most believe that the impetus came from Wingfield and others throughout the state. In Tobin's telling, only he felt free to offer the bill. In difficult economic circumstances, the state legislature easily passed the bill, laying the foundation for a state economy different from any conventional American mode. When the measure passed, Nevada cemented its reputation as the nation's scapegoat, the place where people could engage in behaviors for which they would be sanctioned and even shunned at home.

The Depression drove other states to desperate measures, and Nevada responded to efforts to impinge on its divorce trade, another of the staples of the state economy. In the early years of the Depression, Idaho and Arkansas reduced the wait for a divorce in their states to the same three months that Nevada required. Nevada's response was quick and simple: reduce its own wait from three months to six weeks, making divorce easier in Nevada than in competing states. If an American state intended to profit from vice, Nevada would surely provide fierce competition.

Legalized gambling had a greater long-term effect on the state's fortunes. Initially, it brought an industry that had been operating in the shadows for more than two decades back to the forefront of the state. As a result of the change in law, construction experienced a quick boom that provided hundreds of jobs. Hotels and nightclubs that planned to offer gambling needed remodeling and expansion; the illegal speakeasies and backroom gambling joints moved to the picture windows on the most heavily trafficked streets. In Reno the Bank Club, the city's largest casino, was remodeled, and others were enlarged. On Easter weekend more than 5,000 visitors, many from California, came to gamble in Douglas Alley, the center of Reno's gambling district, affirming the state's decision to legalize wagering.

Las Vegas followed more slowly. The city issued only six licenses in April 1931, mostly to clubs such as the Apache Club or the Northern Club on Fremont Street, but the most significant went to gambler Tony Cornero and his brothers. As a veteran of illegal activities, Cornero recognized the advantages of legalized gambling for operators ahead of anyone else. He also understood the importance of catering to workers at the dam. When he opened the $31,000 Meadows Club on Boulder Highway outside of Las Vegas on May 2, 1931, the plush casino offered entertainment as well. Inside, dam workers in search of recreation could find faro, twenty-one, roulette, craps, and poker to accompany shows by the Meadows Revue and music from the Meadow Larks, a Los Angeles band. Compared to the clubs inside the red-lined district on Fremont Street between First and Third, the Meadows Club was a palace. Even at the inception of legalized gambling in the 1930s, Las Vegas was split between downtown casinos and resort-like properties on its outskirts.

Gambling remained uncomfortable for Nevada, and even as towns such as Las Vegas began to see themselves as tourist towns, they couched the significance of gambling in deemphasizing its importance as a draw. Las Vegas's tourism increased as people came to the dam. Throughout the 1930s, the city marketed itself as a place that had not changed, a city where nineteenth-century mores and values held sway, and chief among those was the right to do as you pleased without government interference. Las Vegas was, it seemed to say, the Old West, where the institutions of progress had not yet taken hold and there was leeway to behave as you chose. No one could tell you how to live, Las Vegas's message imparted, and the old prospectors with their burros in hotel lobbies on Fremont Street added more than local color. Along with the requisite enormous gold nugget that gave so many establishments their names, the combination persuaded visitors that they were engaged in something other than simple sin—that they were, instead, recovering the freedom that had been a mainstay of American life before civilization took hold.

Many were not convinced, and scathing critiques of the state and its communities were commonplace throughout the 1930s. Reno, with its self-adorned nickname, "The Biggest Little City in the World," bore the brunt.

"Reno is a blot on civilization," the *International Society of Christian Endeavor* asserted in a typical example, "a menace to the American home and national prestige." The response was swift and loud, excoriating the Silver State and anyone who supported its unusual version of state's rights. The legal permission to sin did not yet extend to the realm of morality, further accentuating the difference between Nevada and every other state in the Union.

Control of legalized gambling fell to the counties under the new law, and each administered it as its leaders saw fit. Each county empanelled a supervisory board that included three county commissioners, the sheriff, and the district attorney. In most counties, the sheriff handled the day-to-day administration and enforcement proceeded in the local, even idiosyncratic way of small-town government in lightly regulated states. City councils in Reno, Las Vegas, and other incorporated communities added their own licenses to the state's requirements. The state received one quarter of licensing fees; in unincorporated areas, the county received the rest. Inside city limits, the city received half of the revenue and the county's share was reduced to one quarter.

Gambling alone did not alter the state's economic fortunes during the 1930s. In 1933, it generated only $69,000 for the state, not nearly enough to stanch the decline in revenues from failing industries such as mining and agriculture. Cities benefited most; Las Vegas and Reno could each count on about $50,000 in revenue from gambling, a sizable sum for these two small metropolises. Marriage and divorce added to state coffers, but Nevada's economic health remained tenuous throughout the decade. As did nearly every other western state, Nevada relied on federal money.

In this respect, the election of Franklin D. Roosevelt became a pivotal moment in the history of the state. On November 1, 1932, just a few days before the presidential election, Nevada Governor Fred Balzar declared a two-week bank holiday to prop up the state's banking system, but the Wingfield banks were already too far toward insolvency to be rescued by time. Over the objections of his financial experts, Wingfield had made too many loans to ranchers and farmers in Nevada. When they could not repay their obligations as the economy teetered, Wingfield's empire toppled. By June 1932, four banks in the state had failed and the Wingfield flagship, the Reno National Bank, teetered on the brink. Even a $4.8 million loan from the Hoover-era Reconstruction Finance Corporation and a plea for a second loan from Governor Balzar could not save the chain. By Christmas 1932, the state bank examiner had taken control of the Wingfield empire, the pride of Nevada. Receivership followed in

1933. Wingfield's faith in his home state ruined him. As Las Vegas and southern Nevada flourished with the dam, the rest of the state's economy collapsed.

Roosevelt's New Deal resuscitated the state. A wide constellation of programs designed to prime the pump of the national economy by putting people to work, the New Deal sponsored public works projects, gave home loans, guaranteed bank deposits, and provided work or relief for the unemployed. Nevada's position was particularly vulnerable, but its powerful congressional delegation brought home federal dollars. In the end, savvy politicians helped Nevada capitalize like no other state in the Union. The Silver State received more money per person from New Deal programs than any other state. It was also first per capita in loans, Civilian Conservation Corps (ccc), Civil Works Administration (cwa), and expenditures for public roads. Between the establishment of the ccc in April 1933 and June 1939, more than four thousand young men worked in twenty-four ccc camps throughout the state. cwa programs provided short-term employment for thousands of Nevadans who labeled street signs, painted barns, drilled wells, and built historical markers. The dollars that came from such programs became the lifeblood of the state throughout the 1930s.

The state had experience with federally funded projects before the New Deal. As did the representatives of other western states, Nevada's congressional delegation lobbied for federal facilities in the state. The siting of the Naval Ammunition Depot in Hawthorne in 1928 offered Nevada access to federal subsidies the state had never before experienced. The project brought about $5 million in construction alone and laid the basis for later federal developments. In 1930, Senator Tasker Oddie sponsored the Oddie-Colton bill, which compelled the federal government to pay the full cost of roadways through public land and Native American reservations. As a result, the federal government spent almost $30 million during the 1930s on Nevada highways—triple its expenditures during the 1920s, and further accentuating the growing dependence on Washington, D.C., money.

The condition of the state's other industries made Nevada's strategy even more logical. Only the adroit maneuvering of the congressional delegation helped save mining, the state's other primary industry. In 1932, mining hit bottom, producing only $4.2 million, about 15 percent of the annual value before the Depression. Nevada's two senators, Oddie and the alcoholic but powerful Key Pittman, each battled for a specific mineral. During the early years of the Depression, Oddie unsuccessfully pushed for price supports for copper, the most important mineral in the state in the 1910s and 1920s, and

Pittman offered the customary arguments for silver subsidies that were the hallmark of his career. In 1933, playing both sides against the middle, Pittman persuaded Roosevelt to order the purchase of all American silver production at a price more than 20 cents an ounce above the market value, followed in 1934 by the Silver Purchase Act, which put 25 percent of the U.S. monetary reserve in silver and drove prices up even more. Copper soon rose in price as a result of federal legislation, and by 1937, Nevada mining exceeded the production of the best years of the 1920s. Federal dollars and political manipulation eased Nevada's situation during the 1930s.

Nevada was no more grateful for the federal largesse than other western states that prided themselves on their individualism. The vaunted Nevada sense of self provided a crucial dimension of state character, and Nevada identity already demanded a perception of personal independence. The federal funds that sustained it contributed to a complex paradox: people asserted their self-sufficiency ever more loudly as more of their money came from federal programs. Not uncommon in the West, the predicament contributed to an ongoing pattern. Nevadans and other westerners had a hard time acknowledging the source of their sustenance and even resented the hand that fed them. Yet without federal assistance, and especially the federal purchase of silver, it seems unlikely that Nevada would have escaped the 1930s as comfortably as it did. As was the case in many western states, the worst years occurred under the laissez-faire Hoover regime; the New Deal and its many programs improved the lot of ordinary Nevadans. If the state had to swallow a little government assistance, it beat the alternatives during the Depression.

THE NEW DEAL established the dominance of federal money in Nevada. This was not a new pattern, for the state has been beholden to one or another dominant industry since its founding. The fact that government now took the reins, as it did almost everywhere in the West and indeed the nation, offers telling commentary on the state of American business. Private enterprise, which had long been predatory in Nevada, had failed. Federal agencies stepped in, and throughout the 1930s and World War II federal money remained the dominant source of capital in Nevada. After the dedication of the dam, construction dollars and the jobs they supported diminished and Nevadans cast about for a strategy that did not involve government, but nothing significant enough to drive the state economy appeared. Tourism and divorce in the 1930s filled a gap, but alone they were not sufficient to revive the prosperity of the dam years. Mining remained vulnerable, propped up by federal subsidy and the machinations of powerful politicians. Nevada's circumstances were not bad by the end of the decade, but there was little opportunity to improve the state's economic situation as long as the national economy remained stagnant.

Only the attack on Pearl Harbor and the response it inspired rescued Nevada. As tensions worsened in the 1930s, the American government sought to remedy its limited industrial capability in the West. Even before the Japanese attack, officials recognized that the U.S. faced a two-front war. Americans needed more plants, more assembly lines, and more mineral production in the West. The West needed the industrial infrastructure of the East if the nation was to successfully wage war in the Pacific.

As global conflict escalated with Hitler's invasion of Poland in September 1939, President Franklin D. Roosevelt planned for the nation's defense, and facilities in the West became a priority. The entire region had served as a provider of raw materials since the nineteenth century, but little of the industrial infrastructure that characterized cities such as Pittsburgh, Chicago, or Cleveland existed in the Far West. The pattern of extractive industry remained; the region largely produced raw materials and shipped them elsewhere to be milled, processed, and finished. While these circumstances worked well in building a national economy, they had not been conceived for war. The federal government sought a comprehensive industrial infrastructure in the West as soon as it could be achieved.

The effort to build an industrial West had an important impact on the state. Mining received a boost as surveyors searched for industrial grade minerals, and copper prices—long considered a measuring stick for military buildup— rose significantly. As tensions throughout the world increased, Nevadans recognized that their state's minerals were essential in the war effort. The 1936 discovery in Nye County of brucite and magnesite, the essential ores of magnesium, offered another of the mineral finds that defined Nevada's past. The combination of federal dollars and entrepreneurial ingenuity made its development possible. In July 1941, the $150 million Basic Magnesium Incorporated (BMI) factory, located between Las Vegas and Boulder City, was authorized. Construction was completed before the end of 1941. The plant was to transform the raw magnesium mined near Gabbs in Nye County, almost 350 miles from the plant, and furnish 112 million pounds of magnesium each year. The material was used in aircraft wings, incendiary bombs, flares, and tracer bullets. Electricity from Boulder Dam powered the plant. Nevada instantly had an industrial component.

After Pearl Harbor, Nevada became a haven for war-related operations. Away from the coast, it did not face the threat of assault by sea, a prospect so daunting after the Japanese attack that many feared invasion of the West Coast. Industrial development increased at a rapid pace in Nevada. The federal government commandeered an air field north of Las Vegas, ultimately spending more than $25 million on the construction of facilities there. The Las Vegas Gunnery School, as the installation became known, supplied tail gunners for the Army Air Corps, graduating four thousand every six weeks by 1942. North of Reno, Stead Army Air Base trained signal companies. An Army air base came to Tonopah, and Fallon received a Naval Air Station. Hawthorne's ammunition depot grew in significance, size, and expenditures as well; Minden received a huge runway to train pilots, and countless other places participated in the war effort.

Wartime investment became a backbone of the state economy. Not only did the federal government employ thousands, it also brought trainees to the state in significant numbers. They too received a paycheck, and in a state that had made sin legal, the opportunities to spend that money were plentiful. Gambling, saloons open all hours, and legalized prostitution combined to make Nevada a desirable posting for many young soldiers. Nevadans profited not only from the federal outlay to build the facilities for the war, but from the expenditures of individual soldiers as well. The state's unique strategy began to yield dividends.

The consequence of the dominance of federal dollars impinged on the vaunted Nevada sense of individual choice. Local decision-making bodies had little choice but to respond to federal needs, for the basis of prosperity came from construction contracts, service work, or the opportunity to liberate dollars from the pockets of workers. Federal dollars were so crucial that when the Federal Security Agency and the military pressured communities to outlaw prostitution, most gave in to this decidedly non-Nevadan demand. In 1942, Las Vegas closed its red-light district to accommodate the military, and after November 1942, bars and casinos closed from 2:00 A.M. to 10:00 A.M., an otherwise unlikely prospect in southern Nevada. But closure was worthwhile if the consequence of failing to comply was to be off-limits to military personnel.

World War II also gave a powerful boost to labor in Nevada. The state had a strong tradition of organized labor. Nineteenth-century unions had been prevalent and the twentieth-century mining boom fostered labor organizations. In southern Nevada, craft unions received a strong boost from Boulder Dam. A generation of local labor leaders learned their trades at the dam, and they honed them at Basic Magnesium. They represented the American Federation of Labor (AFL), the more conservative craft unions, rather than the Congress of Industrial Organizations (CIO) or the radical industrial unions such as the "Wobblies"—the Industrial Workers of the World (IWW). AFL unions were conservative not only in their cooperative relationship with management; they also routinely denied membership to African Americans. At the dam, only twenty African Americans found jobs among the more than 5,200 workers in spring 1934, and the AFL's racial policies held sway throughout the 1930s despite efforts by the IWW to get in on the work there. By the early 1940s, as the AFL and the CIO grappled for supremacy in American labor, the AFL controlled labor in southern Nevada in close embrace with business, and African American workers were largely excluded from participation.

Wartime demand for labor transformed Nevada's workplace. The state never had enough labor and the demands of war industries sent recruiters across the country to bring workers back to the Silver State. Men and women alike came to BMI from all over the country, a large number of African Americans from the South among them. Discriminated against throughout American society, such workers found protection and even refuge in CIO unionization; at Basic Magnesium, many supported the International Union of Mine, Mill, and Smelter Workers (IUMMSW), an affiliate of the CIO. At BMI, women workers, called "Magnesium Maggies," drove forklifts, handled magnesium ingots and wrapped them for shipping, and engaged in a host of other jobs. They too belonged to unions, and the struggle between the CIO and the AFL made BMI a test case not only for their relative power, but for the protection of organized labor in American law.

In the U.S., organized labor had only been protected in law since 1935, when Congress passed the National Labor Relations Act. The act required that employers recognize a union chosen by the majority of their workers, providing legal protection for workers' rights that had never before existed. With this legislation, the federal government took on the role of labor's protector. The creation of the National Labor Relations Board, the National War Labor Board, and the Fair Employment Practices Commission all served to regulate the relationship between business and labor. This balancing role, labeled the "Broker State" by scholars, was supposed to assure fairness in the wartime workplace.

At BMI, the Broker State broke down, damaging not only the CIO but the position of labor throughout the nation.

In the patriotic fervor that followed Pearl Harbor, both the AFL and the CIO ratified a no-strike pledge for the duration of the war, limiting labor's ability to counteract the power of business. While wartime might not have been an appropriate circumstance for labor action, business regarded the pledge as evidence of labor's weakness and moved to cripple the labor movement. The various federal commissions were supposed to provide redress for labor, but in the case of BMI the inaction of regulatory bodies such as the National Labor Relations Board allowed the AFL to unite with management to crush its rival, the CIO. Determined local resistance trumped the Broker State, rendering the labor bureaucracy impotent and setting back the causes of the integrated workplace and workplace democracy.

Race became a wedge issue at BMI, and wartime Nevada was not an easy place for African Americans, but it was not appreciably worse than many other states. The small number of African Americans in the state and the introduction not only of African American workers but also of their southern white counterparts combined to create racial tension as southerners tried to extend their home region's racial structure to the Far West. The wide open nature of Nevada allowed a larger measure of live-and-let-live than was common elsewhere in the nation, and African Americans could enjoy at least some of those options. But in labor as in much else, Nevada remained segregated into the 1950s.

Race also revealed its ugliest dimensions in the treatment of the Japanese in wartime Nevada. Although Nevada's Japanese numbered only 756 when the attack on Pearl Harbor took place, some were the focus of considerable suspicion. The copper camps of Ruth and McGill retained the heaviest concentration of Japanese nationals, as well as Nissei and Issei, Japanese-born and American-born Japanese. These men had been segregated since their arrival and were resented for their willingness to work for lower wages than white workers would accept. Most were single and they lived in a tightly managed world, with little opportunity to interact with non-Asian workers. Their isolation proved a liability, for they had none of the familiarity or social ties that might attest to their loyalty. The day after the attack, Japanese workers were kept from their jobs in the mines; two Japanese managers were turned over to immigration authorities. Within a week after Pearl Harbor, the Nevada Consolidated Copper Company fired most of its Japanese supervisors, and shortly after, many of the Japanese nationals in Nevada were removed to Salt Lake City. Two

Japanese committed suicide, suggesting the powerful sense of abandonment and futility that accompanied the rise of nationalistic fervor as the war began.

In places where Japanese had longer histories and were integrated into daily life, they received more local support. A number of Japanese families were scattered throughout the state. Their children attended local schools; in the Paradise Valley School District in the early 1920s, one classroom included five Japanese, six Mormons, and an African American child. While no one remembers close social interaction between adults, many communities respected their Japanese neighbors for their hard work and rectitude. That sentiment yielded positive dividends. When the war began, some newspapers cautioned against blaming all Japanese for the attack, and Governor E. P. Carville pleaded with Nevadans not to persecute loyal citizens who were naturalized or native-born. Southern Nevada's Tomiyasu family, who owned a ranch in the Las Vegas Valley, were not threatened; Clark County Sheriff Gene Ward vigorously defended the family from insinuations of disloyalty. In the end, although Utah, California, and Arizona all housed internment camps for Japanese, Nevada did not. It is hard to claim that Nevada was more enlightened than its neighbors; more likely, the small number of Japanese and their integration into communities such as Las Vegas provided them a measure of social support that the isolated men in Ruth and McGill or populous Japanese neighborhoods in California did not have.

The state's politics were altered as well. The demise of Wingfield in the 1930s and the rise of the New Deal guaranteed new influences, for the old bipartisan oligarchy no longer held sway. The election of Pat McCarran to the U.S. Senate by 1,700 votes in the Democratic sweep in 1932 signaled a change in emphasis. McCarran owed his election to the influx of largely Democratic workers at the dam; early in his career, he had been a good friend of organized labor, advocating unions and earning a reputation for resistance to Wingfield and his minions that slowed his political advance in the conservative political structure of the day. Nor did personal rivalry help him. McCarran and Nevada's senior senator, Key Pittman, were old adversaries. In a drunken rage on the streets of Reno, Pittman assaulted McCarran. The antipathy remained fierce, stymieing McCarran until 1932. Only after Pittman's death in 1940 did McCarran emerge as the most powerful politician in the state.

From his seat in the U.S. Senate, McCarran fashioned an empire, but different from the parochialism of previous Nevada senators. Unlike Pittman, who tended to focus more on local matters such as silver, the ruthless McCarran weighed in more frequently on national issues. A conservative Democrat more like those from the South, he opposed FDR in a number of important situations, earning him a reputation and some powerful enemies. McCarran weighed in loudly against the scheme to pack the U.S. Supreme Court in 1937, earning him accolades for his individualism at home but the enmity of the very powerful president. He attacked parts of the New Deal, but strongly supported public works and relief spending, for they helped his bread-and-butter constituents at home. Even as he gained power in the 1930s, McCarran stood out in the Senate for his single-minded capability and firm perspective, always certain he was right. He became the state's most powerful politician and the dollars moved toward him. At the same time, he sponsored countless young Nevada men and helped them through law school in the nation's capital; they rewarded him by becoming "McCarran's boys," his foot soldiers, and later forming the core of the next generation of Nevada's political leadership. If the old bipartisan machine had assured the power of the elite, McCarran's mostly guaranteed his own preeminence.

Even during the war, McCarran's power worked to the state's advantage. Although his adamant defense of silver earned him a reputation for selfishness and his trenchant isolationism seemed out of place after the war, his position on both the appropriations and judiciary committees gave him great reach. McCarran became chair of the District of Columbia committee in 1941 and of the vastly more powerful Judiciary Committee in 1944. With that power, his parochialism served the state well and McCarran became known for delivering for Nevada, sometimes at the expense of the rest of the nation.

But the Nevada he served had become different from the one in which he was raised. By the end of the war, Nevada's direction had shifted. Not only had the state become dependent on federal dollars, it had become more populous as a result of wartime expansion. The beginnings of an industrial base rooted in military need began a transformation from producer of raw materials to something new. Nevada would not yet stand alone, able to create an industrial economy like any other state, but it was no longer the fiefdom of mines and railroads that it had long been. If the state had been run by only a few masters before 1929, it remained a closely held fiefdom at the war's end. Nevada's politicians, especially McCarran, were almost all powerful in the state, but the sources of their power had shifted from alliances with mining to dependence on the federal government. The colonial pattern that characterized Nevada since statehood changed little; only the source of the sustenance was different.

6 The Mob Comes to Nevada

AMERICANS HEAVED a collective sigh of relief at the end of World War II. For the duration of the war, Americans put aside their personal desires in favor of the war effort, and with its end, the nation erupted in a frenzy of joy. It seemed impossible that after five years of war, the conflict had finally come to an end and normal life could resume. People across the country danced in the streets and cheered the return of peace; Nevadans were as excited as anyone else. The war meant sacrifice and the loss of loved ones; it also opened the way for the development of a new society, one in which Nevada was poised to play a considerably more significant role than it had before the 1940s.

World War II revolutionized the United States, creating opportunity, hastening urbanization, and in the West, affirming and even accelerating the dependence of individual states on the federal government. In its aftermath, an economic, social, and demographic transformation of American society gained momentum. The war changed the expectations of Americans as well as how and where they lived, and the postwar era promised that the gains of the war would continue. After a few years of turmoil, indeed they did. Life improved for nearly everybody. Many of those who migrated to cities to work in defense-related industries found that they liked their new urban lives better than their poverty-stricken prewar existence. The range of opportunities and excitement of cities had great appeal, especially in contrast to the worn-out farms and narrow horizons of the Depression era.

The war presaged the transformation of American culture as well. The battle for freedom of peoples, ethnic groups, and nation states all around the globe waged in World War II became a catalyst of the individual rights revolution in the United States. After a terrifying decade at the onset of the Cold War in which civil rights were threatened, it helped create the mentality that argued strongly for individual freedom, accidentally diminishing community goals and encouraging individual rights to flourish at their expense. This change anticipated the transformation of national values that over time made the once sinful activity of "gambling" in the U.S. into "gaming," a legitimate recreational choice. Personal freedom grew in direct response to the horror Americans felt at the tactics of fascist governments.

A nation that fought to keep the world safe for democracy decided over time that it had an obligation to extend freedom to all of its citizens. Following 1945, African Americans accelerated their wartime efforts, vigorously lobbying for their civil rights and beginning the most significant change in the age-old mores of American society. Women reclaimed the delicious new freedom they had tasted during the war and permitted the next generation of American women to stake their claim to social equality. The walls of the pink ghettos of teaching and nursing crumbled; at first ever so slowly, then with accelerating speed. The people who regarded the fight against fascism as their cause fought for the rights of strangers across the seas. Their children learned to embrace individual rights above social goals.

After the war, leisure took on new and greater significance. Americans felt entitled to their leisure even as they worked longer hours. They had more spending money, and being less likely to defer gratification, they enjoyed more ways to spend it. The pace of life quickened. Institutions such as the drive-in and fast-food restaurants developed; they fit the needs of the time, reflecting the emphasis on haste in everything from commuting to eating that characterized the postwar world. Americans wanted more and they wanted it faster. Success in the postwar era depended on remembering this axiom.

All of these changes played into the definition of itself that Nevada long honed. The Silver State always prized individual freedom and independence, and since the end of the nineteenth century, it promoted leisure; sometime ribald, but leisure nonetheless. The state remained small—about 150,000 people in 1950—and the basis of its economy during the 1930s and 1940s, federal spending, had inherent limitations. A long process of trial and error resulted, in which Nevada learned how to cater to the national public as the public learned to regard what Nevada offered as recreation instead of sin.

THE FEDERAL PRESENCE so crucial to Nevada in the 1930s and throughout World War II did not disappear with the war's end. Instead it transformed into a lucrative and extremely dangerous long-term relationship that began with the assumption that the deserts of Nevada and the nation were vast wastelands—uninhabited and unimportant, and available for use, despoliation, and even contamination. Federal agencies administered more than 90 percent of the state, making Nevada the most heavily federal of the then forty-eight states. As a result, the federal government held powerful influence, enhanced by its role as the state's salvation during the Depression and the war. When the United States needed a domestic location to test new atomic and thermonuclear weapons, the Pandora's box that ever after vexed the United States and the world, Nevada became the logical choice. Since it was a pariah—small in population and large in space, most of which was desert—it was easy to see Nevada as a primeval landscape, a great open space devoid of people, a wasteland. The siting in Nevada of the nation's most comprehensive atomic and nuclear testing program followed.

American interest in splitting the atom began as a result of the threat of a Nazi bomb. When World War II began, the Third Reich was far ahead of the Allies in securing a destructive weapon. The U.S. responded with aggressive research that held vast, largely unrecognized consequences for the human species. From the moment Italian expatriate scientist Enrico Fermi began the Atomic Age by manipulating the first exponential pile of uranium and graphite under the stands of Amos Alonzo Stagg Stadium on the University of Chicago campus in December 1942, science opened a new world, made of the basic building blocks of the universe. It was a race against the enemy to harness the power of the atom, and when that genie was out of the bottle, nothing could ever again be the same. In August 1945, the U.S. dropped an atomic bomb first on Hiroshima, a Japanese city with some military significance, and a few days later, on Nagasaki. The power of atomic fission became clear to the world.

The use of atomic power offered a fitting conundrum, one that both expressed the faith that Americans had in science and technology and their revulsion at its power. After the atomic bomb, the world was a different place. The bomb was more powerful than anything the world had ever seen. Its very existence demanded new and different standards of behavior from individuals and nations to assure that the use of atomic weapons did not become a routine feature of warfare. Atomic fission was more than another toy. It required a fundamental rethinking of the way humans did their business.

The atomic conclusion to World War II was only a prelude to the Cold War and the nuclear arms race, in which the U.S. and the USSR engaged in a standoff with missiles pointed at one another, each possessing the capability to destroy the world many times over. Each side achieved deterrence with the threat of response and the only way to demonstrate that either nation could respond was to test newer and more powerful nuclear weapons. Immediately after World War II, the U.S. began a testing program in the South Pacific. Within a few years, the consequences of testing and the scrutiny of the world made federal officials look for a place in the continental United States to continue the testing program. The Nevada desert seemed perfect, and just before dawn on January 27, 1951, an Air Force b-50 bomber dropped an atomic device on the old Las Vegas Gunnery Range, located just beyond the Spring Mountains to the west of Las Vegas. The flash of the explosion woke ranchers north of Salt Lake City; the concussion shattered windows in Arizona. Atomic testing became a constant in the continental United States during the 1950s. Part of the gunnery range and additional lands were renamed the Nevada Test Site and became the primary location for the nation to test its atomic and later thermonuclear arsenal.

The best explanation for the choice of location was that the southern Nevada desert provided large areas of government-held, uninhabited space for which there seemed to be no apparent economic purpose. During World War II, the gunnery range had been a training ground and exploded and unexploded ordnance littered the range. Already given over to military purposes and wholly federal property, the gunnery range became the home of aboveground nuclear testing in the continental United States. Between 1951 and 1963, the Nevada desert was the scene of an aboveground atomic test 126 times, an average of once every three weeks.

Testing added something that Nevada had never before possessed, a claim on a full contribution as an American state. When atomic tests began in the early 1950s, at the height of the Cold War, they were seen as patriotic events, achievements to celebrate. News reporters received security clearance to watch the explosions from a high point on the test site. Tourists streamed in from California to watch the blasts, parking their trailers so they could see the explosion at dawn. Las Vegas hotels sponsored parties and took people to locations where they could see the mushroom cloud rise. Lights came on in time for people to see the explosions in the early morning. Women asked for atomic hairdos, their hair piled high in "beehives" atop their heads, and the Las Vegas Chamber of Commerce printed releases and "cheesecake" photos of attractive young women, sometimes covered only by the outline of a mushroom-shaped cloud. There was even a crowning of "Miss Atomic Bomb." Even nuclear explosions could be packaged as fun.

Yet the tests created considerable anxiety. After each test, a fine layer of dust—fallout—covered everything in whatever direction the wind blew. Small towns in eastern and northeastern Nevada and southern Utah were often blanketed with radioactive debris. Atomic Energy Commission (AEC) men in white protective suits followed with their Geiger counters, checking radiation levels. Most tests occurred with short notice, allowing little time for preparation, and a change in the wind direction or velocity brought unintended consequences. The Utah author Terry Tempest Williams tells of a memory she had of a dream in which she was awakened by an enormous light in the dark; as an adult she discovered that she had been a child asleep in a car on the road when one of the atomic tests occurred. She also refers to her family as the "clan of the one-breasted women," the result of the preponderance of mastectomies among them, a consequence she attributes to exposure to fallout. In May and June 1953, 4,500 of the 14,000 sheep on the range east of the test site died. Although ranchers sued for compensation, they were denied in federal court. One 1959 shot occurred as winds shifted to the north, blowing heavy debris toward Ely and Baker. A few hours later, ranchers in the Baker area stood among dead sheep and other animals in misery as AEC workers in masks and outfits resembling spacesuits tried to assess the damage with their Geiger counters.

The economic impact of nuclear testing cemented the importance of federal dollars in the state. Testing required the creation of an entire community, called Mercury, near the location of the various detonations. It could house as many as 1,200 people and contained a post office, but its only employer was the federal government. Nellis Air Force Base on the outskirts of Las Vegas also supported the nation's military efforts. It became the primary tactical weapons training center for the U.S. military, and throughout the Cold War, the base remained not only a national defense resource, but a source of jobs, revenue, and millions of dollars in local spending. The test site's payroll was vast, equal only to the amount of money paid to contractors of all kinds who worked at the site. In 1969, the base employed 9,000 people at an annual payroll of $60 million, almost 15 percent of the Las Vegas workforce. With more employees than any single hotel, the Nevada Test Site illustrated the federal dependence of Nevada even as gambling became the state's primary pursuit.

The people who worked at the test site made up a segment of migrants to the state that differed from earlier such work-related influxes. Many came to Nevada as a result of World War II and military service. Most made careers of either federal service or one of the test site contractors—EG&G or Wackenhut for security services, or later Raytheon or Bechtel. The test site was applied science personified. Little research took place there. Few PhD-level scientists were permanently located in Nevada, most arriving a few days before a "shot," as the tests were called, and departing soon after. The skilled workforce located in the Silver State typically shared a high school education and peculiar mechanical or engineering aptitude, often honed on the farms of their youth. "Test site families," as they were called, became common. The work provided a secure, solidly middle-class living.

Many test site jobs were typical of one dimension of American labor: work that paid well, despite a lack of demand for skill, because it was dangerous. In an era when $10,000 a year was an ample salary, some of the miners who dug the tunnels for the underground tests made three times that amount as test after test was staged. Poor and minority workers were recruited for the most dangerous tasks; high pay was to be their compensation for risk. Many took the work, not realizing what they were subjected to. The companies that ran the test site recruited African Americans from the South and gave them good wages. Some served as "rad monitors," forward observers, close to the aboveground tests of the 1950s. The only skill they needed was the ability to count to ten. Others cleaned up after the underground tests of the 1960s, 1970s, and 1980s. Their mortality rate was astonishing and led to lawsuits in the 1980s and 1990s; simultaneously their income led to middle-class prosperity otherwise denied African Americans. The tremendous human toll illustrated the brittleness of the bargain.

African American and white test site workers alike were exposed to radiation in their daily endeavors by a callous and disingenuous Atomic Energy Commission and its successors. With casual disregard for the risk to workers and hiding under the cloak of national security, responsible individuals became boys with toys, exploding them with abandon without regard to consequences. They knew more than they told; the public knew less. It could have happened with so little opposition only in a state like Nevada, where power remained in a very few hands, prompting not only the arrogance of the federal government, but that of its officials and the agencies they represented as well. The needs of individual workers and the safety of the community could be neatly tucked into a pocket and forgotten in the name of false ideals of money, power, and national security.

IN 1946, a little red sports car came down US 91 from Los Angeles and pulled into the desert oasis of Las Vegas to inaugurate a new capital regime in Las Vegas, transforming the city and eventually the state. Out of it emerged a disheveled but handsome man with a strong jaw and hard eyes. Benjamin "Bugsy" Siegel, a mobster tied to underworld leader Meyer Lansky, brought different power to Nevada. He had been closely associated with Murder Inc., the 1930s gangland killers in New York, but escaped their fate—death by the electric chair or at one another's hands—by landing in Hollywood. He dabbled in movies and became a man about town. Unable to attain the level of success he desired in Hollywood, Siegel came to Las Vegas—a town he had occasionally visited during World War II—with Lansky's blessing. The two men and their vision of the "dinky little oasis town," as gangster Meyer Lansky called Las Vegas, provided the state with another master: organized crime, the most nefarious in the state's history.

Lansky and his associates eyed Las Vegas in the 1930s and made their first moves as early as 1941, but in most accounts Siegel receives credit for envisioning the complicated relationship between gaming and status that made the Flamingo Hotel and Casino a world-class destination. Siegel's vision transformed Las Vegas from a western, institution-free center of vice into a world-renowned spectacle of gambling, entertainment, and fun by blending the themes of Monte Carlo, Miami Beach, and Havana. In the process, he inaugurated an era in which the capital to fund gaming, which quickly became the state's dominant industry, came first from the pockets of organized crime and later from legitimate money the underworld could control.

The reasons for organized crime's interest in Nevada were obvious. The state was small and poor, and power was there for the taking. Legalized gambling offered mobsters something they could not have anywhere else in the nation: the freedom to operate above ground without interference. The state's nonexistent tax structure and lax law enforcement made it even more appealing. Nowhere else in the nation could illegal gamblers ply their trade, make piles of money, and become respectable citizens. For the gamblers who ran towns such as Newport, Kentucky, or Phenix City, Alabama—known centers of vice that were periodically raided by law enforcement—Nevada had colossal appeal.

The first to recognize the opportunity had been California gamblers, pushed out of Los Angeles by the election of Mayor Fletcher Bowron in the late 1930s. Tony Cornero, who founded the Meadows Club in 1931, settled in Nevada after California Attorney General Earl Warren, who later became chief justice of the United States Supreme Court, began a full-scale legal assault on Cornero's off-shore gambling boats. After Cornero capitulated, he made his way to Las Vegas, and in 1944 he leased the Apache Hotel. Others such as Guy McAfee, a Phillip Marlowe–like Hollywood vice commander who was married to a brothel madam and ran illegal gambling joints in southern California, and Sam Boyd, who operated Bingo parlors in Los Angeles and Honolulu, scurried to Las Vegas for the cover of legalized gambling. But at the time, they were exceptions—regional operators looking for a safe locale for their activities. They capitalized on gaming but did little more, leaving their mark in symbols rather than structures. McAfee ran a number of clubs on Fremont Street and the Pair-o-Dice Club on US 91, which he nicknamed the Strip, after his beloved Sunset Strip in Los Angeles.

This trickle of gambling expertise became a torrent after World War II. Siegel led a generation to Las Vegas that included Gus Greenbaum, an Arizona bookmaker; David Berman, a veteran of ten years in Sing Sing and the former boss of the rackets in Minneapolis, and his dandy of a younger brother, Chickie; Israel "Icepick Willie" Alderman, who ran typical 1930s gaming road-houses called "carpet joints" in Minneapolis; Moe Sedway, a Siegel associate from Los Angeles; Morris B. "Moe" Dalitz, associated with the Mayfield Road Gang in Cleveland; Jack Entratter of the Copacabana in New York and Miami, who arrived in Las Vegas via Havana; Morris Rosen; and countless other figures linked to the underworld and illegal gambling. Reno attracted its share as well. Lincoln Fitzgerald of the Detroit Purple Gang came to Reno and became co-owner of the Nevada Club. Urban gambling in Nevada acquired a decidedly unsavory look.

After Siegel's arrival, mob influence spread quickly. At the end of 1945, Siegel put together a consortium to buy the El Cortez, a 59-room downtown Las Vegas hotel; in six months, he and his partners sold it, reaping an astonishing 28 percent profit. Stunned by their success, organized crime leaders relished a long presence in legalized gambling. Experienced criminals, Lansky and the other behind-the-scenes characters skillfully masked their involvement. The purchase of the El Cortez initiated a pattern; in every subsequent purchase or development of a resort, "connected" illegal gamblers who became legal in Nevada and prominent local citizens joined together. Outside capital and some form of local respectability were closely linked.

After the El Cortez, Siegel searched for a new property, and a development on the edge of town caught his eye. Billy Wilkerson, a man-about-town who founded the *Hollywood Reporter* as well as Ciro's Restaurant in Los Angeles, envisioned Las Vegas as Beverly Hills in the desert. He planned a swank and elegant resort called the Flamingo that transcended the sawdust-covered floors and cowboy boots of the western-themed casinos. Wilkerson's plans outstripped his resources, and with little capital in the state and less chance to borrow from conventional sources, he searched for investors. Siegel and his friends bought two-thirds of the project for $650,000, much of which came from a loan from the Valley National Bank of Phoenix, in which Greenbaum held a stake. After that initial investment, Siegel raised money from his friends in $50,000 shares. Not another dime of legitimate money financed the Flamingo after Siegel took it over.

The Flamingo was not the first hotel on the Las Vegas Strip. In 1940, California hotelier Thomas Hull visited Las Vegas and decided to build one of his El Rancho luxury motor courts south of town. When it opened on April 3, 1941, the western-themed property became the prototype for the roadside resorts that characterized the 1950s and 1960s, the sprawling auto-based culture of the postwar years. The Last Frontier followed in 1942, built by R. E. Griffith, whose family owned 475 movie theaters. Decorated with Navajo artwork and mounted animals, the Last Frontier was attractive, but still regional in its themes. Both combined those important regional themes with a combination of motor court or dude ranch ambiance, a pattern that lasted in Las Vegas into the 1960s. Throughout the era, resorts looked like beachfront hotels, cut low and expansive. It fell to Siegel and Wilkerson to blend the local resort model with the cosmopolitan themes of Monte Carlo or Havana. The gangster managed to envision a complicated relationship between status and leisure that foreshadowed the future of the state.

Capital remained the greatest barrier to Nevada's growth, its absence smoothing the way for criminal operatives such as Siegel. With a few exceptions, banks shunned casinos as investments. In 1946, when Siegel tried to extort $2 million from the Chicago mob to complete construction in a move that likely led to his murder, he had $1 million of his own money in the project and $3 million that his connected friends had invested in $50,000-sized shares. Legitimate money, from people such as Wilkerson, and illegal money joined to build casinos that were run by the underworld, basking in the sunshine that Nevada offered.

This pattern of financing was typical of Nevada casinos and hotels throughout the late 1940s and 1950s. Even resorts with legitimate origins, such as Wilbur Clark's Desert Inn in Las Vegas or the Nevada Club in Reno, became part of vast organized crime networks. Lincoln Fitzgerald and his Detroit partners Raymond "Ruby" Mathis, Dan Sullivan, and Mert Werthheimer bought Ed and

Harry Robbins's Nevada Club, keeping Ed Robbins as a front man. In 1949, the group took over Reno's Riverside Club from an aging George Wingfield, further illustrating how money and power had gravitated to newcomers. In 1947, Bernie Einstoss, Leo Kind, Frank Grannis, and Lou Werthheimer leased the Mapes Hotel and casino from Charles Mapes, maintaining the lease until 1958. When Clark began building the Desert Inn in 1947 with $250,000, he soon found himself short of money. For nearly two years, the framed structure sat in the hot desert sun. In 1949, Clark met Dalitz, and within a few months, Dalitz and his partners contributed $1.3 million in capital and owned 75 percent of the project. Wilbur Clark's Desert Inn opened in April 1950 and local residents called it "the most brilliant social event in the history of the Strip." Clark became a glorified front man at the resort that bore his name. The Desert Inn opened a pipeline of similar money, and hotels such as the Sands, completed in 1952; the Riviera, opening in 1955; the Tropicana, which opened in 1957; and the Stardust, following in 1958; solidified the power of East Coast and Midwest mobs in Las Vegas. Similar financing became the norm throughout the 1950s and 1960s.

The infiltration of mobsters and their money raised eyebrows within Nevada, but such funds were the only resources the state could find to support its aberrant but rapidly growing industry. As the American economy took off after World War II, banks and bond issues funded growth across the country, enhancing existing financial mechanisms. But the line was sharply drawn when it came to even legal vice. Nevada was largely excluded from such funding. Banks would only rarely fund casinos, and when such money could be found, it came from regional and even renegade institutions. The social stigma attached to vice remained too great. Nevada was vulnerable to the machinations of anyone with capital to loan, and the state fell prey to nefarious influences in the process.

The shift in power became more apparent as other industries waned. Mineral production accelerated after World War II, growing as a result of the Korean War and reaching peaks in 1955 and 1956, but dropping by almost 40 percent in the subsequent decade. While mineral production almost matched the rapid growth of gambling revenue between 1946 and 1956, as mining diminished in the subsequent decade, gambling again tripled to almost $337,000,000 in 1966. By the time mining mustered an upturn in the late 1960s, gaming generated at least four times the annual yield of mining. Agriculture and ranching grew in value as well, but their increases, and indeed their position in the state economy, were dwarfed by the expansion of gambling. In the two decades following World War II, Nevada shifted from extracting its raw materials to providing leisure and recreation for the American public. The results transformed the state from a producer of raw materials to a center of leisure.

The change in source of revenue put tremendous pressure on the institutions of Nevada government. The bipartisan machine of the prewar era was dead, and with the death of the mercurial U.S. Senator Pat McCarran during a campaign speech in Hawthorne in 1954, the state lost its most powerful national leader. McCarran had been a divisive figure, despising first Key Pittman and then Pittman's brother, Vail Pittman, who lost to McCarran in the 1944 U.S. Senate primary. Although a Democrat, McCarran had been a supporter of Joseph McCarthy—"Tailgunner Joe," the fraudulent war hero and Republican senator from Wisconsin who conducted communist witch hunts during the early 1950s—an opponent of immigration, and the author of restrictive internal security legislation called the McCarran Act or the Internal Securities Act that suspended some civil liberties. Despite gestures such as the senator's announcement of support for the entire Democratic ticket just before his death in 1954, the factionalism McCarran fomented tore at the party, damaged its viability, and gave Republicans a better chance in statewide elections.

Nevada's political parties responded ineffectively to postwar change, leaving industry in charge of state government as it had been since statehood. When a chance to redefine the character of state politics emerged, politicians abdicated. Instead of crafting powerful democratic institutions, state politicians followed the historical patterns of state politics and let industry dictate terms. Although some, such as Governor Charles Russell and Governor Grant Sawyer, battled the new powers, they found little support. The rural roots of the state gave mining, agriculture, and ranching considerably more power than they merited, and the rapid shift from illegal to legal made gamblers unfamiliar with the ways power works from the inside. In the old days, when they were illegal, gamblers bought politicians. Understanding the difference between that and contributing to political campaigns involved a subtlety that many in the casino industry in the 1950s only slowly grasped.

The conservative nature of state politics also contributed to government's ineffectiveness. Nevada remained fiscally conservative, unlikely to tax its residents, socially Libertarian, permissive about vice in particular, and committed to a limited role for government. The strategy reflected the traits of nineteenth-century Nevada, when mining and rural interests controlled the sparsely populated state, but they were far less viable in a state that experienced most of its growth and change in its cities. The most dramatic shift in population between 1945 and 1960 was the stunning growth of Nevada's two primary cities, Reno and Las Vegas. In 1940, Nevada's population reached 110,247; the state remained more than sixty percent rural and Reno was the largest city at 21,317. Two decades later, sixty-five percent of the state's 285,278 people lived in cities, led by the 64,405 in Las Vegas and the 51,470 in Reno. The state's institutions had been created for a rural state. Their viability in an urban state full of newcomers remained in question.

Political shenanigans at the state level became commonplace in the changing state. The Democratic Party enjoyed a two-to-one advantage in voter registration, but the fractious rivalries in the party diminished its success. In 1950, McCarran undermined Vail Pittman and threw the governor's election to Republican Russell. Two years later, Thomas Mechling, a newcomer without political experience, defeated former state Attorney General Alan Bible in the Democratic primary for U.S. Senate. Mechling was a whirlwind on the Nevada scene, but instead of taking his primary victory and attacking his Republican opponent, incumbent George "Molly" Malone, Mechling challenged Pat McCarran's machine and attacked the U.S. senator personally. McCarran refused to support Mechling at the last moment, and Malone and the Republicans retained the U.S. Senate seat. Personal feelings trumped all else. Nevada politics remained an "Old Boys' Club" regardless of party affiliation; a sandbox where an invitation was necessary to be allowed to play.

Even more, the blending of illegal and legal gambling led to scandal. The first major investigation of gambling came in 1950, when Estes Kefauver, a Tennessee senator with an eye on the White House, sought to root out corruption and focused on Nevada's gaming. He followed the model of the time. The House Un-American Activities Committee began the process of holding traveling hearings in the late 1930s. Senator Joseph McCarthy perfected the form with a series of hearings that pretended to root out alleged communists in government and other positions of power. McCarthy gained great notoriety and even fame from his attacks, and the canny Kefauver thought he found a parallel path to presidential consideration. In November 1950, he brought his road show to Las Vegas.

Kefauver's arrival became a pivotal moment in the transformation of the state. Since the legalization of gambling in 1931, Nevada had remained apart from the nation, but outside entities had not seriously challenged Nevada's right to go its own way. The integration of illegal gamblers into legalized gambling had been one result. Kefauver sought to challenge the corruption he believed that integration harbored, putting Nevada on notice that it could not expect the rest of the nation to allow it to do as it pleased without scrutiny. From 1931 until Kefauver's committee met in Las Vegas on November 15, 1950, Nevada gambling had been an intrastate operation run by local codes and customs; after Kefauver, the practices of the Silver State were part of the larger discussion of American values and mores.

Kefauver's Las Vegas hearing turned into an absurd stage for the conflict in values. Nevada had already institutionalized a process through which people with convictions for illegal gambling elsewhere could be licensed in the state; Nevada, the thinking went, needed their skill to make the most of this new industry that promised to take away the ongoing economic doldrums. To Kefauver—himself no stranger to gambling and nightlife—and the other senators, this tacit acceptance of criminals as paragons of economic virtue was too much to stomach. After a day of hearings in which the committee embarrassed a few local casino men, Kefauver and his friends left Las Vegas. The committee's final report eight months later devoted only four pages to Las Vegas. Nevada's individualist ways, rooted in the idea of state's rights and the lack of any other way for the state to thrive economically, triumphed over national control. In the process, the perverse patterns of the state, the blending of the legal and the illegal, acquired firm sanction. Scandal or not, notorious past or not, Nevada and its newly legal gamblers were inextricably joined.

In the process, Las Vegas took from Reno the dubious crown of most sinful American city, guaranteeing that southern Nevada's future would outshine that of the north. By selecting for itself the motto of "Biggest Little City in the World" in 1929, Reno trimmed its own wings and, in the end, unwittingly consigned itself to secondary status in the state. The decline of industries like ranching and agriculture after World War II contributed to the southern tilt of the state. Reno's role as supplier of Nevada's hinterland, the string of rural communities scattered throughout the northern part of the state, simultaneously diminished. Population growth preceded the economic transformation that gambling wrought, but even in the public image, Nevada's significance shifted southward.

Yet one of the great engines of Nevada's growth, construction on the Las Vegas Strip, slowed in the late 1950s. An enormous burst of construction followed the Flamingo and the Desert Inn. Between 1950 and 1958, the Sahara,

Sands, Dunes, Riviera, Tropicana, and Stardust were all built, creating the first of Las Vegas's many construction booms. The Showboat and the Fremont off the Strip dated from the same era. Construction dollars seeded an increase in visitation, culminating in the 1,000-room Stardust in 1958. But after the Stardust, new construction ceased. During the next eight years, only one new hotel, the nongaming Tally-Ho, was built on the Strip. Considerable renovation of a number of hotels took place, but the dollars that supported the growth of the city once again dried up.

The reasons were simple. In 1950s Las Vegas, most of the money for hotel construction came from the figurative shoe boxes under the beds of mobsters across the country. Ben Siegel had begun the practice with the $50,000 shares he sold in the Flamingo, but the process became more complex as the hotels became more expensive. Siegel's cost ran up as high as $6 million at the Flamingo, resulting from a combination of inexperience; his weird ideas, such as having an individual sewer line for each room; and the light fingers of some of his contractors, who checked materials in the front gate of the construction gate, billed them to Siegel, and promptly drove them out the back door. Throughout the early 1950s, Las Vegas hotels were small. The Sands, which became one of the premier hotels of the 1950s, home to Frank Sinatra and the "Rat Pack," had only 200 rooms when it opened and cost a mere $5.5 million, less than the Flamingo. Mobsters had that kind of money, and they could even finance the Stardust at $14 million. But beyond that amount, the mobsters needed other sources of funding they could control.

The first generation of mobsters-turned-legitimate in Nevada had also grown old. Few were young men when they came to Nevada in the 1940s and 1950s and many did not expect to live long lives anyway. Davie Berman died in surgery in 1956, Gus Greenbaum and his wife were brutally murdered in their Phoenix home in 1958, and others slipped into what passed for retirement. When John F. Kennedy was elected president in 1960, his brother, Robert F. Kennedy, became U.S. attorney general and from that position launched an all-out assault on the mob and its influence on organized labor. Few mobsters had the energy to battle increasing federal pressure such as wiretaps, indictments, and bad publicity, and if they did, it cost them the very money they might be likely to otherwise invest in new hotels. The early 1960s became scandal-ridden stasis for Nevada and its new leading city. The illegitimate money that built the Strip was no longer sufficient to expand it and there were no other sources of capital that might easily fund Nevada's growth.

In a complicated and indirect manner, mobsters were able to secure legitimate capital for the growth of the city, inaugurating the next phase in the growth of the state's preeminent industry. The Teamsters' Central States, Southeast, Southwest Areas Pension Fund, run by Allen Dorfman—the stepson of mobster Paul "Red" Dorfman and an associate of the Chicago mob—became the source of new money for Las Vegas. In the early 1950s, Teamsters boss Jimmy Hoffa handpicked the younger Dorfman, then a college physical education instructor, to handle the Teamsters' insurance to repay a favor to his mobster stepfather. Red Dorfman's muscle assured Hoffa's control of the union. Allen Dorfman rose quickly. The union insurance contract made him a wealthy man; ambitious, he wanted even more. Under Hoffa's tutelage, he became one of the prime movers in the pension fund's investment decisions. In 1967, when Bobby Kennedy's long campaign to imprison Hoffa finally came to fruition, the union boss handed Dorfman complete control over the pension fund's loans.

Moe Dalitz, who knew Hoffa in Detroit when both were young, and St. Louis attorney Morris Shenker, a Hoffa confidante who served as counsel to American National Insurance Corporation, a small Texas insurance company, shepherded pension fund investments into gambling. In the late 1950s and early 1960s, Dalitz received pension fund support for a number of Las Vegas renovation projects. Through him, the fund backed the creation of the La Costa Hotel and Country Club in Southern California. The insurance company had its own nefarious roots in the empire of Texas crime boss Sam Maceo and business mogul W. L. Moody, Jr., both of whom were friends of Nevada Senator Pat McCarran. The Hoover-era FBI described Shenker as the most highly paid mob attorney in the country, ignoring another Las Vegas–affiliated mob attorney, the stunningly discrete Sidney Korshak. American National became a conduit through which capital for casino funding reached Las Vegas. Shenker soon held a stake in a number of casinos. In 1963, the fund had more than $167 million in assets, and more than 60 percent of the fund's resources were invested in real estate, compared to the 2.3 percent typical of similar investing consortiums in that era.

Early Teamsters' Pension Fund forays into Las Vegas had little to do with hotels and gambling. In 1958, *Las Vegas Sun* publisher Herman "Hank" Greenspun, one of a very few American newspapermen to publically challenge Senator Joseph McCarthy's reign of terror and a loud critic of organized crime in his adopted state, received $250,000 to finance a golf course. Teamsters' money funded other social developments as well. On April 14, 1959, the 100-bed Sun-

rise Hospital opened, built by the Paradise Development Company, whose officers included Moe Dalitz, casino executive Allard Roen—who had been indicted
in the United Dye and Chemical stock fraud case—and two young Las Vegas
businessmen, Irwin Molasky and Mervin Adelson. The Paradise Development
Company needed capital and the pension fund provided it, with Hoffa assuring its profitability by delivering the Teamsters' union health care contracts to
the new hospital. A symmetry to construction soon became apparent, seeding
further growth.

The Paradise Development Company's next projects offered southern
Nevada its first modern commercial development boom. With capital in hand,
the company planned the future of nonresort Las Vegas by turning Maryland
Parkway, a two-lane road that paralleled the Strip about two miles to the east,
into the main commercial thoroughfare for the growing city. Nearly everyone in the city with any kind of aspirations, worker and executive alike, came
to live in the area east of the new commercial center. The enclosed Boulevard
Mall, the first modern shopping center in Las Vegas, was the capstone to these
accomplishments when it opened in 1967.

In the mid-1960s, pension fund capital shifted to hotels with a flamboyant
visionary style that traced back to Bugsy Siegel and the Flamingo. After Jimmy
Hoffa was indicted in 1963, the model he devised sunk its claws even deeper
into Las Vegas. Pension fund money provided a clear shift from the first generation of growth, when mobsters reached under their beds for shoe boxes of
money. Instead, the money arrived through a range of legitimate conduits to
banks such as the Bank of Las Vegas, established in 1954 and headed by E. Parry
Thomas, the most important financier in mid-century Las Vegas. Thomas put
the money into local circulation as workmen built the new Strip. The Teamsters' Pension Fund became the grease that created distinctive new hotels,
including Caesars Palace, funded by a loan from the Central States Pension
Fund, and run by Jay Sarno, an eccentric but brilliant entrepreneur.

By the mid-1950s, Sarno was an experienced hotelier who was closely tied
to the Teamsters' Pension Fund. In the late 1950s, he financed hotel projects in
Atlanta and Dallas for his national Cabana chain. A close friendship with Hoffa
led Allen Dorfman to support Sarno's endeavors. In one instance, Sarno was
offered money from the fund at a lower interest rate than he requested, a ges-
ture that led the FBI to treat the hotelier as a mob front man. Sarno was not
deterred. When he conceived of Caesars Palace, he wanted to inject a new level

of glamour into the casino industry. Three decades later, people still regarded his vision as gaming's primary brand name.

Caesars Palace's $19-million price tag was the most ever spent to develop a Las Vegas hotel. It outstripped the first generation of properties and inaugurated a newer, more grandiose era. Caesars was much more than even a resort/ dude ranch with a casino and shows. It was built to reflect dreams back on its patrons in Sarno's idiosyncratic manner. The casino was egg-shaped, following his belief that such shapes relaxed people. A frieze showing the battle of the Etruscan Hills graced the wall next to the Noshorium Coffee Shop, itself a tongue-in-cheek combination of the Yiddish term "nosh" for snack and a Roman-sounding suffix. Classical fountains and statues graced the property and eighteen huge fountains bordered the 135-foot driveway. The 800-seat Circus Maximus Theatre, patterned after the Coliseum in Rome, hosted only the top acts of the day; such superstars as Frank Sinatra and Barbra Streisand were among the headliners.

The Teamsters' Pension Fund became the primary source of capital in 1960s Las Vegas. Besides Caesars, it financed other, less spectacular resorts including the Aladdin—which opened a few months before Caesars Palace and where Elvis and Priscilla Presley married in 1967—the off-Strip Landmark Hotel; the downtown Four Queens; and Circus Circus, Sarno's on-Strip successor to Caesars. Most were more in line with the 1950s Strip than with Sarno's vision, but they were profitable investments that blurred the line between the mob and legitimate business.

In a typical instance of the blending of legal and illegal business, the Landmark began as the project of wealthy Kansas City, Missouri, developer John Carroll, who secured $3.3 million from the Appliance Buyers Credit Corporation, a Whirlpool subsidiary. Short $10 million, Carroll built apartments and a small shopping center and searched for more capital. In the typical partnership between unknowing legitimate fronts and mob-controlled money, the pension fund came up with a $6 million loan in August 1966.

By the time Carroll received the loan for the Landmark in 1966, the pension fund had become the dominant source of development capital in southern Nevada. The rising cost of resort development, particularly after Caesars Palace, demanded sophisticated sources of funding. Even Valley Bank's money was scant in comparison to the needs of the state's leading and fastest growing industry. Las Vegas could easily absorb upwards of $100 million in development capital. The traditional means of capital formation, stock offerings and bonds, were generally blocked. Wall Street was not ready to take a chance on gaming, leaving its potentially lucrative rewards to the pension fund and the organized crime bosses who ran it. Not only in Las Vegas, but throughout the state, the pension fund provided the primary source of capital. The King's Castle at Lake Tahoe was only one among the fund's northern Nevada investments. By the 1960s, the pension fund made Nevada and Las Vegas beholden not to conventional financial powers in America, but to the parasitic forces that preyed upon it.

At the same time, the Teamsters' Pension Fund breathed new life into Nevada's economy. By supporting new hotel construction, it created thousands of jobs, provided the facilities to meet the demands of thousands more new visitors, and built the infrastructure for the largest city in the state. Simultaneously it perpetuated the patterns of oligarchy, of control by only a few hands, that marked the state's history. The difference was that the wealth that underpinned power in the state shifted to men with criminal affiliations and, in some cases, long criminal records of their own. Nevada's political structure faced all kinds of challenges throughout the 1960s.

The influx of mob money posed real problems for Nevada politicians. They were caught between their roles as leaders of the state and their dependence on sources of capital that could sustain the economy. This led to strained relationships within the state and outside its boundaries. Grant Sawyer, who became governor in 1959, faced the state's civil rights crisis head-on, wavering only when he found himself squeezed between the casino industry and the increasingly vocal African American community in southern Nevada. African American numbers increased dramatically during and after World War II, for despite its historical racism, Nevada offered economic opportunity. "Eight dollars a day and working in the shade," Lucille Bryant wrote home to Tallulah, Louisiana, of the opportunities for African American women in postwar Las Vegas. Working as a hotel maid was a step up from picking cotton in the fields of the South.

Nevada's African American population had been small, only 664 people in 1940, but the growth of Las Vegas made it the largest and only substantive African American community in the state. The 178 African Americans in Las Vegas in 1940 became 15,000 by 1955, but better opportunity and pay could not excise the American disease of segregation. Las Vegas had been integrated before 1941 in a frontier, small-town way. In 1930, 150 African Americans lived in Las Vegas, and Clarence Ray, an African American gambler who settled in Las Vegas in 1925, described a community of about fifteen families, all of whom owned property. After 1945, African Americans were consigned to the "Westside," north and west of Las Vegas's downtown, where roads were not even paved until the mid-1950s. They worked at the test site or in service and behind-the-scenes jobs on the Strip, but through the 1950s they were not, figuratively or literally, permitted to enter hotels on the Strip by the front door.

In a city devoted to meeting customers' desires, licentious and otherwise, such rigidity could not hold for long. Even though in the mid-1950s Sammy Davis, Jr., called Las Vegas "Tobacco Road"—after the classic Erskine Caldwell novel that showed the poverty and despair of the dark side of the American South—in 1955 a multi-racial casino-hotel, the Moulin Rouge, opened in Westside, cracking another barrier as the rest of the nation grappled with the *Brown v. Board of Education* decision. Not only did whites and blacks share the stage at the Moulin Rouge, they mingled socially until dawn. For the "Mississippi of the West," as Nevada has been termed since World War II because of its prevalent racial discrimination, even the illusion of social integration—a mixing place where the elites of entertainment could fraternize—was a rapid stride that reflected the city's dependence on its cultural cachet. Las Vegas in the 1950s sought hipness; that trait required a loosening of the noose of segregation that affected the city and the state.

Even more, Las Vegas found itself dependent on African American labor in a manner similar to many cities in the South. Certain kinds of jobs, usually low status and poorly paid, were routinely filled by African Americans. In most places, this arrangement stripped clout and even dignity from African Americans, but in Las Vegas, the story was quite different. As it grew, the city suffered a consistent shortage of labor and employees; even African American ones, in the 1950s, were valued if for no other reason than there was no one to replace them. The combination of necessary labor and celebrity performers gave the African American community influence that it lacked in most other American cities.

The Moulin Rouge projected civil rights to the fore in Las Vegas. With leadership from Dr. Charles West (the city's first African American physician), Dr. James McMillan (the first African American dentist), and a core of NAACP leaders that included David Hoggard Sr., Woodrow Wilson, Lubertha Johnson, and many local ministers, the African American community challenged Nevada's de facto segregation. They lobbied Carson City and founded the Nevada Voter's League, which supported Civil Rights proponent and senatorial candidate

Howard Cannon with more than 1,000 votes in the 1958 election. Gubernatorial hopeful Sawyer, another civil rights proponent, also received support from the Nevada Voter's League. The groundswell announced the presence of a vocal African American community that could influence politics in the state, but little legal change in the status of African Americans followed. African American leadership contemplated more drastic measures.

In 1960, McMillan, West, and others planned massive street protests in downtown Las Vegas and on the Strip to highlight the predicament of African Americans. Following the model of Civil Rights leaders such as Rev. Dr. Martin Luther King Jr., McMillan and his friends planned marches and did not rule out the passive resistance that was the hallmark of the era. They threatened marches similar to those that would become so famous throughout the South. Hotel owners were caught; they were not excited about integration, a fact that stymied changes in law despite African American support for Sawyer and other politicians, but they could not afford the bad publicity that marches would bring. Images of street battles in Las Vegas brought local leadership to the table. The threatened marches meant a linkage to civil rights protests in the South that did little to promote the image that Las Vegas leaders sought for their city. Despite efforts to intimidate McMillan, on March 26, 1960, just before the deadline for direct action, the city and Strip operators agreed to integrate public places. For the first time since World War II, Las Vegas's African Americans could enter the hotels where they worked through the front doors.

It would be hard to classify Nevada in 1960 as a progressive state by any measure, nor did any other state look at Nevada as a model, but the active and energized Las Vegas African American community achieved the first goal of the Civil Rights movement—freedom of accommodations—without much of the legal and often street struggle that marked the nation for the ensuing decade. As African Americans entered Strip hotels and enjoyed shows, meals, and gambling, southern cities remained rigidly segregated; the courts had to end the practice in the South, while economic reasons contributed to its demise in the Silver State. Even liberal cities like San Francisco struggled with similar civil rights issues. Four years passed before Berkeley students, inhaling the heady fumes of the civil rights movement, forced the San Francisco Sheraton to hire its first African American behind-the-scenes employees. Las Vegas's hotels were, at least in theory, open to all.

Yet the political structure of the state played little part in this crucial change. Even Sawyer and Cannon, both beneficiaries of African American voters, neither created integration law nor fashioned resolution of the crisis, although Sawyer pushed the legislature as hard as he thought he could. Under Sawyer in 1961, the state legislature established a commission to see if discrimination existed— a laughable objective even as legal segregation came to an end. The appointment of Bob Bailey, an African American entertainer who became a broadcaster, as chair was the most aggressive step associated with the commission. Sawyer's and Cannon's efforts did not impede civil rights, but neither could they deliver. Canny politicians both, they may have been content with symbolic action. As had nearly one hundred years of Nevada politicians, they knew where the power lay—in this case in the gambling industry—and did not risk more than a superficial challenge to the norms of the time.

Politicians were also weakened by the ongoing assault on Nevada's practices from outside the state. Mid-century America remained committed to a hypervigilant moralism, and even as divorce passed from sin to accepted practice, gambling remained a stigmatized activity. After Kefauver, the intimation of organized crime influence dogged the state and every year, it seemed, a new scandal that compromised state authority emerged. The most definitive came in 1954, when Lieutenant Governor Clifford A. Jones was implicated in gambling and prostitution-related corruption and resigned as Democratic National Committeeman, assuring that Republican Charles Russell would triumph in the 1954 gubernatorial election. Despite efforts by two-term Governor Russell to keep corruption from state politics, the rest of the nation still scorned Nevada and its leading industry.

Throughout the 1950s, state officials sought to demonstrate that Nevada was free of corruption. Two of the state's responses, changes made to the gaming laws in 1955 that required shareholders in casinos to pass gaming board scrutiny, and the creation of the "Black Book"—the List of Excluded Persons designed to keep cheaters and criminals away from casinos in 1960—were designed to show the nation that state government could keep illegal activity out of the gambling industry. In the end such efforts were public relations measures rather than substantive attempts to break the bonds between politics and the underworld. Newspapers and law enforcement officials regarded Nevada's political structure as corrupt, compelling Governor Sawyer and many others to protest the unfair treatment of their state.

This righteous indignation compromised Nevada politics, for the rumors had a basis in truth. Throughout his two terms as governor from 1959 to 1966, Grant Sawyer battled the widespread perception that state authority was a handmaiden to organized crime control of the state. Beginning his career as one of "McCarran's Boys," Sawyer became district attorney in Elko. According to legend, in 1958 he drove to Carson City to file the papers to run for any of three statewide offices—governor, U.S. senator, or attorney general—deciding on the governor's office on the way. The decision was fortuitous; it opened the way for Howard Cannon to become senator and he remained in the U.S. Senate from 1959 to 1983. Sawyer found himself the subject of an unusual alliance in Nevada politics. The state's small but influential liberal cadre found him a substantive alternative to conventional Nevada politics, while unions and Strip hotel owners eventually settled on him as their candidate as well. In an upset, Sawyer breezed to victory in the primary. He trounced incumbent Charles Russell by 16,000 votes in the general election, landing in the governor's mansion at the moment that Nevada faced another challenge to its sovereignty as a state.

Sawyer faced a difficult situation. Even as he tried to liberalize Nevada with support for civil rights, he found that U.S. Attorney General Robert F. Kennedy, who had begged Sawyer to deliver the state's delegation to John F. Kennedy in 1960, now looked on the governor, as Sawyer recalled, "as someone who had just stepped out from behind a crap table." Sawyer campaigned under the slogan "Nevada is not for sale," but from the moment he took office, he faced not only suspicion but the suggestion that Nevada's political structure was inherently corrupt. Sawyer's first attempts at a cleanup focused on gaming regulations. The aftermath of Governor Russell's ninety-day moratorium on gaming licenses in 1955 demonstrated that Nevada granted its oversight responsibilities some seriousness. The creation of statewide entities to monitor gaming became a first step in a series of regulatory mechanisms. Sawyer added to them.

Sawyer established the Nevada Gaming Commission as the primary state regulatory agency for gaming. The commission superseded the tax commission's role by evaluating applicants for gaming licenses, collecting tax revenue from the casinos, and enacting gaming regulations. Sawyer took the division of power one step further. From 1945 to 1959, the governor had served as the head of the tax commission, playing a direct role in licensing and enforcement. Sawyer removed the governor from the Nevada Gaming Commission in an effort to assure the separation of powers. Yet the governor still appointed members of the commission, retaining considerable influence for Sawyer and his successors.

The Gaming Control Board, the enforcement arm of the Nevada Gaming Commission, informally created the Black Book, a registry of people who were not to be permitted in casinos at the risk of the casinos losing their state gaming licenses. The process developed informally, with eleven initial members; mostly of the Chicago, Kansas City, and Los Angeles syndicates, not the Cleveland and New York ones so prominent in Nevada gaming. They included Carl and Nick Civella, Kansas City bosses; Louis Tom Dragna, the mob boss of Los Angeles; and Sam Giancana and Marshall Caifano of the Chicago outfit. After a court challenge, the Black Book was upheld as a legitimate exercise of police powers.

Yet the mechanism was never really effective. The excluded people were well-known figures, but often their crimes did not exceed those of earlier license holders. In this respect, the Black Book, renamed the "List of Excluded Persons," served better as a public relations device than a true regulator of the gaming industry. The best that could be said about it was that the Black Book raised the bar for acquiring a gaming license, assuring that central control prevented the most public hoodlums from doing business in the state.

The wrangles between state authority and the federal government continued. Since the mid-1950s, rarely did a year pass without published reports of skimming, mob influence, or charges of corruption. Federal officials did not trust state or local government, seeing it as protecting gaming at all costs. This enraged Sawyer, who argued that the state had to "project an image to the rest of the country that Nevada was not rolling over for organized crime" and was simply a convenient scapegoat. In 1961, Robert Kennedy approached Nevada Attorney General Roger Foley and asked him to deputize sixty-five federal agents for a raid on every major casino in Las Vegas and Reno. Sawyer visited President John F. Kennedy, pleading the state's case that the Gaming Control Board had made great inroads in removing illegal operators and begging that the U.S. government not humiliate the Silver State. Although the president made no promises, the raid never took place.

In 1966, another in the seemingly endless series of scandals in Las Vegas broke wide open, pitting the state against the FBI and the federal government. The FBI operated a series of illegal wiretaps of casino offices and found that skimming continued unabated. Information from the wiretaps magically appeared in newspapers like the *Chicago Sun-Times* before state officials were informed. Nevada followed with its own investigation, but federal law enforcement refused to share its information with the state. The FBI simultaneously impugned the integrity of state oversight of gaming and offended Nevada's Libertarian tendencies.

This was the scenario that Paul Laxalt inherited when he defeated Grant Sawyer in 1966. Although he campaigned as a new kind of Republican—young, fresh, and vital—Laxalt found himself in the middle of a complex situation that played to his advantage. Sawyer's leadership alienated the gaming community: taking on Frank Sinatra, who gave up his gaming license over the presence of Black Book member Sam Giancana at his Cal-Neva Resort at Lake Tahoe was one thing, but when Sawyer's regulators went after the Desert Inn group, Moe Dalitz and Ruby Kolod arranged for more than $200,000 in contributions to defeat the governor. The campaign grew vicious as Laxalt carefully negotiated the simultaneous building of a power base on the Strip while assuring the FBI he would not oppose them as they tried to clean out organized crime. The FBI was so taken with Laxalt that Director J. Edgar Hoover, at the peak of his power and before the nation knew of the immense corruption his agency harbored, wrote a letter with stinging criticism of Sawyer. Hank Greenspun, who detested Sawyer, published the letter on the front page of the *Las Vegas Sun*, providing a public outlet for the behind-the-scenes struggle. Laxalt's brother, Robert Laxalt, the state's most well-known writer—succeeding Walter Van Tilburg Clark—was enlisted to the cause.

There would be another major contributor to the Laxalt campaign, a shadowy figure of American business who operated a vast business empire held apart from public scrutiny. In a way, such an empire was tailor-made for Nevada: it allowed the injection of private but aboveground legal money into the world of casinos and, in the end, contributed to making organized crime irrelevant in the future of the state. Yet the money, as clean as it appeared, came with thick ropes attached. It belonged to the eccentric billionaire, Howard Robard Hughes, the next of the many masters who sought to own Nevada.

The Corporate Era

EARLY ON THE MORNING OF THANKSGIVING 1966, at the Carey siding in North Las Vegas, an ailing old man was transferred from a private railcar to a makeshift ambulance for a trip to the penthouse of the Desert Inn. The occupant, Howard R. Hughes, was the most mysterious figure at the pinnacle of American business, and by the 1960s, was equally famous for his eccentric behavior. Once a moviemaker and aviator, the sixty-one-year-old Hughes had become a disease-ridden, paranoid recluse, but he singlehandedly controlled billions of dollars in assets. With more than enough money to buy the Strip, Hughes was offered goodwill by the state of Nevada, and in some accounts, its integrity as well. Hughes's stamp served as legitimation of gambling and accelerated the process that made it into "gaming." His purchases of casinos throughout the state gave Nevada a new image and opened the way for legitimate capital and corporations to invest in gaming as American mores loosened in the 1970s and early 1980s.

Hughes was seriously ill and deranged by the time he arrived in Nevada in 1966. Born into a family that invented a drill bit essential in the oil drilling common in his native Texas early in the twentieth century, Hughes was orphaned at eighteen. Showing a debonair sophistication that he ever after sought for his public image, Hughes promptly bought out his father's relatives and became sole owner of the Hughes Tool Company. The drill bit became the basis of the Hughes empire, which included aviation, movies, and a major role as a defense contractor beginning in World War II and continuing into the Cold War. At one point, Hughes held more government contracts than any other entity, most of them involving secret research. The CIA was one of his primary sponsors, and more than any other enterprise, his relationship with the government created Hughes's enormous wealth. The defense work his companies undertook provoked intense criticism from those who saw Hughes's efforts as an elaborate and expensive boondoggle designed to enrich only him.

Such suspicions along with personal misfortune contributed to Hughes's solitude. Injured in the crash of a prototype spy plane in 1946, Hughes lived in pain for the rest of his life and developed an intense phobia about germs and dirt. Rich beyond conception by the mid-1950s—his companies having profited from Cold War contracts—he retreated from the outside world into his own private hell and became addicted to drugs. A coterie around him handled his affairs as he fell deeper and deeper into madness. Hughes had mythic power, but by 1966, the myth far exceeded the capabilities of the torn and addled old man who stood at the helm of his empire.

Hughes's mythical business skill offered Nevada something the Silver State desperately craved: respectability. Nevada gambling remained tarnished, and Governor Grant Sawyer's efforts to change that image did little to alter public perception. Mobsters, skimming scandals, and risqué entertainment defined the state in the popular imagination, and even as the harsh neo-Victorian attitudes of mid-century softened, Nevada remained a little too far out for large segments of the nation. Hughes trumpeted a loud patriotism and virulent anti-communism during the Cold War; his image as a relentless and shrewd businessman strongly suggested that American business should take another look at the opportunities of the Silver State. If Hughes found Nevada interesting, many believed, ordinary business leaders should look too.

When he settled in Las Vegas in 1966, Hughes's ties to Nevada stretched back almost thirty years. He had visited Las Vegas since the late 1930s, admiring both the open social climate and the lack of restriction on business. In that era, before he pulled back from the outside world, Hughes enjoyed Lake Tahoe and Las Vegas nightlife and often talked of moving his business empire to the desert. In 1953, already reclusive, he moved into a five-room bungalow called the "Green House" next to the Desert Inn on the Las Vegas Strip. When he left after a year, he had the house sealed in case he decided to someday return; he never did. In 1957, Hughes married starlet Jean Peters at the old Mizpah Hotel in Tonopah, two hundred miles from Las Vegas.

While still mentally healthy, Hughes was an astute businessman, and living in Nevada led him to explore opportunities in the state. During the Korean War, Hughes acquired enormous chunks of the southern Nevada desert, in one memorable instance exchanging five large tracts totaling seventy-three thousand acres in northern Nevada for approximately twenty-six thousand acres, forty square miles, called "Husite" in the western Las Vegas Valley. Hughes's longtime Washington, D.C., lawyer and later Secretary of Defense Clark Clifford and Senator Pat McCarran engineered the exchange on the grounds that Hughes planned a classified missile base on the land. He never built anything on the land—or anything else of consequence in Nevada. Forty years later, Husite became Summerlin, the largest master planned community in the world.

Sequestered in the penthouse of the Desert Inn, Hughes provided a symbol of change. The most successful legitimate businessman in the world had chosen Nevada. Hughes and his entourage occupied the entire floor of penthouse suites reserved for the high rollers on which the casino depended. After a few weeks, the management of the Desert Inn reviewed the arrangement. They expected an increase in gambling revenue to result from Hughes's presence, but were sorely disappointed. Hughes had so far cost them money; they couldn't put the high rollers in the penthouse because Hughes took up the entire floor. Gamble or leave, they told Hughes's representatives. Instead of doing either, Hughes bought the place for approximately $13 million a few months later and remained cloistered in the penthouse for four years.

The purchase of the Desert Inn initiated the grandest buying spree in the history of the state. Before Hughes was finished, he bought the Frontier for approximately $14 million, the Sands at $14.6 million, the Castaways at $3 million, the $17 million Landmark and its nearly $9 million Teamsters' Pension Fund loan, and the Silver Slipper. Hughes added a television station, airlines, small airport facilities, one hundred residential lots at the Desert Inn Country Club, and thousands of acres of undeveloped land to his empire. Hughes also made overtures to purchase Caesars Palace, the Riviera, the Dunes, and the Stardust in Las Vegas as well as Harrah's in Reno and Lake Tahoe until federal officials began examining antitrust issues. Even before the Nixon administration overruled Justice Department objections to Hughes's purchase of the famous Harold's Club in Reno and the Landmark Hotel—a decision that was later exposed as the consequence of a bribe and helped topple presidential friend Charles "Bebe" Rebozo—the tycoon controlled about one-seventh of the state's gaming revenue, one-quarter of Las Vegas's cash flow, and more than one-third of the revenue generated on the Las Vegas Strip. In a brief moment, he became the single most important person in the state, the sole proprietor of an enormous proportion of the state economy.

Howard Hughes's entrance into gambling began the long road that turned what had once been sinful behavior into "gaming," a legitimate recreational choice. Unquestionably the forerunner of a new era, Hughes arrived at an ideal moment. His illegal-to-legal predecessors had begun to give way. Moe Dalitz had beaten back tax evasion charges in 1964; Meyer Lansky and others tired of the constant federal surveillance and other hassles of trying to move from the fringe to the center of American culture. Selling out to Hughes, whom they treated as a sucker, seemed a good idea. The day the Hughes organization took over the Desert Inn, April 1, 1967, no one from the new ownership group made a count of the winnings. According to legend, the employees helped themselves while the inexperienced Hughes executives wondered how to run a casino.

In a strange way, Howard Hughes resembled the gangsters he replaced more than the corporate America that revered him. Hughes was a confirmed risk taker who flaunted rules all his life; he was beholden to no one, and even more important, owed no one. Because he was the sole owner, only he had to undergo gaming board investigation. With the help of Governor Laxalt, who was committed to bringing legitimacy to gaming, a man of Hughes's stature and wealth had little problem manipulating state regulatory bodies. As was the case with the development of the first hotels on the Strip, the source of capital upon which Hughes relied was private and personal. The reclusive and idiosyncratic billionaire differed from his predecessors. Despite occasional scrutiny from Congress and whistle blowers, his vast empire had little public association with organized crime. A forerunner of the new Las Vegas whose patterns resembled the old, Hughes's interest helped legitimize investment in the casino industry.

As the new governor, Laxalt based his campaign on the principle that he would provide a new direction for Nevada, and he believed that Hughes offered him an ideal solution to the state's misfortunes. Hughes solved Nevada's capital woes. He provided a source of legitimate money that the state desperately needed and might be able to use to attract more. This led Laxalt and state regulators to allow Hughes to be licensed without a hearing or real investigation. This accommodation influenced the creation of the Corporate Gaming Act, which removed barriers to corporate investment that had been enshrined in the 1955 regulations. Laxalt's predecessor, Grant Sawyer, opposed their removal out of fear that organized crime would gain an inroad into legitimate business. Dirty money, he believed, would mix with clean money, tainting both. Laxalt did not share this concern, and in 1967, he and his supporters, William F. Harrah and Barron and Conrad Hilton, persuaded the legislature to pass the Corporate Gaming Act. The law eliminated the requirement that each stockholder of an entity that owned a casino pass a Gaming Control Board investigation. There were risks: as Sawyer believed, legitimate money could be co-opted by behind-the-scenes mobsters, but it was equally true that the existing regulations did little to deter skimming and other violations. Nevada's need for a bigger pool of investors made the change in law attractive; Hughes's presence assured positive public relations. Passage of the law opened the door for an infusion of corporate capital and raised the stakes in gaming.

The relationship between the Hughes empire and Laxalt grew closer as the governor gave the billionaire everything he needed to turn Nevada into a private empire. The governor became the tennis partner of Hughes's public face, a former FBI and CIA operative named Robert Maheu. Laxalt flew on Hughes's private jet and Hughes himself even wrote that he envisioned a relationship between the two men that would put Laxalt in the White House. The Hughes public relations machine promised jobs, recreational facilities, a medical school, and countless other amenities to the Nevada public, putting at ease most worries about a shadowy boss. He became one of the most powerful people the state had ever known.

Hughes's control of Nevada came apart as a result of his inability to understand the outside world. Hughes's cash funded Nevada politics, and it inspired arrogance and even contempt for state law. After funding the governor's law firm, Hughes felt no qualms about calling Laxalt at the governor's mansion in the middle of the night. He dictated public policy, advocating unusual and even bizarre ideas often closely related to his fear of germs. Hughes was also a racist even by mid-century standards, fearing the African American presence in Las Vegas. His downfall stemmed from his perception that the law was for sale and that no one had the fortitude to stop him.

By the time the story of Hughes's bribe to Nixon's friend Charles "Bebe" Rebozo surfaced in 1971, the reclusive tycoon had left Nevada for good. Four years to the day after his arrival, on Thanksgiving Eve 1970, Intertel—a wholly owned subsidiary of another gaming company, Resorts International—descended on Las Vegas to take charge of the Hughes casinos. Resorts International's roots were tied into organized crime as well, but in this case, they came because of an odd situation: of all the major casinos in Nevada, only Hughes's lost, even hemorrhaged, money. Hughes's long-time legal counsel believed that Maheu and his cronies were stealing from the Hughes empire and called in Intertel to seize the casinos and account for their assets. Despite Maheu's close relationship with Laxalt, which prompted the response of the full force of Nevada's weak government on his behalf, Intertel whisked Hughes away to the Bahamas. Hughes never returned to Nevada; Laxalt left the governorship after one term, returned to the practice of law, faced criticism over the funding of his family's Ormsby House casino and hotel in Carson City, and represented a number of clients with close ties to the underworld.

Yet Hughes's impact on Nevada was lasting. His legitimacy, as tainted as it appeared in hindsight, gave the state something it had not possessed in almost a century: a claim to respectable status. Since the Kefauver hearings of the 1950s, Nevada had been the target of journalistic and political venom from across the country. The state seemed to endure a scandal a week, and as had been the case for most of the twentieth century, Nevada seemed the most tainted and disreputable of American states. Hughes's image and presence stopped that cold, paving the way for legitimate investment in gaming from conventional sources and pushing the state toward a future driven by the objectives of multinational corporations.

HUGHES DID OPEN THE WAY for new capital to enter the state and like most of the development after 1945, it centered in the south, in Las Vegas. The new capital became pivotal in a number of ways, shifting power and population to the south at an even greater rate and dividing the state in a new way. Once it had been rural Nevada against the city, Reno; as Las Vegas grew, it stood alone against not only the rural counties, but against Reno and Carson City as well. Once a state centered in the north, Nevada began to develop a new center of power, far to the south, tied to the emergence of gaming and leisure in American society and apart from the agriculture, ranching, mining, and even federal expenditure that had once driven the state. Nevada began to turn its limits into advantages, initiating the move from pariah status to the mainstream.

The changes also upset power relations within the gaming industry. Underworld money diminished in importance as a result of Hughes's investment, and the cost of building hotels and casinos increased. New entrepreneurs arrived in the state, in this instance seeking to build empires not in the land, but atop it in gambling and real estate development. These too centered in the south, the most prominent among them being the son of an Armenian immigrant and a former boxer just past his fiftieth birthday, Kirk Kerkorian.

Kerkorian was a quintessential American success story. The son of a fruit peddler in Fresno, California, he dropped out of eighth grade. Obsessed with flying, the young Kerkorian earned a pilot's license, became a crop duster and then a flight instructor, and flew bombers for the Canadian Royal Air Force during World War II. After the war, he bought a small plane and ferried gamblers from Los Angeles to Las Vegas, expanding into carrying defense cargo for the military. The company became Trans International Airways. By the mid-1950s, he was well-off and looking to invest. Las Vegas caught his eye, and between 1955 and 1962 he acquired considerable Las Vegas land. The most important piece, a tract on the Strip near the corner of Flamingo Road, cost him $960,000 in 1962; he sold it to Caesars Palace in 1968 for $5 million.

All of this was prelude to Kerkorian's efforts to make Las Vegas his own. He planned to build the largest hotel in the world on eighty-two acres of Paradise Road just off the Las Vegas Strip. The $80 million, 1,512-room International Hotel was a tour de force, another rite of passage in the ongoing upscaling of Las Vegas that began with Teamsters' Pension Fund money and had now progressed to more conventional capital. Kerkorian bought the Flamingo as well, but only to train his workers for the opening of the International. Kerkorian, who had been known as a high roller in 1940s and 1950s Las Vegas, provided one major advantage over other possible buyers; unlike corporations such as the Fujiya Nevada Corporation—a Japanese company that contended for the sale—or Sheraton, Kerkorian was the sole stockholder of his company and the only person who had to pass gaming board inspection. As a result of his success at the Flamingo, which turned ten times the profit under legitimate ownership than it had under the mob, Kerkorian received Securities and Exchange Commission permission to offer 17 percent of the company's stock to the public.

The public offering of stock in a casino was a dramatic shift that heralded a new era in the gaming industry. The capital markets had been shy about funding casinos, assuring that illegal money became a leading source of Nevada's post-1945 development. An initial public offering by the Golden Nugget fell flat in the 1940s; among casino owners, only the Del E. Webb Corporation, which owned the Sahara after 1960 through a complicated set of holding companies, was a publicly held corporation. Kerkorian was the first to take advantage of the options provided in the Corporate Gaming Act, and his success opened the way for hotel corporations to enter the gambling industry.

The Hilton Corporation, then considered among the top-flight hotels in the world, led the way. In 1970, just a year after the opening of the International, the Hilton chain purchased the Flamingo and the International. Kerkorian aspired to more grandiose properties, planning a new world-class resort, the MGM Grand Hotel, which exceeded even the International in number of rooms when it opened on December 5, 1973. The sale of the International and the Flamingo to Hilton had two enormous consequences: not only did it move Ker-

korian closer to his personal goal, it also fully opened the way for hotel corporations in Las Vegas. If they had felt a stigma before, Kerkorian and Hughes
had erased it. After the arrival of Hilton and as a result of its enormous success in Las Vegas—by 1976, 43 percent of the gross revenues of the 163-hotel
chain came from its two Las Vegas properties—legitimate capital had an inroad
that became progressively more important. Holiday Inn and Ramada followed
close behind Hilton, and a new form of financing supported the development
of Nevada gaming.

Hilton made Nevada acceptable to the hotel industry, with dramatic results
for the state. Hilton's payroll in Las Vegas topped $35 million by the end of the
1970s, more than half the peak payroll at the Nevada Test Site in its two hotels
alone. The three thousand jobs it provided heralded a new era in Nevada, for
an enormous hotel required a much larger staff. As gaming revenues increased
and the dollars that came from rooms, shows, and other services grew, traditional industries such as mining suffered. Copper ceased to be a viable part of
the state's mineral economy during the 1970s and new technology made mining far less labor intensive. Although the revenues from mining remained high,
the position of extractive industries in the state diminished. Mining ceased to
be the dominant employer and in the end, its power as a political force shrank.
As early as the 1970s, Nevada began to take on the traits of the New West, making its money in service instead of extraction. The shift led to other significant
changes in the state as well.

One such shift was the transformation of organized labor. Organized labor
had a strong history in Nevada, both north and south. In the 1920s powerful
Reno and little Las Vegas were both heavily unionized, the Reno Chamber of
Commerce gushing in 1927 that "strikes are unknown in Reno. . . . All trades
are on a union basis." A Fourth of July 1949 strike in Reno set in motion the
creation of the Committee of One Thousand, which set out to break the strike.
Even though the 1949 strike was settled quickly, with power broker Norman
Biltz tending bar and announcing he would donate his wages from the work to
the strikers, the Committee of One Thousand took its initiative from this strike
and the anti-union Taft-Hartley Act of 1947 to organize a petition drive. In a
1952 referendum ballot, Nevada became a right-to-work state, when a slim
majority of voters approved an open shop law. In this, the Silver State mirrored
its western and southwestern neighbors, almost all of which did not permit
unions to compel employees in unionized workplaces to join. Yet Nevada was
different than states such as Arizona or Utah. The state had a long history of

unions in mining and its small population gave organized labor great power. Along with its many other shortcomings, Nevada lacked the labor force to support the growth of almost any industry. As a result, unions held an important position as suppliers of labor as corporations built bigger hotels and needed more workers.

In southern Nevada, the Culinary Union became the anchor of post-1945 organized labor. Its roots dated to the 1930s, but the Culinary Union remained small, only becoming influential after World War II, when the dapper Elmer "Al" Bramlet arrived in Las Vegas in 1946. Born on a farm near Jonesboro, Arkansas, the small slight man came from the poverty-stricken southern plains, a historically impoverished region that got worse during the Depression. By the time he reached fourteen, Bramlet left Arkansas for good. In 1931, he began work as a dishwasher in Joliet, Illinois. After World War II, he found work as a bartender in Los Angeles, joined the bartenders' union, and became its business agent. In 1946, the bartenders' union sent him to Las Vegas to help the fledgling Culinary Union, and he and the city found each other. He had the traits the young city prized: toughness, competence, energy, and flamboyance. Bramlet built from the ground up, organizing workers and finding new ones for the rapidly growing city. Bramlet traveled on long recruiting trips, returning with the labor that Las Vegas so desperately needed. A delivery system began, carload by carload, catapulting Bramlet to real power. By 1954, he'd become the general secretary of the Culinary Union Local 226 in Las Vegas.

Bramlet found Nevada's greatest need as its economy changed: consistent, dependable labor. In Las Vegas, hotels accepted the union in return for a steady supply of labor. Labor was in such demand that Bramlet established a hiring hall in Las Vegas, an unusual occurrence in a right-to-work state. In return for the industry's cooperation, the union screened workers and vetted their credentials, weeding out undesirables at little cost to the hotels. Throughout the 1950s and early 1960s, the relationship was smooth. The hotels needed the union as much as the union needed the hotels. Funding for the city's growth, which during the 1960s came from Teamsters' Central States Pension Fund, helped cement hotel-union relationships.

In a comfortable and tightly intertwined relationship with the hotels, Bramlet excelled at contract negotiations. He met with the hotel owners, men much like himself, and negotiated one-on-one. Bramlet recognized that his workers could easily be replaced or made to do each other's jobs, so firm work rules, specific duties for different jobs, limits on what employers could ask of their workers, and—because many of the occupations depended on tips—a guaranteed minimum tip per customer, became the hallmarks of a Bramlet contract. Bramlet simply ensured that the workers got a piece of the pie. Since the cost wasn't terribly important to the bosses, the negotiations were often easy. No one signed contracts. Bramlet shook hands and a deal was in place. No one, neither management nor workers, broke the deal.

Bramlet was tough with labor problems. In an open shop state, he had only solidarity to guarantee the union's success. His people toed the line and he leaned on business owners who didn't want to go along. Bramlet threatened restaurant owners who would not accept the union, in one case keeping pickets outside a restaurant for almost twenty years. Uncooperative owners were fewer and fewer, and Bramlet found himself one of the power brokers in one of the most unusual states in the nation.

Bramlet earned his power the hard way. He built the union into a sizeable and powerful organization and turned it into a political force. He had great support among African Americans because he fought for wages and decent work conditions. When Bramlet became general secretary in 1954, membership stood at about two thousand. In 1967, when the first major culinary union strike in Las Vegas occurred, membership topped sixteen thousand. A partnership evolved between labor and management that worked to everyone's advantage.

The system worked very well as long as Las Vegas retained much of its old flavor. Workers and owners had much in common, even during the first major walkout, the Downtown Strike in 1967. This walkout reflected quintessential old Las Vegas, impenetrable to the outside world. Benny Binion, the hard-nosed Texas gambler who opened the Horseshoe in 1951 and became a real power in the city, brought food out to workers who struck his hotel. Italo Ghelfi, the owner of the Golden Gate, snuck cold drinks and smokes out to the strikers, hiding from his own security force. The familial relationships at the core of 1950s and 1960s Las Vegas, the mythic mob-run town, prevailed even over economic tension.

The onset of the corporate era altered the tacit labor arrangement. Unionization worked because gaming made the hotels so consistently profitable, and the union's ability to produce labor contributed to their success. The Corporate Gaming Act of 1967 and its amended version in 1969 allowed corporations with pre-existing assumptions about labor-management relationships to own hotels. Hilton, Holiday Inn, Ramada, and their successors focused on making each sector of the hotel profitable. They were willing to battle the union. Hughes's Summa Corporation was the leading antagonist, refusing to negotiate. This show of corporate force highlighted new power but it closed the door to the easiest solutions to most labor disputes. Quickly the familiarity between management and labor diminished. The handshake contracts soon disappeared. All the documents bore signatures. In 1968, the Culinary joined the Teamsters and the bartenders' union in a strike pact. In any strike, the unions would not cross each other's picket lines. The two sides watched each other warily.

The new climate led to ongoing testing of the boundaries of the labor-management relationship. During the early 1970s, posturing on both sides led to conflict. A wage dispute triggered a strike against three hotels in 1970. The Nevada Resort Association, the trade organization for about half of the unionized casinos, retaliated by closing the three hotels and declaring a lockout. Everyone faced the consequences. Not only did the Strip lose more than half a million dollars each day during the four-day lockout, the city, county, and state each lost considerable money in tax revenue each day. The costs dampened the taste for battle, leading to a three-year contract in 1973 without incident. When that contract expired without resolution in 1976, the Culinary Union struck over a wage increase and the terms of a "no-strike, no-lockout" clause. In this first major citywide strike, the union stayed out for sixteen days, and Nevada Governor Mike O'Callaghan, the one-legged Korean War veteran, school teacher, and former Boys Club boxing coach who was one of the most popular politicians in Nevada history, mediated. Labor-management relations in gaming had become important enough for the governor's attention.

The emerging corporate presence in Las Vegas had a profound impact on the union. After 1970, power shifted to legitimate corporate capital. This money made the old arrangements increasingly anachronistic, as the availability of enormous sums created a new scale for local development, and the union's unique position became more difficult. The Culinary Union had built its position on the charisma of one man and on the peculiarities of Las Vegas's situation in the 1950s and 1960s. When the circumstances changed, the union found itself in a more complicated environment.

ORGANIZED CRIME'S ROLE diminished at the same time. As companies that were traded on the New York Stock Exchange invested heavily in Nevada casino-hotels, organized crime suddenly became financially obsolete. Hotel chains pioneered the way and financial markets slowly changed their view of gaming as an investment. Wall Street could muster a great deal more money than organized crime ever could; the nearly $300 million that the Teamsters had invested in Nevada in the late 1960s might have remained the largest single pool of capital in the Silver State, but it had ceased to represent the growth sector of gaming. In an instant, the passage of the revised Corporate Gaming Act set the stage for the redistribution of power away from organized crime and toward Wall Street.

But organized crime remained a powerful force in the state, the primary source of campaign contributions, and a major influence on political decisions. Replacing its investment and clearing it from the state remained very different kinds of propositions. The first seemed easily accomplished; the latter was far more complicated. A fifteen-year long struggle to rid Nevada of the influence of organized crime ensued.

By the early 1970s, the mob had gotten arrogant and slipshod, especially in Las Vegas. Since the 1950s, when Las Vegas became an open city—which meant that any organized crime outfit could have a "franchise" there—mobsters had run the city and the state with occasional scandals but little interference in the business of making money. Skimming continued unabated, and while U.S. Attorney General Robert F. Kennedy successfully sent mob friend Jimmy Hoffa to jail and even secured a few indictments of people in the casino industry, organized crime treated the state of Nevada much as it had any other government: it bought what it could, which was often a great deal, and endured the rest. The legality of gambling in Nevada simply did not change the ways of thinking of mobsters who went legal. Even Hughes's and Kerkorian's entries did not change the characteristic patterns of the industry. By the early 1970s, the elaborate shell around mob control began to collapse. Organized crime's complacency made it simultaneously vulnerable and inflexible.

Once Hilton and other hotel chains became comfortable in Las Vegas, the advantages of corporate capital became increasingly apparent. After he sold the International, Kerkorian built the first MGM Grand, again the biggest hotel in the world at more than two thousand rooms. When it opened in 1973, the hotel employed 4,500 people, another enormous addition to the state's labor force. The difference in scope and scale suggested the possibility of a new reality. But the mob presence stood in the way—still crucial as an economic force and deeply entrenched in state politics. The transformation to legitimate capital markets needed a catalyst, a mistake by organized crime that would allow it to be kicked out of Nevada gambling once and for all.

Smug and smarter about crime than changing national culture, mobsters provided an opportunity simply by continuing to operate as they had since 1945. In 1974, Allen R. Glick, a fresh-faced unknown from San Diego, received a $62.7 million loan from the Teamsters' Pension Fund to purchase Recrion Corporation, which owned the Stardust, the Fremont, and the Marina in Las Vegas. The sale to Glick was an attempt to whitewash the company. Glick served in Vietnam and returned to try his hand at real estate. He bought the bankrupt Hacienda Hotel and Casino at the southern end of the Strip. Glick's takeover of another bankrupt casino in Lake Tahoe brought him into the orbit of the Teamsters' Pension Fund. Soon after, the young entrepreneur sought to pounce on Recrion and needed money fast. After efforts to raise it elsewhere, he came to the Teamsters at almost the same time they sought out his clean-cut image.

This marriage generated predictable consequences. In college, Glick had become friendly with Joseph Balistrieri, son of Frank Balistrieri, Milwaukee's mob boss. After the sale was complete and Glick created the Argent Corporation to manage his new holdings, Balistrieri instructed Glick to sell half the company to the mobster's son for $25,000 as a token of appreciation for receiving the funding. Compromised, Glick had little choice. At the Stardust—under the watchful eyes of the chairman of Argent Corporation's executive committee—Frank Rosenthal, a gambler, utilized the skills of famed slot cheat turned counting room boss Jay Vandermark. Supported by the enforcement power of mob underboss Tony Spilotro, Rosenthal and Vandermark conducted a 1950s-style mob-skimming operation. By some estimates, the skim took as much as $7 million a year from the Stardust's slots alone.

By the mid-1970s, the climate had begun to change, and the Stardust situation offered an opening for those who wanted to move gambling onto more legitimate footing. Argent Corporation drew negative publicity from the day Glick took over. Two murders that came close to Glick, one in San Diego and the other in the Caesars Palace parking lot, raised considerable questions about the state's new licensee. Rosenthal's presence at the Stardust attracted even more attention. Rosenthal was known as a mob associate and had been convicted of trying to fix a college basketball game in the 1960s.

Glick and his behind-the-scenes bosses carried on as casinos in Las Vegas had since the 1940s. The skim continued, orchestrated by Vandermark. Before Rosenthal's licensing hearing Glick gave him a ten-year, $250,000 per year contract that stipulated that Rosenthal would be paid whether or not he received a gaming license. In January 1976, the Gaming Control Board decided that Rosenthal did not meet Nevada's standards for a gaming license. In May 1976, a Gaming Control Board raid on the Stardust counting room uncovered a skim in process. Vandermark disappeared to Mexico the next day.

The pressure continued. After his ouster as CEO at the Stardust, Rosenthal received his $250,000 annual salary from Argent and served as entertainment director. He hosted a local television show and played man-about-town, still trying to secure a gaming license. Rosenthal questioned the state's right to deny him work in the gaming industry, challenging the state's right to regulate the industry at all. Turned back by the courts and permanently denied a gaming license at a 1979 Gaming Commission hearing, Rosenthal lost his composure and verbally attacked public officials and the media.

Rosenthal's outburst obscured the salient event: the Gaming Commission denied his license. Suitability for licensing was, like beauty, in the eye of the beholder. Rosenthal would have easily cleared the Gaming Commission during the 1960s, but his application in the 1970s took place in a far different climate. As Rosenthal tried to attain licensing, the mainstreaming of gaming and the casino industry, and with it the state of Nevada, took shape. Atlantic City legalized gaming in 1976, an enormous step that contributed to Nevada's legitimacy. State lotteries began in many states and were under consideration in more. Entrepreneurs such as Donald Trump began to look for ways to invest in casinos. Nevada no longer stood alone. Licensing standards evolved and became less flexible. The burden of proof fell on the applicant for a gaming license.

Throughout the 1950s and 1960s, gaming regulators routinely licensed a range of thugs to run casinos. During the 1950s, Joseph "Doc" Stacher held a gaming license. His record of arrests dated from the 1920s and included New York and Nevada convictions during the 1950s and a grand jury appearance in Los Angeles in 1962. L. B. "Benny" Binion arrived in Las Vegas in 1946 with an arrest record in his home town of Dallas, Texas, that dated back to 1923. In 1951, Binion was granted a gaming license. He was convicted of tax evasion and suspected of murder soon after. Publicly listed shareholders in hotels in 1963 included Moe Dalitz, Ruby Kolod, Morris Kleinman, and Sam Tucker, all connected to the Mayfield Road Gang from Cleveland, at the Desert Inn; Edward Levinson, an associate of Meyer Lansky who managed the skim from Las Vegas casinos in the 1950s and owned pieces of a number of casinos, at the Fremont and Horseshoe; Ben Goffstein and the Gus Greenbaum estate at the Riviera; and Jack Entratter at the Sands. These legal listings were the tip of an iceberg. Even at the end of the 1960s, all kinds of people were licensed to own and work in casinos. The standards the commission applied to Rosenthal heralded a new level of regulation. In the process, they helped turn "gambling," a deviant behavior, into "gaming," a legitimate recreational option.

Clearing out the mob was easier said than done. It occurred in fits and starts. In 1979, after a nearly three-year battle to rid the Aladdin of James Tamer, an affiliate of the Lebanese underworld, and Sorkis Webbe, its legal counsel, the Gaming Commission suspended the Aladdin's state gaming license. Later the Gaming Commission gave the Aladdin a sell-or-close-it order. On August 6, 1979, gaming control agents entered the Aladdin casino and sealed the slot machines and the tables. It was a sad fate for the hotel. If the standards applied at Rosenthal's licensing hearing were remarkable, closure of a mob casino simply for being a mob casino was revolutionary. A little more than a decade after the Corporate Gaming Act, Nevada state government made unprecedented efforts to rid its primary industry of organized crime.

Another decade completed the process of excising the mob. The arrival of FBI agent Joe Yablonsky as special-agent-in-charge of southern Nevada led to a half decade of vigorous prosecution. The city became tense, and city leaders screamed that Yablonsky had a vendetta against them. One who was targeted was Harry Claiborne, a U.S. district court judge and longtime Las Vegan who was later impeached and removed by Congress for tax evasion. U.S. Senator Paul Laxalt, who returned to politics in 1974 and later became a close confidant of President Ronald Reagan, squawked so loudly about Yablonsky that it attracted attention to corruption in Nevada instead. A scandal at the Tropicana led to further prosecutions, and the mob's hold—always tenuous—convulsed and released. Yablonsky's organized crime task force put the mob truly on the run and by the middle of the 1980s Las Vegas was largely free of mob ownership of casinos even though dozens, even hundreds, of high-level executives in various casinos had ties to or experience with the mob. Legitimate capital had replaced the underworld and all the tough guys in the world couldn't change that. Yet the presence of corporate capital did not solve all the problems of access for casino development.

Throughout the 1970s, large national banks shied away from casino gambling. Only the legalization of casino gambling in Atlantic City and the large profits that investors attained persuaded East Coast and California banks to invest. Through the auspices of the Del Webb Company, the Sahara received $135 million in 1979 from New York banks for improvements to the resort. The sum was $25 million more than the hotel requested. At about the same time Aetna Insurance Company loaned $60 million to Caesars World, the parent corporation of Caesars Palace. Soon after, First Interstate Bank began to develop a sizeable casino and gaming loan portfolio. By 1980, the five dominant gaming organizations in Nevada—Harrah's, MGM, Del Webb, the Hilton, and Caesars World—were all publicly held corporations.

As this change in the basis of the state economy occurred, much of the rest of the state mirrored the problems of the interior West. Rural Nevada remained sparsely populated and devoted to the traditional western economy. In many of the so-called "cow counties," agriculture, ranching, and mining formed the basis of the economy. In some, local-option legalized prostitution contributed to coffers, but most of Nevada remained as it had always been, a loosely connected hinterland removed from the cities of the state and the region. It shared the loss of population, declining economy, and general malaise of the rest of the rural West.

Since 1945, rural counties throughout the intermountain West had been in decline. From Colorado to the Sierra Nevada, many lost population and income. Most of the traditional industries collapsed and those that did not usually passed from local hands to multinational corporations. When new opportunities arose, they had danger attached, as did the uranium boom on the Colorado Plateau in the 1950s and 1960s. Mining, timber, and agriculture, all essential to regional identity, faced serious problems. Not only did these pursuits become less lucrative, they also caused environmental problems that inspired the ire of the growing American environmental movement.

In Nevada, Lake Tahoe became the focus of environmental efforts. This high-mountain jewel, perhaps the most beautiful lake in the U.S., had become inundated with tourists as a result of the development of casinos. By the mid-1960s, as many as 150,000 came to the lake on a busy weekend. Interstate 80 increased winter travel, for it made ski resorts such as Squaw Valley easily accessible. The Winter Olympics at Squaw Valley in 1960 helped promote skiing, and the new residents of California, as many as 1,500 each day in the early 1960s, clamored for skiing and other forms of recreation. Urban growth around the lake provided an early example of sprawl. The lake that Mark Twain once called "the fairest picture the whole earth affords" was severely threatened.

Bistate jurisdiction complicated the situation. Half of Lake Tahoe was in California, and the Golden State had its own rules and regulations, far more stringent than antigovernment Nevada. California embraced the ideas of environmentalism while Nevada salivated over growth. With questions of growth, water pollution, sewage disposal, and erosion dogging the lake, some kind of joint administration of the region was necessary. After difficult jockeying by proponents of different results, the Tahoe Regional Planning Agency (TRPA) was established in 1970. While it heralded the beginning of an era of multistate administration, it faced a number of difficult circumstances.

Lake Tahoe's popularity made most of its problems far worse. As visitation grew, newcomers followed. Real estate values climbed—a benefit for some sectors of the population, but hard for families—and speculation became rife. Growth exceeded the systems to manage it and public officials were charged with finding a solution. Besieged by competing interests on all sides, the TRPA suffered the fate of most planning efforts. It weakened under pressure, granted variances, caved in to developers, and in the end failed to slow urbanization. The *San Francisco Chronicle* called the agency an "impotent pygmy"; The *Los Angeles Times* announced that all TRPA could plan were casinos and shopping centers. Under attack from California, Nevadans tried to bolster support for management of the lake, but in the end, the bistate concept failed. Nevada officials believed they had done their part by restricting the expansion of casinos and wanted California to cede more control to the Silver State. Californians did not trust Nevada to protect the lake and demanded more control. In the end, California officials sought a national recreation area at Lake Tahoe, but without the support of Nevada for the project, federal agencies would not intervene. By 1979, the idea of a national recreation area at Lake Tahoe was dead, victim of political warfare.

Yet the battle over Lake Tahoe stirred Nevada in new ways. A strong liberal contingent in the north, often associated with the university, actively supported protection of Lake Tahoe, and the lake became a symbol of the changing state. "Save Lake Tahoe" became a rallying cry in urban Nevada, tying the changing state to larger national trends. Nevada's cities became a hotbed of support and the state's first environmental groups spurred a small awakening. As Nevada's cities grew and the state's economy shifted even more heavily to gaming and tourism, protecting assets such as Lake Tahoe made economic as well as social sense. The fact that tourism had caused the problems of Lake Tahoe complicated the situation, but not necessarily the response in the state. Saving Lake Tahoe became a social good in some circles, opponents said, regardless of the impact on the economy of the region.

Even as urban Nevada rallied to save its stunning lake, rural Nevada became enmeshed in a backlash against change in American society. Agriculture and ranching enjoyed disproportionate influence in the state legislature, and as the economic condition of rural Nevada worsened, legislators fashioned a response. Early in the 1970s, as a result of complaints from Nevada ranchers who claimed that the Bureau of Land Management—the weakest of federal land management agencies—threatened their livelihood, the Select Committee on Public Lands of the Nevada legislature pursued the transfer of federal lands in the state. Local control had always been appealing in Nevada; the fact that almost 90 percent of the state remained in federal hands had long been a source of conflict between the state and the U.S. government. The call for transfer of land gathered momentum, and leaders challenged the legality of a number of federal statutes that they believed infringed on their rights. These sagebrush rebels sought new relations between state and federal governments, and political leaders such as Barry Goldwater, U.S. senator from Arizona, and John L. Harmer, the lieutenant governor of California during Ronald Reagan's governorship, wholeheartedly supported their view. States should have more control over what went on within their boundaries.

The Sagebrush Rebellion was not really new; it merely reshaped the objections of the nineteenth century in late twentieth-century terms. Proponents believed that mining, ranching, and agriculture still drove the state, but the federal government controlled so much land that it held Nevadans back. New legislation added a twist to their objections. Sagebrush rebels were Nevada Libertarians at their most strident. Heir to a long tradition that argued for local control, the Sagebrush Rebellion sounded like characteristic griping, but struck a chord in the changing West. Advocating an updated version of "states' rights," the idea that state authority supersedes federal authority, the Sagebrush Rebels fashioned local government as the most—and sometimes only—important form of democracy.

This philosophy was hardly new; instead it was a challenge to the way the United States has operated since the Civil War. That war had been about the concept of union as much as the issue of slavery; its aftermath had been proof of the supremacy of the federal system in the United States. Although federal authority suffered numerous attacks throughout the late nineteenth century and the first half of the twentieth, federal supremacy held into the 1970s on questions of federal land. Despite the antiauthoritarian cast of the 1960s, even that tumultuous decade saw the expansion of federal power and the use of it to protect land from development rather than to allow it to move from national to local hands. In this context, the Sagebrush Rebellion seemed anachronistic, a relic of an earlier America.

The larger trends in American society did little to dissuade rural Nevadans, themselves threatened not only by the changing economic climate but by the changing culture of American society. Rural Nevada prided itself on its self-reliant traditions, rarely recognizing the role of federal subsidies for water, electricity, and even grazing that underpinned their independence. "Culture and custom," the code words for the insistence that time-honored use of public lands conveyed de facto ownership to long-time users, underpinned the Sage-brush Rebellion. Hardly different from "squatters' rights," this idea lacked a basis in law. Nevada gave up its public lands as a condition of statehood, and like many western states, it had never even owned the land that they targeted for transfer. This was not local land, as sagebrush rebels liked to insist. It was merely "locally located," proximate to people who had made long use of it under federal terms.

The Sagebrush Rebellion spoke to deep-seated regional fears that crystal-lized in Nevada. The individual rights revolution of the 1960s, the growing distrust of authority and the federal government in particular, and the impact of environmental regulation inspired fear and disgust at what some western-ers self-righteously believed was a powerful federal leash. The strident cries of the rebels reminded the nation of the fears of rural westerners, and many who found inspiration in the romantic mythology of the American West offered at least tacit support.

The Nevada legislature, ever iconoclastic, lent support to the Sagebrush Rebellion. In 1979, Nevada passed legislation that targeted Bureau of Land Management holdings in Nevada for transfer to state hands, asserted state control of mineral rights and surface access, advocated a multiple-use per-spective for management, and protected existing leases made by individuals with the federal government. Other western politicians embraced the action. Senator Orrin Hatch of Utah introduced a similar bill in the U.S. Senate in 1979 and became one of the leaders of the revolt, and Nevada's senators Paul Laxalt and Howard Cannon were joined by Dennis DeConcini and Barry Goldwater of Arizona, Alan Simpson and Malcolm Wallop of Wyoming, and Jake Garn of Utah. Archconservatives Senator Ted Stevens of Alaska, Senator Jesse Helms of North Carolina, and Senator Richard Jepsen of Iowa added their names to the long list of supporters.

The campaign year of 1980 became the high water mark of the Sagebrush Rebellion. Not only did the honorary sagebrush rebel Ronald Reagan trounce the incumbent Jimmy Carter for the presidency, Wyoming, Utah, and New Mexico followed Nevada with bills that claimed sovereignty over BLM lands within state boundaries. Wyoming claimed national forest land as well as that managed by BLM. Arizona joined the Sagebrush Rebellion when a general referendum overrode a gubernatorial veto. Governors Jerry Brown of California and Richard Lamm of Colorado vetoed similar bills, while one measure in Washington state passed the legislature, but was voided by a 60 percent "no" vote in a referendum. Although Sagebrush Rebellion bills went down to defeat in Montana, Idaho, and Oregon, the movement had real momentum. Powerful senators from western states who opposed it fell, and Cannon—a moderate, four-term Nevada Democrat—felt the residual effects two years later when conservatives united to defeat him for reelection. The Sagebrush Rebellion attracted wide support in many western states as well as among opponents of federal power and jurisdiction, Libertarians, other advocates of the fictional free market, and a range of fringe interests across the nation.

The rebels tapped a reservoir of distaste for the changes of the twentieth century. In Nevada and the West, rural areas wielded much more power than their economic production or their population merited. Rural leaders tried to use political power to reinstate a nineteenth-century economic regime. Their successes in 1979 and 1980 masked significant problems for their movement. Nevada ranchers did not represent urban and suburban Nevada, which far outnumbered the rural areas. Yet when President-elect Reagan expressed his support—a telegram with the powerful words: "I renew my pledge to work toward a sagebrush solution"—to the second conference of the League for the Advancement of States' Equal Rights in November 1980, Sagebrush rebels could believe they stood in the vanguard of a new—if also old—American movement.

In Nevada, they certainly enjoyed political power. Both U.S. senators embraced the movement, and Governor Robert List, elected in 1978, faced the impact of the Sagebrush Rebellion and of Proposition 13 in California, the 1978 referendum that cut and capped property tax rates and damaged California's ability to provide services to its people. A referendum that capped property taxes in Nevada at 1 percent of real value had already passed; it came up for its second and binding vote in 1980. List tried to circumvent it by proposing a property tax cut, a repeal of the sales tax on food, and tax deferral for the elderly. In 1981, with the help of the legislature, he succeeded with a tax package that cut 50 percent from the property tax rate and raised the sales tax from 3.5 percent to 5.75 percent.

List's measure was a disaster that changed state revenue forever. Sales tax is a regressive tax, borne equally by anyone who purchases, regardless of income. Property tax and income tax both require that those who make more pay more. The result of List's policy was to unequally redistribute the tax burden in two ways: from the well-off to the less so; and from the north, where many of List's friends owned large ranches, to the south, where property was much smaller. The rationale was simple: the sales tax was shared by Nevada's 12 million tourists, all of whom bought goods and services, and this meant that an increase in sales tax was palatable in ways that a property tax was not. It spread the pain to visitors. But sales tax revenue rose and fell and was difficult to predict with accuracy. As much as 75 percent of the state's revenue came from sales and gaming taxes, assuring unstable revenue, dependent on the level of expenditure within the state. This made state funding susceptible to economic recession in dramatic ways. Without a stable tax structure, Nevada could not depend on its major source of revenue. The result since has often been chaos, as government expenditures rise and fall with increases or decreases in consumer spending.

The change in taxation made the state even more dependent on tourism and gaming. Nevada's traditional sources of income all shrunk in relationship to the ever-growing gaming take. Gross gaming revenue topped $1 billion in 1975 and $2 billion in 1980. It crossed the $3 billion threshold in 1985. In 1980, the gross yield from mining topped $390 million, rising to more than $640 million in 1983. Even more, mining became increasingly technological; it used fewer workers to accomplish every task than it had a generation before, cutting into its advantage for the state. Gaming was labor-intensive in a manner than modern mining was not, and every year a larger percentage of Nevada workers were employed in gaming and tourism. Gaming had become the dominant industry in the state—even if the state legislature did not always recognize this reality. The power of rural Nevada remained intact; the revenue of the state was increasingly generated in the cities.

Las Vegas had become the economic center of the state, but the early 1980s were its lowest point. During the late 1970s, inflation and interest rates rose to record levels, shutting down economic growth and creating what President Jimmy Carter called "a crisis of confidence." The remedy, a national recession in 1981 and 1982 caused by Ronald Reagan's policies, cut into leisure spending at a time when much of the revenue and an overwhelming percentage of employment in Nevada depended on tourism. The state's leading city, Las Vegas, faced hard times as well. Two enormous hotel fires, one at the MGM and the other at the Las Vegas Hilton, damaged the city's reputation. In the MGM fire, eighty-four people died. Little new construction occurred after the MGM opened in 1973, and the city seemed tired, worn, and a little tawdry. The effort to remove organized crime from the casinos was well underway, but corporate capital investment slowed. Money became widely available for renovation, but no major new hotels opened on the Strip. Las Vegas seemed to be losing its appeal. Visitation actually dropped in 1981 and 1982, a reversal that the city had never before experienced. Sin City seemed to lose its edge and its ability to communicate with a changing American public.

Yet by the mid-1980s, Nevada's most marketable asset, gambling, had begun to spread across the nation. In 1976, New Jersey legalized gambling in Atlantic City, and beginning with New Hampshire, numerous states initiated state lotteries. As other conventional prohibitions broke down in the aftermath of the 1960s, the widespread cultural objection to gambling receded, and people regarded the activity in a new way. With states invested in the activity as a way to raise scarce revenue, it became more difficult even for straight-laced states to disdain gambling. States without lotteries found that their residents would cross the border to adjoining states to buy hundreds, even thousands, of lottery tickets. Dog racing became legal in a number of states, and America became a nation of legal gamblers.

For Nevada, this new circumstance provided a genuine opportunity, a way to package what had once been vices and had now become typical activities. With the influence of organized crime on the wane and gambling rapidly becoming gaming, Nevada's amenities appealed to a wider market than ever before. But the state faced its same, eternal question: where would the money to support growth come from? There were no sources of indigenous capital in the state, no enormous local investors to shore up the state's industries, and even with the growing interest of banks and the financial markets, Nevadans still feared that their aspirations would remain unfunded. A transformation required a combination of ingenuity and fortitude merged with considerable capital. As it always seemed in Nevada, this change came from an unexpected source.

8 The Mirage Phase and the New Nevada

THE OPENING of the Mirage Hotel and Casino on the Las Vegas Strip on Thanksgiving 1989 heralded the beginning of the newest phase of gaming, the economic and cultural engine that had come to define Nevada, and its increasingly close cousin, entertainment. This $630 million property, $500 million more than had ever been spent on the construction of a hotel/casino, transformed Las Vegas from a city that marketed gaming and gave away almost everything else to a comprehensive resort that, within a decade, became the most visited tourist destination in the world.

The Mirage was the first of eleven megaresorts built in Las Vegas between its opening and the start of the new century. In the process, Las Vegas hotel rooms more than doubled in number to 125,000, twice that of any other city in the United States. Its population also doubled to more than 1.5 million, and in a way that no one could have imagined Las Vegas became a normal American city that typified one dimension of postindustrial America. Even more, Las Vegas came to entirely represent Nevada to the rest of the world, even if political power in the state still lay in the north. Where once Nevada had been associated with silver and mining, it now meant entertainment in every sense of the word. With 70 percent of the state's population, and generating an even higher percentage of its revenue, Las Vegas became Nevada's cash cow, its proceeds fought over by other parts of the state.

Wall Street financing transformed Las Vegas and with it Nevada. Impresario Steve Wynn, a protégé of banker Parry Thomas, raised the stakes in the casino industry, laying the foundation for the transformation of the town from Sin City to the queen of resorts. Bond and bank financing allowed Las Vegas to become more than simply glitzy excess, fodder for the nation's gossip columnists. Once the dollars that built Las Vegas's resorts came from Wall Street, the city's attractions could be shaped to the tastes of the mainstream public.

Las Vegas had always provided a segment of society with a luxury experience at a middle-class price; the Mirage Phase allowed it to reach for the entire middle class, American and global alike. The ongoing easing of the stigma attached to gaming and the willingness to merge gaming with conventional postwar attractions on the scale of Disneyland gave Las Vegas access to nearly every segment of American and even world society. Not only did people who wanted to gamble come to the transformed desert town, so did people who wanted to experience the spectacle and have a vacation in a classic but updated sense of the word. Sin City became more palatable and maybe even a little less sinful.

Born in 1942, Wynn came to the gaming industry naturally. His father had run bingo parlors in the East, and from early in life, Wynn understood the power of ownership of games of chance. In 1967, he and his wife Elaine moved to Las Vegas, where he purchased a small percentage of the Frontier Hotel. By most accounts, at that time the Frontier was connected to organized crime. Wynn's partner, Maurice "Maury" Friedman, fronted for the mob and testified against his cohorts in a scandal that brought down the Frontier's management team. Wynn himself was not accused of wrongdoing, but the property was in chaos, and everyone associated with it was suspect.

When Howard Hughes purchased the casino during his remarkable buying spree in the late 1960s, Wynn was bought out. The young entrepreneur used the proceeds to purchase a liquor distributorship, a valuable concession in southern Nevada, and accumulated enough savvy and wealth to engineer the purchase of the only piece of land that Hughes ever sold. Hughes hated to sell land, but once Wynn demonstrated that it cost money to keep the piece, the tycoon's representatives relented. Some have seen the hand of Thomas, Nevada's primary financier at the time and Wynn's mentor, in the transfer. The tract was a dubious sliver next to Caesars Palace, so narrow that it seemed to offer little. Caesars Palace managers thought little of the purchase until Wynn threatened to build the narrowest casino in the world on it. Caesars Palace chairman Clifford Perlman was furious and refused to deal with the young upstart. He later relented and bought the property, netting Wynn a $766,000 profit.

Wynn turned that payday into controlling interest in the downtown Golden Nugget. By June 1973 vice president Wynn ran the casino, taking it from the margins to the leading position on Fremont Street. The Golden Nugget quadrupled its profit in the first year that Wynn took the reins; in 1977, he added a 579-room tower to the hotel, raising the stakes in downtown Las Vegas and increasing the hotel's profits to $12 million within a few years. In the space of a decade, Wynn became known as the most astute operator in the casino business.

Wynn had plans that far exceeded the Golden Nugget, but he faced uncertain financial markets. Even though the Teamsters' Pension Fund had been a primary source of casino funding in Las Vegas since the 1960s, most banks and Wall Street houses still frowned on investing in gaming. Even after the opening of Atlantic City in 1976 and the growing number of states with legalized lotteries in the late 1970s and 1980s, the business was not quite respectable. Wynn explored a number of routes, stumbling upon complicated and unconventional formulas for casino financing. Wynn met financier and later convicted felon Michael Milken, and persuaded the powerful Milken and his Wall Street firm, Drexel Burnham Lambert, to back his ventures with junk bonds, risky but high-yield financial instruments. Milken financed Wynn's move into Atlantic City in 1978, when Wynn used junk bonds to buy and renovate the Strand, a decrepit hotel on the Atlantic City Boardwalk. With $160 million in funding, he rebuilt it as the 506-room Atlantic City Golden Nugget. Within a few years, Wynn's casino became the most profitable in Atlantic City, securing his ties with a major source of development capital.

But Wynn's aspirations were in Las Vegas and Milken remained the most dependable source of capital to replace what had come before. Throughout the 1980s, Wynn planned the pinnacle casino that became the Mirage. Through Milken and Drexel Burnham Lambert, Inc., Golden Nugget Inc., Wynn's parent company, borrowed $535.1 million in what observers of the financial markets called "a work of art." Milken's junk bonds underpinned the project.

In the process, Drexel Burnham Lambert became the dominant financial force in the Nevada economy, far surpassing other investors and even mining as a source of Nevada's economic success. By 1989, the $2.57 billion DBL invested in the Silver State represented the single largest amount of capital expenditure ever in the state. As many as 100,000 new Nevada jobs and much of the population growth during the 1980s resulted from that money. Thomas, the original banker to the Strip who built his small enterprise into a $270 million conglomerate by the mid-1970s, recognized the impact. In 1989, he observed that "Milken has been the primary mover [in Nevada] for the last several years." In a nod to the difficulties of acquiring capital in the old days, Wynn suggested that Milken's influence paralleled that of Thomas during the 1960s and 1970s.

The Mirage was like no previous hotel casino anywhere. It turned a casino experience into entertainment. "Fantasy become reality" served as its theme; a fiery volcano erupted hourly, cooled by precious water in the desert. Illusionists Siegfried and Roy and their famed white tigers contributed to this ambience, as did a tank of live dolphins, and later the nouvelle circus Cirque du Soleil, an act that Wynn raved about and brought to the mainstream public. The Mirage created a script that put the visitors at the center of any experience on the property; it let customers feel that they were special and even unique and that what happened during their visit revolved around them. In the process, it reflected back onto American culture its essence in an age of self-indulgence. The Mirage became the pinnacle that Las Vegas could offer a tourist: an invented reality that only occasionally demanded the suspension of disbelief.

The Mirage opened at a fortuitous time for Las Vegas. In 1988, the Indian Gaming Regulatory Act attempted to resolve the increasing disputes between states and tribes about gaming. It allowed Native Americans to offer gaming on reservation lands under certain circumstances. After a 1990 court decision that allowed Indian casinos in states that allowed only lesser forms of gaming, Indian casinos opened in a dozen states during the next few years. In response to the drain on state revenues, a number of state governments responded with their own gaming. In states without legal gaming, revenue began to transfer to Indian reservations or nearby jurisdictions with legal gaming, yet the social cost was left to those entities that did not receive profits from gaming. The result was a massive upswing in legal gaming in the nation, a reflection both of new law and the cultural shift away from the neo-Victorianism of mid-century.

Nevada initially regarded Indian gaming as a threat, but the opening of the Mirage helped turn more gaming in other places into an advantage for the Silver State. The Mirage reemphasized entertainment, a motif from Las Vegas's past that had been in decline since the 1970s. Buildings such as the Mirage made Las Vegas into the first postmodern spectacle, something Americans of the late twentieth century just had to see. The volcano, the shows, and even the ambiance of the hotel drew people who might never have come to Las Vegas before. Las Vegas was a wonder, an experience trophy Americans had to mark off on their list of lifetime accomplishments.

The difference between Las Vegas and the new Indian casinos was not lost on Americans. If anything, Indian gaming and its state-run counterparts seeded Las Vegas and brought it more visitors. Countless people, exposed to gaming for the first time in these smaller venues, thought: "now we really need to see Las Vegas." Everything was so much more spectacular in the desert. The Mirage's air handling system made it so that visitors never smelled stale smoke. Most Indian casinos were prefabricated warehouse buildings that reeked of cigarettes. In Las Vegas, the drinks tasted better, there were buffets and other amenities, the slot machines were looser, and the shows more spectacular. To a society obsessed with the self and indulgent of its own whims, the new Las Vegas was a kind of paradise.

The "Mirage Phase," the rush to build that followed Wynn's announcement of the Mirage, altered not only the skyline of the Strip but the culture of Las Vegas as well. The Excalibur followed in 1990, and throughout the 1990s, new hotels were completed nearly every year. After the Excalibur opened, the Luxor, Treasure Island, and the second MGM Grand opened in 1993. In 1995 the Hard Rock Hotel debuted a few blocks off the Strip. In 1996, three new hotels—the Stratosphere Tower, Monte Carlo, and New York, New York—opened, followed by the Bellagio in 1998, Mandalay Bay, the Venetian, and Paris Las Vegas in 1999, and the new Aladdin in 2000. Together they turned the city into a metropolitan area of a mere 1.5 million people with twice the number of hotel rooms of New York or Los Angeles. The exotic decadent Rat Pack—era themes of earlier resorts—the Dunes with its Sahara sultan motif, the Tropicana's pre-Castro Cuban atmosphere, Caesars Palace and its Greco-Roman theme, the Rio and its Carnival decor, and others—were pushed aside by an iconography derived from contemporary popular culture that appealed to a younger generation. Once again, Las Vegas made from its past a new future, carrying the state with it.

During the Mirage Phase, Las Vegas chased a new respectability. In the early 1990s, Wynn, Kirk Kerkorian of the MGM, William Bennett of Circus Circus, and others recast the town as a family entertainment resort. Many of the new properties opened with enormous theme parks; roller coasters became common as well. The opening of the Grand Slam Canyon—a theme park at Circus Circus—the Luxor, Wynn's Treasure Island resort, and the MGM Grand in 1993 signaled an effort to provide mainstream visions with fantasy and leisure. "This is part of a major metamorphosis in Las Vegas," then Mayor Jan Laverty Jones said as the MGM debuted. "Las Vegas is changing from just adult entertainment to a resort destination."

In the decade that followed the opening of the Mirage, Las Vegas became the premier resort destination in the world. The skyline of the Strip in 2000 was dominated by eleven major resorts that had not been there ten years before. These resorts redefined what Las Vegas meant to visitors. By 1998, 300,000 people per day walked along the Strip near its intersection with Tropicana Boulevard. Major corporations of all kinds invested in the city; developers, retailers, and entertainment companies prominent among them. When visitation topped 35,000,000 in 2000, Las Vegas could truly claim that it had become the only city in the world devoted to the consumption of entertainment.

The exuberance of American society during the 1990s enhanced Las Vegas's appeal. The phenomenal rise in the stock market between 1992 and 2000 made the nation seem prosperous and people were free with their money in ways that they might never have been in a different economic climate. More luxury cars were leased and purchased across the nation than ever before. More new homes with fabulous amenities graced subdivisions from Long Island to Seattle. People spent money on rest and recreation; Las Vegas's brand seemed palatable and au courant.

Las Vegas's fortuitousness was more than its packaging of leisure. The presence of gifted entrepreneurs such as Wynn who intuited the core of American desires in a moment of prosperity turned the American scapegoat into a national center of leisure and pleasure.

Las Vegas also came to mean opportunity in a changing economy. Throughout the 1980s, the semi-skilled but high-paying working class jobs that had been the backbone of industrial prosperity were no more. Steel nearly disappeared as an American industry. The U.S. ceased to make electronics; the last mass-market American-made television was assembled in Springfield, Missouri, in 1979. The nation nearly lost the auto industry to imports as well, rescued only by the rise of the sport utility vehicle. In the California recession that followed the end of the Cold War, thousands of middle-class aerospace industry workers lost their jobs, and few opportunities with anything resembling similar pay existed.

Las Vegas provided one answer. As the court of last resort for unskilled and semi-skilled workers, it gave those with barely a high school education a chance to earn a middle-class income. The Culinary Union helped keep wages high even as its numbers swelled to more than 50,000 workers. Las Vegas provided solid pay for unspecialized work, a refuge for many as the industrial economy faded.

After a decade of predictions that each new hotel opening would cause the state's economy to collapse, the Mirage Phase suddenly ended. Steve Wynn found his stock at a low point early in 2000 and MGM's Kirk Kerkorian made a $6.4 billion offer. The Wynn empire—the Bellagio, Mirage, Treasure Island, and Golden Nugget, along with properties elsewhere—changed hands in an instant, bringing to an end a golden age of capital development in Nevada. Reticence on Wall Street contributed to the slowing. The financial markets were more than glad to take profits from Las Vegas, but they were not quite willing to let Las Vegas be Las Vegas. By the end of 2000, capital for construction became harder to find, new construction and expansion plans were on hold, and the market seemed very fragile.

As the twenty-first century gathered momentum, Las Vegas finally shared greater commonality with the rest of the nation. It depended on the same sources of capital that other communities did and had accepted many of the same rules and regulations. It was not only that the rest of the nation had moved toward normalizing the behaviors that used to make Las Vegas exceptional; in its hierarchy, distribution of wealth and status, demography, and stratification of its labor force, Las Vegas had become more like the rest of the nation as well. Once a pariah, Las Vegas had become a paradigm of the postindustrial economy.

As gaming spread throughout the nation—often run by Las Vegas companies—the colony was transformed. Las Vegas became a colonizer, exporting its version of the new economy to New Orleans, Detroit, and elsewhere. Las Vegas had always reflected America onto itself. It had always been the mirror people held up to their faces to see what they hoped for and what they feared. As it became normative, the entire historical equation of the city was thrown on its head. Las Vegas became the first city of the new century, the one that owed its allegiance to the shape of the new universe, to the signs and symbols of a culture of entertainment.

LAS VEGAS'S GROWTH had an overwhelming impact on Nevada, overshadowing almost every other issue in the state. As population centered in the south, the balance of power began to shift away from Reno and Carson City in the north, where it had resided since statehood. A preponderance of state officials came from Las Vegas and Clark County, and only skillful handling of state politics throughout the 1980s and 1990s allowed the north to retain its longstanding control. The recent arrival of almost half of the state's population in a single decade—Nevada grew from 800,508 in 1980 to 1,201,675 in 1990 and 2,018,828 in 2000—contributed to the ability of the north to retain power in the state. Many of the newcomers simply did not care enough about local issues to go to the polls.

The growth in Nevada's population was reflected in the addition of congressional seats. In 1982, Nevada added its second seat in the U.S. House of Representatives. Barbara Vucanovich, who first arrived in Nevada in 1949 in search of a divorce and stayed in the Silver State, was elected and retained the seat for more than fourteen years before retiring. Vucanovich was the first woman elected to federal office in the Silver State. This addition illustrated the change in state politics. Since statehood in 1864, Nevada's two senators outnumbered the state's congressional representative. After 1982, the state enjoyed equal numbers in both houses.

Yet the addition of a representative did little to increase the state's clout in national politics. As Barbara Vucanovich took her seat in Congress, Nevada was represented in the U.S. Senate by Democrat Howard W. Cannon's successor, Republican Chic Hecht, in one seat, and in the other, by Paul Laxalt, a close confidant of Ronald Reagan who spent most of his time protecting the gaming industry from federal scrutiny. Despite Laxalt's power, his proximity to Reagan worked against the state in important ways. The Reagan revolution promoted unfunded mandates, sending programs formerly funded by the federal government to the states without accompanying resources. The "first friend," as Laxalt was called, could not be seen as asking for funding that his president was trying to end. Laxalt was also compromised by his loud protests against Joseph Yablonsky, the FBI special-agent-in charge in Las Vegas who engaged in a strident campaign to expose organized crime infiltration of the casino industry. The louder Laxalt protested, it seemed, the more it became plausible that criminal involvement in many casinos continued.

The combination of Laxalt's distraction and Republican dominance of the state's congressional delegation led to a weakness that exposed the state's vulnerability. Before the beginning of the Mirage Phase, Nevada remained a backwater, looked down upon by other states and regarded as a physical wasteland. Its status as consisting of almost 90 percent federal land and its history of hosting atomic and nuclear testing made it seem a likely candidate for greater involvement in the nuclear industry. In 1983, the process of siting the first national high-level nuclear waste dump honed in on the Silver State, illustrating the ongoing marginal status of Nevada and its colonial position.

The rise of nuclear power changed American sources of energy. By 1967, nuclear power provided 46 percent of the 60 million kilowatts of electric power orders placed by domestic industry. But this so-called clean energy came with consequences. Active reactors throughout the country produced radioactive waste. In the early 1980s, Congress determined that permanent storage facilities for all high-level nuclear waste were essential. On December 13, 1980, Congress passed the Low-Level Nuclear Radioactive Waste Policy Act, designed to fashion a solution to the question of the disposal of low-level radioactive waste, the spent but still radioactive materials used in hospitals, universities, and laboratories. The passage of the Nuclear Waste Policy Act of 1982 (NWPAA) on December 20, 1982, tackled the far more difficult problem of high-level waste, the spent fuel rods and other radioactive materials that were left from the process of creating nuclear energy.

The act directed the selection of five sites to be studied for the location of a permanent high-level waste storage facility. From the five, two would be selected—one east of the Mississippi River and the other west. The process was supposed to be a reflection of the best science had to offer, state-of-the-art facilities to protect Americans from the byproducts of their opulent lifestyle. The legislation directed that science serve as the guide for the choice of location; under its terms, high-level nuclear waste could only be located in geological formations certain to withstand any disaster for more than 10,000 years, the amount of time necessary before the radioactive waste material ceased to be a threat to humanity.

Science was never a determinant in the decision-making process. Power and politics instead shaped the choices. In December 1984, when the Department of Energy selected three sites as the preferred choices to be examined for the first repository—Deaf Smith County in desolate west Texas; Yucca Mountain, northwest of Las Vegas; and the Hanford Reservation in central Washington state—it violated the first of its regulations. No locations east of the Mississippi River were recommended for study. Much to the pleasure of the public east of the Mississippi River and the powerful congressional representatives and senators who represented them, the selection of eastern locales had been delayed until the second proposed repository.

In 1983, the three sites that were chosen seemed like good candidates for "national sacrifice zones," places where nuclear waste could be housed without a threat to a significant percentage of the public and where the state was too weak or too disorganized to resist federal entreaties. Hanford had been the place where plutonium was milled, the blue-collar factory town of the military nuclear industry. It had been the site of numerous spills and releases of radioactive gasses. Yucca Mountain, adjacent to the Nevada Test Site, was a central part of the history of above- and below-ground atomic and nuclear testing. In the 1980s, the Nevada Test Site remained a viable operation, employing thousands of workers and generating millions of dollars in income in the state. The nearly vacant Deaf Smith County, Texas, was a few hours from the Pentax weapons plant at Amarillo, Texas. A spill there seemed likely to affect almost no one.

Rather than look at the science of the process, federal officials supposed that people in all three places were unlikely to strenuously object to a repository or would be unable to muster sufficient influence to fight.

The three initial choices were as far as the process went. Shortly after the initial selection, the Department of Energy "indefinitely deferred" the search for the second site. Protests in Texas against the choice of Deaf Smith County and the vast power of the Texas congressional delegation made it hard to force the repository on a large and powerful state. Hanford was in a populated, agricultural area along the Columbia River. Washington's senators, the powerful Henry "Scoop" Jackson, who died in 1983, Daniel J. Evans, who succeeded Jackson, and Slade Gorton, enjoyed great influence, and the Northwest had long been the home of strident environmentalism. That left Yucca Mountain, in the middle of a federal weapons range, in a state that remained a colony of everywhere, a place dependent on other places for nearly everything it needed to survive. Combined with weak political representation, Nevada's history and its fundamental nature made it a target for a nuclear waste repository.

Yucca Mountain was marginally viable from a geological standpoint, but from a political perspective it was ideal. In 1987, Senator Bennett Johnston (D-LA) and Senator James McClure (R-ID) introduced legislation to assess only Yucca Mountain, ending the search for any other location. Even if there had been safeguards, the record of the Department of Energy and the huge sums necessary to "characterize" the site, to assure its adequacy as a repository—estimated at more than $1 billion in 1988 but rising to more than twenty times that sum by 2000—all but guaranteed that Yucca Mountain would be chosen. With passage of the bill, the planned scientific process had become strictly political. Johnston's Yucca Mountain legislation became known as the "Screw Nevada" bill.

The bill became a galvanizing factor in Nevada, something that made each Nevadan, urban or rural, into a sagebrush rebel of a sort. The federal government once again oppressed Nevada. The Nevada legislature united to oppose NWPAA and the Yucca Mountain project with the passage of Assembly Bill 222 in 1989, which made it illegal to dispose of high-level nuclear waste in Nevada. Despite widespread efforts to purchase the goodwill of the Nevada public—in one instance, a well-known television news correspondent put his hard-won credibility at the service of the Department of Energy and Yucca Mountain for a hefty sum; in another in 2001, former governor Robert List sullied his name and his reputation when he was hired as a lobbyist of the nuclear industry—and the creation of the Yucca Mountain Science Center in Las Vegas to "educate" the public, Nevadans saw the "Screw Nevada" bill as an affront to the state and a breach of its sovereignty. They opposed the siting of the dump with as much ferocity as a state with limited faith in government and large numbers of newcomers could. Bumper stickers that read "Nevada is not a wasteland" became common. Nevadans even boycotted the Yucca Mountain Science Center. "The only people who visit," a high-level official remarked, "are family and friends," testimony to both the distaste for federal authority and the widespread fear of nuclear waste in a state that produced none of its own, but had long been the national sacrifice zone for nuclear weapons testing.

Laxalt's successor, Democrat Harry Reid, who entered the Senate in 1987, and Richard Bryan, another Democrat who replaced Hecht in 1989, represented the next generation of leadership, but by the time they arrived in the Senate chambers the damage had been done. Although both were more effective than their predecessors, the new senators alone could not stymie the effort to locate the dump in Nevada. The state's two U.S. representatives had little influence. Rapidly growing and politically weak, Nevada found itself unable to fend off the ignominious fate of being selected for the nation's only nuclear waste dump.

Yet the in-migration of thousands of people every month created the potential to block the dump no matter what bills were signed or proclamations issued. When the original siting process took place, Nevada's population barely topped 800,000. Its people were Libertarian by inclination; albeit blindly patriotic in most circumstances, they expected little from government and wanted it only to leave them alone. The state lacked the political influence and organization to stave off the initial siting. The tremendous change in the state more than doubled its population to 2 million by 2000 and many of the newcomers brought a different set of expectations than their predecessors held.

By 2006, the battle against Yucca Mountain was almost over. Despite the George W. Bush administration's support of the dump, Nevadans had successfully mobilized to thwart the federal government. Senator Harry Reid, long an opponent of making Nevada a nuclear wasteland, had taken the lead; as Senate Minority Leader after 2004, he made cutting the Yucca Mountain budget a personal cause. A number of scandals in the certification process led to more questions about the suitability of Yucca Mountain as a repository for high-level nuclear waste. Transportation of nuclear waste also contributed to the demise. Under plans that the Department of Energy filed, as much as 83 percent of the national population was likely to have nuclear waste pass through their imme-diate vicinity. The dump was supposed to open in 2008; by 2006, the date had been pushed back to 2017 and few expected Yucca Mountain to ever receive nuclear waste.

Rapid population growth led to other changes in Nevada politics. As the state grew, the distribution of voters shifted. During the 1990s, registration of Democrats and Republicans in Nevada evened out; by the end of the decade, both parties were almost equally represented among registered voters. They were distributed unevenly throughout the state. The north and rural Nevada voted predominantly Republican. Las Vegas's suburbs leaned heavily Repub-lican, while the city of Las Vegas, North Las Vegas, and much of urban Clark County were heavily Democratic. The result was an ongoing struggle for either party to attain dominance.

Nevada's politics had always been unusual, and the growth of population did little to change their fundamental nature. As had been the case since statehood, small groups of powerful leaders met behind closed doors and created the structure that led to elective office. This made a candidate's political affiliation mean less than his or her willingness to support platforms such as a refusal to raise the gaming tax, the lowest in the nation, that benefited the state's leading industry. Although not quite the bipartisanship of the early twentieth century, this arrangement assured that power remained in a few hands.

At the same time, the nature of Nevada politicians began to change. Nevada politicians had long been cut from the mold of the rural West. They had been folksy and diffident—"aw shucks" kind of guys who seemed to meet the people on their own terms. But as the state's population changed, so did its represen-tatives. The new leaders were blow-dried in that California way, sometimes thoughtful and often merely vacuous. Carpetbaggers had long been a major problem in Nevada; people who had money and a short history in the Silver State found the ease of campaigning through television too much to resist. The mercurial Aaron Russo, who ran for the Republican gubernatorial nomina-tion in 1998, was typical. In the Republican primary, Russo threw a scare into the more staid Kenny Guinn, who later went on to a resounding victory in the general election. Russo was a Californian with a short history in Nevada but with plenty of wealth, and he was able to parlay his knowledge of media into an effective if sometimes bizarre challenge. Russo clearly exploited the transience of Nevada's population. As U.S. Senator Harry Reid found out in the 1998 elec-tion, when more than 30 percent of the state's voters had not been residents during his previous campaign, incumbency was neither an advantage nor a disadvantage, and he won by just over four hundred votes statewide. Instead, it was a cipher that diminished the value of experience and made elections a popularity contest.

When Guinn took office in 1998, he inherited one of the best economic climates in the state's history. The Mirage Phase was still going strong; the Bellagio opened the month before the election, followed by the Venetian and Paris Las Vegas, assuring strong visitation and full coffers. Casinos started to slump in 2000, prior to the vicious attacks on the U.S. that took place on September 11, 2001. Although Reno, primarily a driving destination, felt little impact, Las Vegas, still the state's cash cow, took a much harder hit. As much as 65 percent of Las Vegas's visitation arrived by air, and in the aftermath of the atrocities Americans were afraid to fly. Foreign travel, especially from the Far East, precipitously declined as well. For the first time in a generation, Nevada's economic strategy suffered genuine setbacks.

In the aftermath of September 11, state revenues plummeted, many of the major hotels laid off employees, and the rosy climate of the 1990s dissipated overnight. Surprisingly, population growth did not significantly slow, exacerbating the gap between state expenditures and the needs of the state's population. After reelection in 2002, Governor Guinn took on the state's greatest problem: its inability to generate enough revenue to prevent a slow but steady decline in the quality of life.

The state faced new challenges. Never before had Nevada seen the influx of so many people, many of whom were in need of government assistance. Las Vegas had become the place everyone thought could rescue them from the doldrums of the American industrial economy, and thousands of potential workers—many with families in tow—arrived in the Silver State. A significant percentage was Spanish-speaking, bringing a historic diversity back in a new way. The state's mechanisms were not set up to provide the level of social service the new residents needed. Even worse, the state's taxation system did not allow the generation of new revenue at the rate necessary to provide for the needs of newcomers.

There were other problems. Although Las Vegas quickly recovered from 9/11, Reno was not so fortunate. The "Biggest Little City in the World" had always been a driving destination. This shielded it from the full brunt of 9/11, but not from encroachment onto its primary market. Many of Reno's customers came from Sacramento and the San Francisco Bay Area. The spread of Indian gaming had a direct impact on Reno. By the early 2000s, some Indian casinos matched the amenities that Reno offered. When Thunder Valley opened on the route from San Francisco and Sacramento, Reno suffered.

Indian gaming remained controversial in Nevada. Although Las Vegas remained the pinnacle of entertainment, the first wonder of the postmodern world, it too had to consider the implications of Indian gaming. Especially in the San Diego area, new casinos that sported Las Vegas–style shows sprouted in the new century. They promised experience, exactly what Las Vegas sold its visitors. But they lacked the cachet of Las Vegas, the symbolic significance of being at the new center of postindustrial capitalism, the place where money and power met in the twenty-first century. Las Vegas continued to thrive.

In the first half decade of the twenty-first century, Las Vegas turned into a real estate market in a way no one could have anticipated. Housing prices rose dramatically, in some areas tripling in value in less than one year. This proved the axiom that all tourist towns are ultimately real estate markets, but it also put pressure on the working class that made up the backbone of the economy. Las Vegas became pricey, and in the process, a push for vertical housing began to take shape. Americans remained in love with the single-family dwelling, and Las Vegas was an unlikely place to throw off that obsession. Although a number of condo towers were built, many projects shut their doors before ever breaking ground. Yet with almost $20 billion in construction planned in 2005, Las Vegas remained one of the hottest real estate markets in the nation.

Las Vegas's success belied deeper issues. In many ways, Nevada's traditions and its future collided head-on. In the old Nevada people thought they did for themselves, without a handout from government. That was easy in a state with 150,000 people, as had been the case in 1950. But as the state became more urban and passed the two million mark, the old ways seemed archaic. The new Nevada had greater needs than the mythic Silver State of old. They manifested themselves in many ways.

Nevada had long been at the bottom of most social service measures in the U.S. The state's education system ranked in the bottom five nationally, close to Arkansas, Louisiana, Mississippi, and Alabama. Teenage pregnancy was among the highest in the nation, as was teenage suicide, drug use, the number of high school dropouts, and other similar measures. Nevada even had the highest rate of smoking in the nation. For a state that saw itself as the vanguard of the twenty-first century, this was an untenable state of affairs.

There were reasons for some of Nevada's shortcomings. The transience of the population accounted for some of the problems, but many argued that the lack of investment in the state led to its perennially low rankings. The question became how to change the state's direction at a time when every sector of government was bombarded with demands for service that they could not meet. It was a paradox: how to do more with not nearly enough at the same time that antitaxation sentiment reached a fever pitch.

Governor Guinn had cast himself as a visionary. He saw the renovation of the state as his primary objective. Under Guinn, the state had embarked on the millennium scholarship program, guaranteeing any student who graduated from a Nevada high school with a B average $10,000 to attend any Nevada institution of higher education. This brilliant idea had the potential to solve one of Nevada's ongoing problems. The Silver State's high school graduates attended college at the lowest rate in the nation. For Guinn, the public acceptance of the role of government in supporting higher education became a springboard for a package of reforms that promised to reshape the state.

At the same time, anti-government forces were flexing their muscles. Much of the sentiment stemmed from people who were new to the state and who had chosen Nevada because it was largely a tax-free climate. An amendment to the state constitution forbade a state income tax. Casino and sales tax made up 75 percent of the state's revenue collection, and both were notoriously unstable. Despite the run-up of the Mirage Phase, sales tax and casino tax were prone to fluctuation. Many had forgotten how volatile such sources of revenue could be.

The growth in the retirement population contributed to the growing anti-tax sentiment. By 2002, retirees comprised one-quarter of the population of Clark County and almost one-fifth of the state. The next largest population segment was people between the ages of 55 and 64, who would soon be moving into retirement. Many of those people were newcomers who lived their working lives elsewhere and did not want to invest in their new homes. Seniors became a powerful coalition against spending even for services they used in abundance. In 2002, a Henderson library bond issue failed by a 62 percent–38 percent margin. Seniors overwhelmingly voted against a measure that would bring new libraries closer to their homes. They were the single biggest users of the library system.

The different ways of thinking collided in the 2003 legislative session. The state reached a crisis, with the legislature unable to agree on a budget, thanks mainly to an initiative requiring a two-thirds vote of the legislature to approve any tax increase. For almost two weeks, a group of Republican legislators labeled the "Mean Fifteen," just one more than one-third of the assembly, held up a new taxation measure that promised to set the state right. They battled against their governor, who had proposed the measure, creating a rift in state politics that cut through the Republican Party and led to countless internecine fights within it. The tax measure, which amounted to $836 million, was the largest ever enacted in state history. Most Nevadans never felt it, for they did not experience the tax increase in any direct fashion. As always, the Silver State taxed visitors first and then the gaming and leisure industry. Only afterward, when the easy targets had been acquired, did ordinary Nevadans feel any pain. Most never experienced the tax increase of 2003.

The battle over the tax increase illustrated how far apart the different segments of the state had become. Many cheered the tax package because they felt it addressed deep-seated needs in the state and created upward mobility for those left out of the prosperity of the previous decade. An equal number saw the package as treason, a betrayal of the Silver State's promise of low taxes— even though the taxes rarely affected individuals. The state had severed into different camps, each of which had its own value system and ultimately, its own web site.

In the end, Nevada remained the quintessential purple state. On the maps that television used to illustrate political trends, Republican states were red and Democratic blue. Nevada blended the colors. It had a bright blue core in the heart of Las Vegas, surrounded by a purple suburban belt. Most of the rest of the state was bright red, especially in the rural counties. In Washoe County and Carson City in the north, there were a few blue dots, Reno and Carson City in particular. In a strange way, where the need was the greatest, in the rural counties, the antigovernment sentiment was the strongest.

From its early roots, Nevada had come a long way. The Silver State had become something different, the state that made most of its income putting smiles on the faces of its visitors. No other American state relied on tourism to the extent that Nevada did. No other state had Nevada's checkered history. Nevada had once been an outcast among American states. It had been scorned for its practices, exploited for its natural attributes, and dismissed as inconsequential. A colony of everywhere, it had seen its promise delivered to people outside the state's boundaries.

The twenty-first century is Nevada's time to shine. Perfectly positioned to take advantage of the social and cultural trends of American society, Nevada has almost unlimited possibilities. Its investment in a tourist economy, born out of necessity, has proven valuable beyond anyone's wildest dreams. It has a clear charter to an exciting future, one that the rest of American society cannot envision and will certainly envy. The future of the Silver State is brighter than it has ever been.

INDEX

All small town and county names refer
to places in Nevada unless otherwise
indicated

Adams, John Quincy, 3
Adams-Oñis Treaty of 1819, 3–4
Adelaide Mine, 66
Adelson, Mervin, 116
Aetna Insurance Company, 140
African Americans: boxing and, 65, 77; civil
    rights and, 102, 118–21; labor unions
    and, 97, 98, 134; Nevada Test Site and,
    106; the Strip and, 119, 120, 129
agriculture: difficulties of, 1, 76, 78,
    89; economic value of, 110–11, 140;
    irrigation, 83–84; land transfer and,
    141–44; monetization of silver and,
    59–60; railroads and, 58–60
Aladdin, 117, 139, 151
Alderman, Israel "Icepick Willie," 108
All-American Canal, 85
Allsop and Company, 35
American Federation of Labor (AFL), 71,
    97, 98
American National Insurance Corporation,
    115
American River, 9, 15
Anasazi people, 83
Apache Club/Hotel, 91, 107
Appliance Buyers Credit Corporation, 117
Argent Corporation, 137, 138
Arizona, 85, 104, 144
Arkansas, 66, 90
Armijo, Antonio, 10
Assembly Bill 222 of 1989, 156
Atlantic City, 138, 139, 146, 149
Atlantic City Golden Nugget, 149
atomic bomb testing, 103–6

Atomic Energy Commission (AEC), 105, 106
Austin, 63
automobile travel, 76, 159

Bailey, Bob, 121
Baker, 105
Balistrieri, Frank, 137
Balistrieri, Joseph, 137
Balzar, Fred, 92
Bank Club, 91
"Bank Crowd." See Bank of California
Bank of California, 44–47, 48, 49, 50,
    51–53, 54, 55, 56
Bank of Las Vegas, 116
Bank of Nevada, 53, 54–55
Banquet Saloon, Golconda, 66, 67
Barren River. See Humboldt River Valley
Bartleson, John, 13
Basic Magnesium Incorporated (BMI), 95,
    97, 98
Bear Flag Revolt, 16, 19
Bear River, 12
Beatie, Hampton S., 21
Beatty, 65, 66
beavers, 7, 8, 9, 14
Bechtel, 87, 105
Belcher Mine, 53
Bellagio, 151, 152, 159
Bennett, William, 151
Benton, Thomas Hart, 13
Berman, Chickie, 108
Berman, David, 108, 114
Bible, Alan, 112
Bidwell, John, 13
"Big Bonanza," 53, 59
Big Four (railroads), 57
"Big Four of the Comstock." See "Bonanza
    Crowd"

Jackson, David, 8
Jackson, Henry "Scoop," 156
Jack's Valley, 22
Japanese workers, 98–99
Jefferson, Thomas, 3, 9
Jeffries, James J., 65, 77
Jepsen, Richard, 143
J. F. Shea and Pacific Bridge, 87
Johnson, Jack, 77
Johnson, Lubertha, 119
Johnston, Bennett, 156
Jones, Clifford A., 121
Jones, Jan Laverty, 151
Jones, John P., 53

Kaiser Paving Company, 87
Kefauver, Estes, 112–13, 121, 130
Kennedy, John F., 114, 122, 123
Kennedy, Robert F., 114, 115, 122, 123, 136
Kentuck Mine, 49, 51
Kerkorian, Kirk, 130–32, 136, 151, 152
Kimberly, 73
Kind, Leo, 110
King, Martin Luther, Jr., 120
King's Castle, 118
Klamath Lake, 16
Kleinman, Morris, 138
Knight, William, 32
Kolod, Ruby, 124, 138
Korean War, 110, 126, 135
Korshak, Sidney, 115

labor unions: African Americans and, 97, 98, 134; "Broker State" and, 97–98; hotel workers and, 132–35, 152; mining and, 50–51, 70–72, 74, 75, 97, 132–33; mobsters and, 115–18; during World War II, 96–98. See also Culinary Union; Teamsters' Pension Fund
La Costa Hotel and Country Club, 115
Lake Tahoe, 118, 124, 126, 127, 137; environmental efforts for, 140–41
Lamm, Richard, 144
Lander County, 63
Landmark Hotel, 117, 127
Lansky, Meyer, 107, 108, 127, 138
Last Frontier. See Frontier
Las Vegas, x, 6, 15; development of, 1970s, 130–32, 136, 137–38, 139–40;

development of, 1980s, 145–46; Fremont Street, 91, 108, 148; Hoover Dam and, 81, 85–86, 89, 93; Howard Hughes era, 125–30; Indian gaming and, 150–51, 160; labor unions and, 133–35, 152; legalization of gambling and, 91, 92, 107–8, 112–13; Mirage Phase, 147–48, 149–52, 154, 159, 161; Mormons and, 24, 26; Nevada Test Site and, 104, 105; politics in 1990s to 2000s, 153, 158, 159, 162; population, 112, 153, 161; postwar gambling development, 106–10, 113–18, 120–24; railroads and, 66, 85; real estate and, xi–xii, 148, 160; Tonopah mining strike and, 65, 66; Westside, 119; World War II and, 95–97, 98, 99; Yucca Mountain and, 155, 156–57. See also mobsters; the Strip
Las Vegas Gunnery Range/School, 96, 104
Las Vegas Hilton, 146
Las Vegas Sun, 115, 124
Las Vegas-Tonopah Railroad, 66
"Law of the River." See Colorado River Compact
Laxalt, Paul, 124, 128–30, 139, 143, 154, 157
Laxalt, Robert, 124
lead, 74
League for the Advancement of States' Equal Rights, 144
Levinson, Edward, 138
Levi Strauss, 21
Lewis, Meriwether, 3, 6, 9
Lincoln, Abraham, 19, 38; Nevada statehood and, 1, 39–40, 42
List, Robert, 144–45, 156
List of Excluded Persons. See "Black Book"
Lord, J., 75
Los Angeles, 83, 84
Los Angeles Times, 83, 141
Lost City. See El Pueblo Grande de Nevada
Louisiana Purchase, 3, 4, 6, 7, 9, 13
Low-Level Nuclear Radioactive Waste Policy Act of 1980, 154
Luxor, 151

Maceo, Sam, 115
Mackay, John W., 51, 52, 53, 54, 55
magnesite, 95
magnesium, 95–96, 97–98